Air Fryer Cookbook for Beginners

1500 Mouthwatering Days of Quick & Easy Recipes
| Healthy low-fat cooking |
By Orlando Green

Copyright 2023 by Orlando Green

Table of Contents

Breakfast Recipes

Crispy Southwestern Ham Egg Cups

Prep time: 5 minutes **Cooking time:** 12 minutes
Servings: 2

Ingredients
4 (1-ounce) slices deli ham
4 large eggs
2 tablespoons diced white onion
2 tablespoons diced red bell pepper
2 tablespoons full-fat sour cream
1/4 cup diced green bell pepper
1/2 cup shredded medium Cheddar cheese

Directions

Set one slice of ham on the bottom of four baking cups. In a large bowl, whisk eggs with sour cream. Stir in green pepper, red pepper, and onion.

Pour the egg mixture into ham-lined baking cups. Top with Cheddar. Place cups into the fryer basket. Adjust the temperature to 320F and set the timer for 12 minutes or until the tops are browned. Serve warm.

Buffalo Egg Cups

Prep time: 10 minutes **Cooking time:** 15 minutes
Servings: 2

Ingredients
4 large eggs
2 tbs buffalo sauce
2 ounces full-fat cream cheese
1/2 cup shredded sharp Cheddar cheese

Directions

Crack eggs into two (4") ramekins. In a small microwave-safe bowl, mix cream cheese, buffalo sauce, and Cheddar. Microwave for 20 seconds and then stir. Place a spoonful into each ramekin on top of the eggs.

Place ramekins into the air fryer basket. Adjust the temperature to 320F and set the timer for 15 minutes Serve warm.

Quick and Easy Bacon Strips

Prep time: 5 minutes **Cooking time:** 12 minutes
Servings: 2

Ingredients
8 slices sugar free bacon

Directions

Place bacon strips into the air fryer basket. Adjust the temperature to 400F and set the timer for 12 minutes. After 6 minutes, flip bacon and continue cooking time. Serve warm.

"Banana" Nut Cake

Prep time: 15 minutes **Cooking time:** 25 minutes
Servings: 6

Ingredients
1 cup blanched finely ground almond flour
1/2 cup powdered Erythritol
1/2 teaspoon ground cinnamon
1/4 cup unsalted butter, melted
1/4 cup chopped walnuts
2 tablespoons ground golden flaxseed
2 teaspoons baking powder
1/4 cup full-fat sour cream
2 large eggs
2 1/2 teaspoons banana extract
1 teaspoon vanilla extract

Directions

In a large bowl, merge almond flour, Erythritol, flaxseed, baking powder, and cinnamon.

Stir in butter, banana extract, vanilla extract, and sour cream. Add eggs to the mixture and gently stir until fully combined. Stir in the walnuts.

Pour into 6" nonstick cake pan and place into the air fryer basket. Adjust the temperature to 300F and set the timer for 25 minutes.

Cake will be golden and a toothpick inserted in center will come out clean when fully cooked. Allow to fully cool to avoid crumbling.

Nutty Granola

Prep time: 5 minutes **Cooking time:** 1 hour **Servings:** 4

Ingredients

1/2 cup pecans, coarsely chopped
1/4 cup unsweetened flaked coconut
1/4 cup flaxseed or chia seeds 2 tablespoons sunflower seeds
2 tablespoons melted butter 1/4 cup Swerve
1/2 cup walnuts or almonds, chopped
1/4 cup almond flour
2 tablespoons water
1/2 teaspoon ground cinnamon
1/2 teaspoon vanilla extract 1/4 teaspoon ground nutmeg 1/4 teaspoon salt

Directions

Preheat the air fryer to 250F (121C). Divide a piece of parchment paper to fit inside the air fryer basket.
In a large bowl, toss the nuts, coconut, almond flour, ground flaxseed or chia seeds, sunflower seeds, butter, Swerve, cinnamon, vanilla, nutmeg, salt, and water until thoroughly combined.

Spread the granola on the parchment paper and flatten to an even thickness. Air fry for about an hour, or until golden throughout. Detach from the air fryer and allow to fully cool. Break the granola into bite-size pieces and store in a covered container for up to a week.

Portobello Eggs Benedict

Prep time: 10 minutes **Cooking time:** 14 minutes
Servings: 2

Ingredients

1 tablespoon olive oil
1 cloves garlic, minced
1/4 teaspoon dried thyme
Salt and ground black pepper, to taste
2 large eggs
1 teaspoon truffle oil (optional)
2 Portobello mushrooms, stems removed and gills scraped out
2 tablespoons grated Pecorino Romano cheese
1 tablespoon chopped fresh parsley, for garnish
2 Roma tomatoes, halved lengthwise

Directions

Preheat the air fryer to 400F (204C). In a small bowl, merge the olive oil, garlic, and thyme. Brush the mixture over the mushrooms and tomatoes until thoroughly coated. Flavor to taste with salt and freshly ground black pepper. Arrange the vegetables, cut side up, in the air fryer basket.

Set an egg into the center of each mushroom and sprinkle with cheese. Air fry for 10 to 14 minutes until the vegetables are tender and the whites are firm. When cool enough to handle, slice the tomatoes and set on top of the eggs. Scatter parsley on top and drizzle with truffle oil, if desired, just before serving.

Broccoli-Mushroom Frittata

Prep time: 10 minutes **Cooking time:** 20 minutes
Servings: 2

Ingredients

1 tablespoon olive oil
6 eggs
1/4 cup finely chopped onion
1/4 cup Parmesan cheese
1/2 teaspoon salt
1 1/2 cups broccoli florets, finely chopped
1/4 teaspoon freshly ground black pepper
1/2 cup sliced brown mushrooms

Directions

In a nonstick cake pan, combine the olive oil, broccoli, mushrooms, onion, salt, and pepper. Stir until the vegetables are thoroughly coated with oil. Place the cake pan in the air fryer basket and set the air fryer to 400F (204C).

Air fry for 5 minutes until the vegetables soften. Meanwhile, in a medium bowl, whisk the eggs and Parmesan until thoroughly combined. Merge the egg mixture into the pan and shake gently to distribute the vegetables. Air fry for another 15 minutes until the eggs are set. Detach from the air fryer and let sit for 5 minutes to cool slightly. Use a silicone spatula to lift the frittata onto a plate before serving gently.

Lemon-Blueberry Muffins

Prep time: 5 minutes **Cooking time:** 25 minutes
Servings: 6

Ingredients

1 1/4 cups almond flour
3 tablespoons Swerve
3 tablespoons melted butter 1 tablespoon almond milk
1 teaspoon baking powder
2 large eggs
1 tablespoon fresh lemon juice
1/2 cup fresh blueberries

Directions

Preheat the air fryer to 350F (177C). Lightly coat 6 silicone muffin cups with vegetable oil. Set aside.
In a bowl, merge the almond flour, Swerve, and baking soda. Set aside.

In a separate bowl, merge together the eggs, butter, milk, and lemon juice. Attach the egg mixture to the flour mixture and stir until just combined. Roll in the blueberries and let the batter sit for 5 minutes.
Set the muffin batter into the muffin cups, about two-thirds full. Air fry for 20 to 25 minutes, or until a toothpick inserted into the center of a muffin comes out clean. Detach the basket from the device and let the muffins cool for about 5.

"Everything" Seasoning Air Fryer Asparagus

Prep time: 15 minutes **Cooking time:** 20 minutes
Serve: 1

Ingredients

1-pound thin asparagus	1 tablespoon everything
1 tablespoon olive oil	bagel seasoning
4 wedge (blank)s lemon	1 pinch salt to taste
wedges	

Directions

Rinse and trim the asparagus, removing any woody ends. Drizzle olive oil over asparagus on a platter. Toss with the bagel seasoning until well

blended. Arrange the asparagus in a single layer in the air fryer basket. If necessary, work in bunches.

Preheat the air fryer carefully carefully to 390°F (200 degrees C). 5–6 minutes, flipping with tongs halfway through, until slightly soft. If necessary, season with salt. With lemon slices, **Serve:**.

Air Fryer Fingerling Potatoes with Dip

Prep time: 20 minutes **Cooking time:** 25 minutes
Serve: 1

Ingredients

12 ounces fingerling potatoes, halved lengthwise	1 teaspoon garlic powder, ¼ teaspoon paprika salt and ground black pepper to taste
1 tablespoon olive oil	1 ½ tablespoons ranch
⅓ cup reduced-fat sour cream,	dressing mix (such as Hidden Valley Ranch®)
2 tablespoons mayonnaise	1 tablespoon white vinegar
2 tablespoons finely grated Parmesan cheese	
1 tablespoon chopped fresh parsley	

Directions

Preheat an air fryer carefully for 5 minutes at 390 degrees F (200 degrees C).

Combine the potatoes, olive oil, garlic powder, paprika, salt, and pepper in a mixing bowl. Transfer the potatoes to the air fryer basket after tossing until coated.
Cook, shaking the basket halfway through until the potatoes are cooked through and crispy, 15 to 17 minutes in a preheated air fryer.

In a separate bowl, combine sour cream, mayonnaise, Parmesan cheese, ranch dressing mix, and vinegar while the potatoes are boiling.

Transfer the cooked potatoes to a platter and sprinkle with parsley. **Serve:** right away with dipping sauce.

Keto Air Fryer Jalapeno Poppers

Prep time: 15 minutes **Cooking time:** 20 minutes
Serve: 1

Ingredients

6 jalapeno peppers, halved and seeded	7 ½ ounces garden vegetable cream cheese (such as Philadelphia®)
6 bacon strips, halved lengthwise	

Directions

Preheat the air fryer carefully to 390°F (200 degrees C).
Fill each half of jalapeño with cream cheese and wrap a split bacon strip. To secure, tuck in the bacon ends or use toothpicks.

Place the jalapeno poppers in the air fryer basket, working in batches as necessary to minimize congestion.

Cook in a preheated air fryer for 10 to 12 minutes, or until the bacon is done to your preference.

Air Fryer Shortbread Cookie Fries

Prep time: 15 minutes **Cooking time:** 18 minutes
Serve: 1

Ingredients

1 ¼ cups all-purpose flour	½ cup butter
⅓ cup strawberry jam	⅛ teaspoon ground dried
3 tablespoons white sugar	chipotle pepper (Optional)
⅓ cup lemon curd	

Directions

In a medium mixing bowl, combine the flour and sugar. Using a pastry blender, cut in the butter until the mixture resembles fine crumbs and begins to cling. Make a ball out of the
Ingredients and knead it until smooth.

Preheat an air fryer carefully to 350°F (190 degrees C). On a lightly floured surface, roll out the dough to 1/4-inch thickness. Cut into 3- to 4-inch-long 1/2-inch-wide "fries." Sprinkle with more sugar if desired.

Arrange the fries in the air fryer basket in a single layer. Cook for 3 to 4 minutes, or until gently browned. Allow cooling in the basket until hard enough to transfer to a wire rack to finish cooling. Rep with the remaining dough.

To make strawberry "ketchup," use the back of a spoon to push jam through a fine-mesh sieve. Next, stir in the chipotle powder. Next, whip the lemon curd until it is dippable for the "mustard." Serve the strawberry ketchup and lemon curd mustard with the sugar cookie fries.

Breakfast Mushroom Quiche

Prep time: 10 minutes **Cooking time:** 10 minutes
Servings: 4

Ingredients

1 tablespoon flour	1 tablespoon butter, soft
2 button mushrooms, chopped	3 eggs
1 small yellow onion, chopped	9 inch pie dough
	A pinch of nutmeg, ground
	2 tbsp ham, chopped
Salt and black pepper to the taste	1/4 cup Swiss cheese, grated
1/2 teaspoon thyme, dried	1/3 cup heavy cream

Directions

Dust a working surface with the flour and roll the pie dough. Press in on the bottom of the pie pan your air fryer has. In a bowl, mix butter with mushrooms, ham, onion, eggs, heavy cream, salt, pepper, thyme and nutmeg and whisk well.

Add this over pie crust, spread, sprinkle Swiss cheese all over and place pie pan in your air fryer. Cook your quiche at 400 degrees F for 10 minutes. Slice and serve for breakfast. Enjoy!

Duo-Cheese Roll

Prep time: 10 minutes **Cooking time:** 20 minutes
Servings: 12

Ingredients

2 1/2 cups shredded Mozzarella cheese	1 cup blanched finely ground almond flour
2 ounces (57 g) cream cheese, softened	1/2 teaspoon vanilla extract
1/2 cup Erythritol	1 tbsp ground cinnamon

Directions

In a large microwave-safe bowl, combine Mozzarella cheese, cream cheese, and flour. Microwave the mixture on high 90 seconds until cheese is melted. Add vanilla extract and Erythritol, and mix until a dough forms.

When the dough is processed to work with your hands, about 2 minutes, spread it out into a 12-inch × 4-inch rectangle on ungreased parchment paper. Evenly sprinkle dough with cinnamon.

Begin at the long side of the dough; roll lengthwise to form a log. Slice the log into twelve even pieces. Divide rolls between two ungreased 6-inch round nonstick baking dishes. Place one dish into air fryer basket. Adjust the temperature to 375F (190C) and set the timer for 10 minutes. Cinnamon rolls will be done when golden around the edges and mostly firm. Repeat with second dish. Allow rolls to cool in dishes 10 minutes before serving.

Sausage with Peppers

Prep time: 15 minutes **Cooking time:** 15 minutes
Servings: 4

Ingredients

1/2 pound (227 g) spicy ground pork breakfast sausage	4 ounces (113 g) full-fat cream cheese, softened
1/4 cup canned diced tomatoes and green chiles, drained	4 large eggs
	8 tablespoons shredded pepper jack cheese
1/2 cup full-fat sour cream	4 large poblano peppers

Directions

In a skillet medium heat, crumble and brown the ground sausage until no pink remains. Detach sausage and drain the fat from the pan. Crack eggs into the pan, scramble, and cook until no longer runny.

Place cooked sausage in a large bowl and fold in cream cheese. Mix in diced tomatoes and chilies. Gently fold in eggs.
Cut a 4-inch–5-inch slit in the top of each poblano, removing the seeds and white membrane with a small knife. Separate the filling into four **Servings:** and spoon carefully into each pepper. Top each with 2 tablespoons pepper jack cheese.

Place each pepper into the air fryer basket.
Adjust the temperature to 350F (180C) and set the timer for 15 minutes.

Peppers will be soft and cheese will be browned when ready. Serve immediately with sour cream on top.

Chocolate Chip Muffin

Prep time: 5 minutes **Cooking time:** 15 minutes
Servings: 6

Ingredients

11/2 cups finely ground almond flour	4 tablespoons salted butter, melted
1/3 cup granular brown Erythritol	2 large eggs, whisked
	1 tbsp baking powder
	1/2 cup low-carb chocolate chips

Directions

In a large bowl, combine all Ingredients. Evenly pour batter into six silicone muffin cups greased with cooking spray.

Place muffin cups into air fryer basket. Adjust the temperature to 320°F (160ºC) and set the timer for 15 minutes. Muffins will be golden brown when done.

Let muffins cool in cups 15 minutes to avoid crumbling. Serve warm.

Cheesy Bell Pepper Eggs

Prep time: 10 minutes **Cooking time:** 15 minutes
Servings: 4

Ingredients

4 medium green bell peppers ounces (85 g) cooked ham, chopped
1 cup mild Cheddar cheese

1/4 medium onion, peeled and chopped
8 large eggs

Directions

Cut the tops off each bell pepper. Remove the seeds and the white membranes with a small knife. Place ham and onion into each pepper.

Crack 2 eggs into each pepper. Top with 1/4 cup cheese per pepper. Place into the air fryer basket.

Adjust the temperature to 390F (199C) and air fry for 15 minutes. When fully cooked, peppers will be tender and eggs will be firm. Serve immediately.

Bacon-and-Eggs Avocado

Prep time: 5 minutes **Cooking time:** 17 minutes
Servings: 1

Ingredients

1 large egg
Fresh parsley, for serving (optional)

1 avocado, halved, peeled, and pitted slices
bacon
Sea salt flakes, for garnish (optional)

Directions

Set the air fryer basket with avocado oil. Preheat the air fryer to 320F (160C). Fill a small bowl with cool water.
Soft-boil the egg Place the egg in the air fryer basket. Air fry for 6 minutes for a soft yolk or 7 minutes for a cooked yolk. Bring the egg to the bowl of cool water and let sit for 2 minutes. Peel and set aside.

Use a spoon to carve out extra space in the center of the avocado halves until the cavities are big enough to fit the soft-boiled egg. Place the soft-boiled egg in the center of one half of the avocado and replace the other half of the avocado on top, so the avocado appears whole on the outside.

Starting at one end of the avocado, wrap the bacon around the avocado to completely cover it.

Place the bacon-wrapped avocado in the air fryer basket and air fry for 5 minutes. Flip the avocado over and air fry for another 5 minutes or until the bacon is cooked to your liking. Serve on a bed of fresh parsley, if desired, and sprinkle with salt flakes, if desired. Best served fresh.

Double-Dipped Mini Cinnamon Biscuits

Prep time: 15 minutes **Cooking time:** 13 minutes
Servings: 8

Ingredients

2 cups blanched almond flour
1/4 cup unsweetened, unflavored almond milk
1 teaspoon baking powder
1/2 teaspoon fine sea salt
1 large egg
Glaze

1/2 cup Swerve confectioners'-style sweetener or equivalent amount of powdered sweetener

1/2 cup Swerve confectioners'-style sweetener or equivalent amount of liquid or powdered sweetener
1/4 cup plus 2 tbsp(3/4 stick) very cold unsalted butter
1 teaspoon vanilla extract
teaspoons ground cinnamon
1/4 cup heavy cream or unsweetened, unflavored almond milk

Directions

Preheat the air fryer to 350F (177C). Line a pie pan that fits into your air fryer with parchment paper.

In a medium-sized bowl, mix together the almond flour, sweetener (if powdered; do not add liquid sweetener), baking powder, and salt. Cut the butter into 1/2-inch squares, and then use a hand mixer to work the butter into the dry Ingredients.

In a small bowl, pour together the almond milk, egg, and vanilla extract (if using liquid sweetener, add it as well) until blended. With a fork, merge the wet Ingredients into the dry Ingredients until large clumps form. Attach the cinnamon and use your hands to swirl it into the dough.
Form the dough into sixteen 1-inch balls and place them on the prepared pan, spacing them about 1/2 inches apart. (If you're using a smaller air fryer, work in batches if necessary.) Bake in the air fryer until golden, 10 to 13 minutes. Detach from the air fryer and let cool on the pan for at least 5 minutes.

While the biscuits bake, make the glaze Place the powdered sweetener in a small bowl and slowly stir in the heavy cream with a fork.

When the biscuits have cooled somewhat, dip the tops into the glaze, allow it to dry a bit, and then dip again for a thick glaze. Serve warm or at room temperature. Store unglazed biscuits in an

airtight container in the refrigerator. Reheat in a preheated 350F (177C) air fryer for 5 minutes, or until warmed through, and dip in the glaze as instructed above.

Air Fryer Hasselback Potatoes

Prep time: 15 minutes **Cooking time:** 18 minutes
Serve: 1

Ingredients

4 medium Yukon Gold potatoes	1 tablespoon olive oil
3 cloves garlic, crushed	3 tbsp melted butter
salt and ground black pepper to taste	½ tbsp ground paprika
	1 tablespoon chopped fresh parsley

Directions

Preheat an air fryer carefully to 350°F (175 degrees C). Make 1/4-inch or 1/2-inch slices across the full length of each potato, making sure the knife only cuts through to the bottom 1/2-inch, leaving the bottom of the potato intact.
Combine the butter, olive oil, garlic, and paprika in a small mixing bowl. Brush some of the mixtures into the slits of each potato. Season with salt and pepper to taste.

Cook the potatoes in the air fryer basket for 15 minutes. Brushing the potatoes with the butter mixture again, being careful to get it all the way down into the fanned-out slices to prevent them from drying out. Cook for another 15 minutes, or until the potatoes are tender.

Remove the potatoes from the basket and brush with any leftover butter mixture. **Serve:** immediately garnished with chopped parsley.

Air Fryer Ranch Pork Chops

Prep time: 10 minutes **Cooking time:** 18 minutes
Serve: 1

Ingredients

4 boneless	cooking spray
2 teaspoons dry ranch salad dressing mix	
aluminum foil	

Directions

Place the pork chops on a dish and coat both sides lightly with cooking spray. Allow both sides to remain at room temperature for 10 minutes after sprinkling with ranch seasoning mix.

Preheat an air fryer carefully to 390 degrees F and coat the
basket with cooking spray (200 degrees C). Place the chops in the preheated air fryer, working in batches if required to avoid overcrowding.

5 minutes in the oven Cook for another 5 minutes on the other side. Allow it to rest for 5 minutes on a foil-covered dish before serving

Air Fryer Meatloaf

Prep time: 18 minutes **Cooking time:** 20 minutes
Serve: 1

Ingredients

1-pound lean ground beef	3 tablespoons dry breadcrumbs
1 egg, lightly beaten	
1 tablespoon chopped fresh thyme	ground black pepper to taste 2 mushrooms, thickly sliced
1 teaspoon salt	
1 tablespoon olive oil, or as needed	1 small onion, chopped

Directions

Preheat an air fryer carefully at 392°F (200 degrees C). Combine ground beef, egg, breadcrumbs, onion, thyme, salt, and pepper in a mixing bowl. Knead and completely combine.

Smooth the top of the beef mixture in a baking pan. Coat the mushrooms in olive oil and press them into the top. Insert the pan into the air fryer basket and place it in it. Set the air fryer to 25 minutes and roast the meatloaf until it is well browned.

Allow the meatloaf to rest for at least 10 minutes before slicing it into wedges and serving it.

Air Fryer Portobello Pizzas for Two

Prep time: 15 minutes **Cooking time:** 20 minutes
Serve: 1

Ingredients

2 tablespoons olive oil	1 tbsp Italian seasoning
2 portobello mushroom caps, gills removed	6 tablespoons pizza sauce
	2 tbsp sliced black olives
5 tablespoons shredded mozzarella cheese, divided	8 pepperoni slices

Directions

Preheat an air fryer carefully to 350°F (175 degrees C). 1 tablespoon olive oil, rubbed on each mushroom. Fill each with 1/2 teaspoon Italian spice.
Place the mushrooms, cap sides up, in the air fryer basket. 3 minutes in the air fryer Turn the mushrooms over in the basket so that the cap is facing down.

Divide the pizza sauce evenly between the two mushrooms. 2 tablespoons shredded mozzarella and 1 tablespoon chopped olives on top 3 minutes in the air fryer Cover each pizza with 4 pepperoni pieces and the remaining mozzarella cheese. The pepperoni must be weighed down with cheese, or the fan will blow them off the pie. Air fried for 2 minutes, or until the cheese is melted and the pepperoni is browned.

Simple Ham and Pepper Omelet

Prep time: 5 minutes **Cooking time:** 8 minutes
Servings: 1

Ingredients

2 large eggs
1/4 teaspoon fine sea salt
1/8 teaspoon ground black pepper
2 tablespoons diced green onions, plus more for garnish
1/4 cup diced red bell peppers
Quartered cherry tomatoes, for serving (optional)

1/4 cup unsweetened, unflavored almond milk
1/4 cup diced ham (omit for vegetarian)
1/4 cup shredded Cheddar cheese (about 1 ounce / 28g) (omit for dairy-free)

Directions

Preheat the air fryer to 350F (180C). Grease a 6 by 3-inch cake pan and set aside.
In a bowl, use a fork to whisk together the eggs, almond milk, salt, and
pepper. Add the ham, bell peppers, and green onions. Pour the mixture into the greased pan. Add the cheese on top (if using).
Set the pan in the basket of the air fryer. Cook for 8 minutes, or until
the eggs are cooked to your liking.
Detach the omelet from the sides of the pan with a spatula and place it on a serving plate. Garnish with green onions and serve with cherry tomatoes, if desired. Best served fresh.

Ham with Avocado

Prep time: 5 minutes **Cooking time:** 10 minutes
Servings: 2

Ingredients

1 large Hass avocado, halved and pitted
2 tablespoons green onions, plus more for garnish
1/4 cup Cheddar cheese (omit for dairy-free)

2 large eggs
2 thin slices ham
1/4 teaspoon ground black pepper

1/2 teaspoon fine sea salt

Directions

Preheat the air fryer to 400F (205C). Place a slice of ham into the cavity of each avocado half. Crack an egg on top of the ham, then sprinkle on the green onions, salt, and pepper.

Set the avocado halves in the air fryer cut side up and cook for 10 minutes. Top with the cheese (if using) and cook for 30 seconds more, or until the cheese is melted. Garnish with chopped green onions. Best served fresh.

Sausage Eggs with Smoky Mustard Sauce

Prep time: 20 minutes **Cooking time:** 12 minutes
Servings: 8

Ingredients

1 pound (454 g) pork sausage
1 large egg
2 tablespoons milk
1/4 cup mayonnaise
1 tablespoon Dijon mustard
1 teaspoon chipotle hot sauce

8 soft-boiled or hard-boiled eggs, peeled

1 cup crushed pork rinds
2 tablespoons sour cream
Smoky Mustard Sauce

Directions

Preheat the air fryer to 390F (199C) Divide the sausage into 8 portions. Take each portion of sausage, pat it down into a patty, and place 1 egg in the middle, gently wrapping the sausage around the egg until the egg is completely covered. (Wet your hands slightly if you find the sausage to be too sticky.) Repeat with the remaining eggs and sausage.

In a small bowl, merge the egg and milk until frothy. In another shallow bowl, place the crushed pork rinds. Working one at a time, dip a sausage-wrapped egg into the beaten egg and then into the pork rinds, gently rolling to coat evenly. Repeat with the remaining sausage- wrapped eggs.

Set the eggs in the device, and lightly spray with olive oil. Air fry for 10 to 12 minutes, pausing halfway through the baking time to turn the eggs, until the eggs are hot and the sausage is cooked. To make the sauce In a bowl, merge the mayonnaise, sour cream, Dijon, and hot sauce. Whisk until thoroughly combined. Serve with the Scotch eggs.

Pecan and Almond Granola

Prep time: 10 minutes **Cooking time:** 5 minutes
Servings: 6

Ingredients

2 cups pecans, chopped
1 cup almond slivers
1/3 cup sunflower seeds
1/4 cup golden flaxseed
2 tablespoons unsalted butter
1/4 cup granular Erythritol

1 cup unsweetened coconut flakes
1/4 cup low-carb, sugar-free chocolate chips
1 teaspoon ground cinnamon

Directions

In a large bowl, mix all Ingredients. Place the mixture into a 4-cup round baking dish. Place dish into the air fryer basket. Adjust the temperature to 320F (160C) and set the timer for 5 minutes. Allow to cool completely before serving.

Air Fryer Roasted Bananas

Prep time: 15 minutes **Cooking time:** 25 minutes
Serve: 1

Ingredients

1 banana, sliced into 1/8-inch-thick diagonals
avocado oil cooking spray

Directions

The parchment paper should be used to line the air fryer basket.

Preheat an air fryer carefully to 375°F (190 degrees C). Place the banana slices in the basket, ensuring they don't touch; cook in batches if required. Avocado oil should be sprayed on banana slices.

Cook for 5 minutes in the air fryer. Remove the basket and carefully turn the banana slices (soft). Cook for another 2 to 3 minutes, or until the banana slices are browning and caramelized. Remove from the basket with caution.

Air Fryer Crab Rangoon

Prep time: 20 minutes **Cooking time:** 25 minutes
Serve: 1

Ingredients

1 (8 ounces) package cream cheese
1 teaspoon soy sauce
2 tbs chopped scallions
2 tbs Asian sweet chili sauce
4 ounces lump crab meat
1 serving nonstick cooking spray
1 teaspoon Worcestershire sauce
24 each wonton wrappers

Directions

In a mixing bowl, add cream cheese, crab meat, scallions, soy sauce, and Worcestershire sauce, whisk until well blended. Preheat an air fryer carefully to 350°F (175 degrees C). Coat the air fryer basket with cooking spray. Warm water should be placed in a small dish.

On a clean work area, arrange 12 wonton wrappers. 1 teaspoon cream cheese mixture should be placed in the center of each wonton wrapper. Wet the sides of each wonton wrapper with your index finger after dipping it into the warm water. Crimp the wrapper corners upwards until they meet in the middle to make dumplings.

Spray the tops of the dumplings with cooking spray and place them in the prepared basket. Cook dumplings for 8 to 10 minutes, or until desired crispness is achieved. Transfer to a plate lined with paper towels. While the first dumplings are cooking, construct the remaining dumplings using the leftover wrappers and filling.
Serve: with sweet chili sauce as a dipping sauce.

Air Fryer Fish Sticks

Prep time: 15 minutes **Cooking time:** 20 minutes
Serve: 1

Ingredients

1 pound cod fillets
½ cup panko breadcrumbs
1 egg
1 tablespoon parsley flakes,
1 teaspoon paprika
¼ cup all-purpose flour
¼ cup grated Parmesan cheese
½ teaspoon black pepper
cooking spray

Directions

Preheat an air fryer carefully to 400°F (200 degrees C). Pat the fish dry using paper towels before slicing it into 1x3-inch pieces.

In a small bowl, combine the flour and salt. In a separate shallow dish, beat the egg. In a third shallow dish, combine panko, Parmesan cheese, parsley, paprika, and pepper.
Each fish stick should be coated in flour, then dipped in beaten egg, and then coated in seasoned panko mixture.
Spray the air fryer basket with nonstick cooking spray. Arrange half of the sticks in the basket, ensuring none of them is a contact. Cooking spray should be sprayed on the top of each stick. Cook for 5 minutes in a hot air fryer. Cook for a further 5 minutes after flipping the fish sticks. Rep with the rest of the fish sticks.

Air-Fryer Asparagus Fries

Prep time: 15 minutes **Cooking time:** 22 minutes
Serve: 1

Ingredients

1 large egg
1 cup panko breadcrumbs
12 asparagus spears,
¼ cup stone-ground mustard
1 pinch cayenne pepper (Optional)
1 teaspoon honey
½ cup grated Parmesan cheese
¼ cup Greek yogurt

Directions

Preheat an air fryer carefully to 400°F (200 degrees C). In a long, thin bowl, whisk together the egg and honey. In a separate dish, combine panko and Parmesan cheese. Coat each asparagus stalk in the egg mixture before rolling in the panko mixture to coat.

Cook 6 spears in the air fryer for 4 to 6 minutes, or until desired brownness is achieved. Rep with the remaining spears.

Combine the mustard, yogurt, and cayenne pepper in a small bowl. Serve with asparagus spears and dipping sauce.

Cheesy Cauliflower Tots

Prep time: 15 minutes **Cooking time:** 12 minutes
Servings: 16

Ingredients

1 large head cauliflower	1 cup shredded Mozzarella cheese
1/2 cup grated Parmesan cheese	1/4 teaspoon dried parsley
1 large egg	1/4 teaspoon garlic powder 1/8 teaspoon onion powder

Directions

On the stovetop, set a large pot with 2 cups water and place a steamer in the pan. Bring water to a boil. Divide the cauliflower into florets and set on steamer basket. Cover pot with lid.

Allow cauliflower to steam 7 minutes until fork tender. Remove from steamer basket and place into cheesecloth or clean kitchen towel and let cool. Squeeze over sink to remove as much excess moisture as possible. The mixture will be too soft to form into tots if not all the moisture is removed. Beat with a fork to a smooth consistency.

Put the cauliflower into a large mixing bowl and add Mozzarella, Parmesan, egg, garlic powder, parsley, and onion powder. Stir until fully combined. The mixture should be wet but easy to mold.

Take 2 tablespoons of the mixture and roll into tot shape. Repeat with remaining mixture. Place into the air fryer basket.

Adjust the temperature to 320F (160C) and set the timer for 12 minutes. Turn tots halfway through the cooking time. Cauliflower tots should be golden when fully cooked. Serve warm.

Cauliflower with Lime Juice

Prep time: 10 minutes **Cooking time:** 7 minutes
Servings: 4

Ingredients

2 cups chopped cauliflower florets	1/2 teaspoon garlic powder
2 tbsp coconut oil, melted	1 medium lime
2 tbsp chopped cilantro	2 teaspoons chili powder

Directions

In a bowl, merge cauliflower with coconut oil. Sprinkle with chili powder and garlic powder. Set seasoned cauliflower into the air fryer basket.

Set the temperature to 350F (180C). Cauliflower will be juicy and begin to turn golden at the edges. Set into serving bowl. Divide the lime into quarters and squeeze juice over cauliflower. Garnish with cilantro.

Cheesy Cauliflower Rice Balls

Prep time: 10 minutes **Cooking time:** 8 minutes
Servings: 4

Ingredients

1 (10-ounce / 283-g) steamer bag cauliflower rice, cooked according to package instructions	1/2 cup shredded Mozzarella cheese
	1 large egg
2 ounces (57 g) plain pork rinds, finely crushed	1/2 teaspoon Italian seasoning
1/4 teaspoon salt	

Directions

Place cauliflower into a large bowl and mix with Mozzarella. Whisk egg in a separate medium bowl. Place pork rinds into another large bowl with salt and Italian seasoning.

Separate cauliflower mixture into four equal sections and form each into a ball. Carefully dip a ball into whisked egg, and then roll in pork rinds. Repeat with remaining balls.

Place cauliflower balls into ungreased air fryer basket. Adjust the temperature to 400F (205C) and set the timer for 8 minutes. Rice balls will be golden when done.
Use a spatula to move cauliflower balls to a large dish for serving carefully. Serve warm.

Broccoli with Sesame Dressing

Prep time: 5 minutes **Cooking time:** 10 minutes
Servings: 4

Ingredients

6 cups broccoli florets	2 tablespoons sesame seeds
1 tablespoon olive oil	2 tablespoons rice vinegar
2 tablespoons coconut aminos	1/2 teaspoon Swerve
	1/4 teaspoon salt
1/4 tbsp red pepper flakes	2 tablespoons sesame oil

Directions

Preheat the air fryer to 400F (205C). In a bowl, merge the broccoli with the olive oil and salt until thoroughly coated.
Transfer the broccoli to the air fryer basket. Pausing halfway through the cooking time to shake the basket, air fry for 10 minutes.

Meanwhile, in the same large bowl, whisk together the sesame seeds, vinegar, coconut aminos, sesame oil, Serve, and red pepper flakes (if using). Transfer the broccoli to the bowl and toss until thoroughly coated with the seasonings. Serve warm or at room temperature.

Tomato Salad with Arugula

Prep time: 10 minutes **Cooking time:** 10 minutes
Servings: 4

Ingredients

4 green tomatoes
1 large egg, lightly beaten
1/2 cup peanut flour
1 cup mayonnaise
1/2 cup sour cream
2 tablespoons finely chopped fresh parsley
1/2 teaspoon garlic powder
1 (5-ounce / 142-g) bag arugula Buttermilk Dressing

1/2 teaspoon salt
1 tablespoon Creole seasoning
2 teaspoons fresh lemon juice
1 teaspoon dried chives
1/2 teaspoon salt
1/2 teaspoon onion powder
1 teaspoon dried dill

Directions

Preheat the air fryer to 400F (205C). Divide the tomatoes into 1/2-inch slices and sprinkle with the salt. Let sit for 5 to 10 minutes. Set the egg in a small shallow bowl. In another small shallow bowl, combine the peanut flour and Creole seasoning. Soak each tomato slice into the egg wash, and then dip into the peanut flour mixture, turning to coat evenly.

Working in batches if necessary, arranges the tomato slices in a single layer in the air fryer basket and spray both sides lightly with olive oil. Air fry until browned and crisp, 8 to 10 minutes.

To make the buttermilk dressing In a small bowl, whisk together the mayonnaise, sour cream, lemon juice, parsley, dill, chives, salt, garlic powder, and onion powder.
Serve the tomato slices on top of a bed of the arugula with the dressing on the side.

Herb Tomato Egg Cups

Prep time: 10 minutes **Cooking time:** 12 minutes
Serve 6

Ingredients

5 eggs
½ cup tomatoes, chopped
Salt

1 medium onion, chopped
2 tbsp fresh parsley, chopped
2 tbsp fresh basil, chopped Pepper

Directions

Preheat the air fryer to 300 F. In a mixing bowl, whisk eggs with pepper and salt. Add onion, basil, parsley, and tomatoes and stir well. Pour egg mixture into the silicone muffin molds. Place muffin molds into the air fryer basket and cook for 10-12 minutes. Serve and enjoy.

Tasty Egg Bites

Prep time: 10 minutes **Cooking time:** 12 minutes
Serve 6

Ingredients

6 eggs
2 green onions, sliced
2 bacon slices, cooked & chopped
Pepper Salt

¼ tsp mustard powder
1 tbsp milk
¼ cup cheddar cheese, shredded
1 tbsp heavy cream

Directions

Preheat the air fryer to 350 F. In a bowl, whisk eggs with mustard powder, cream, pepper, and salt until fluffy.

Add green onions, cheese, and bacon and stir well. Pour egg mixture into the silicone muffin molds. Place muffin molds into the air fryer basket and cook for 10-12 minutes or until eggs are set. Serve and enjoy.

Cheese Sandwich

Prep time: 10 minutes **Cooking time:** 5 minutes
Serve 2

Ingredients

4 bread slices
4 oz cheddar cheese slices
2 tbsp butter

¼ tsp garlic powder
1 tomato, cut into slices

Directions

Preheat the air fryer to 350 F. Spread butter on one side of each bread slice. Take two bread slices and top with cheddar cheese slices and tomato slices.

Cover with remaining bread slices. Make sure buttered side up. Sprinkle garlic powder on top of sandwiches. Place sandwiches into the air fryer basket and cook for 4-5 minutes. Serve and enjoy.

Easy French Toast

Prep time: 10 minutes **Cooking time:** 10 minutes
Serve 2

Ingredients

2 eggs
¼ tsp cinnamon
½ cup milk

4 bread slices
1 tbsp sugar
1 tsp vanilla

Directions

Preheat the air fryer to 380 F. In a shallow bowl, whisk eggs with milk, sugar, vanilla, and cinnamon. Dip bread slices in egg mixture from both sides.

Place bread slices into the air fryer basket and cook for 4 minutes. Turn bread slices and cook for 6 minutes more. **Serve:** and enjoy.

Air Fryer Keto Thumbprint Cookies

Prep time: 15 minutes **Cooking time:** 22 minutes
Serve: 1

Ingredients

1 cup almond flour	2 ounces cream cheese,
1 egg	softened
3 tablespoons low-calorie	1 teaspoon baking powder
natural sweetener (such as	3 ½ tablespoons reduced-
Swerve®)	sugar raspberry preServe:s

Directions

In a mixing bowl, combine the flour, cream cheese, sweetener, egg, and baking powder until a moist dough forms.

Place the bowl in the freezer for 20 minutes or until the dough is cold enough to shape into balls.

According to the manufacturer's instructions, preheat an air fryer carefully to 400°F (200°C). Then, using parchment paper, line the basket.

Roll the dough into ten balls and set them in the prepared basket. In the center of each cookie, make a thumbprint. Fill each indentation with 1 spoonful of preServe:s. Cook for 7 minutes in a warm air fryer until the edges are golden brown.

Cool the cookies entirely before removing them from the parchment paper, about 15 minutes, or they will crumble.

Air Fryer Spicy Roasted Peanuts

Prep time: 10 minutes **Cooking time:** 18 minutes
Serve: 1

Ingredients

2 tablespoons olive oil	3 teaspoons seafood
salt to taste	seasoning
½ teaspoon cayenne	8 ounces raw Spanish
pepper	peanuts

Directions

Preheat an air fryer carefully to 320°F (160 degrees C). Combine olive oil, seafood seasoning, and cayenne pepper in a large mixing bowl. Stir in the peanuts until they are equally coated.

Place the peanuts in the air fryer basket. Cook the peanuts for 10 minutes in the air fryer. Cook for a further 10 minutes, tossing occasionally.

Remove the air fryer basket and season the peanuts to taste. Cook for 5 minutes more after tossing the peanuts one last time. Allow the peanuts to cool on a dish lined with paper towels

Air Fryer Roasted Salsa Verde

Prep time: 18 minutes **Cooking time:** 20 minutes
Serve: 1

Ingredients

1-pound tomatillos	1 serrano pepper, halved
1 jalapeno pepper, halved	and seeded
and seeded	1 serving cooking spray
½ large white onion, cut	4 cloves garlic, peeled
½ cup chopped cilantro	½ lime, juiced, or more to
1 pinch salt to taste	taste

Directions

Preheat the air fryer carefully to 390°F (200 degrees C).
Remove the husks from the tomatillos and rinse them; cut the tomatillos in half. Place the tomatillos and peppers in the air fryer basket, skin side down. Add the onion. To aid in the roasting process, lightly coat veggies with cooking spray. 5 minutes in the air fryer.

Open the basket and place the garlic cloves inside. Spray lightly with cooking spray and continue to air fry for 5 minutes.

Allow 10 minutes for the veggies to cool. Transfer to a food processor bowl. Combine the cilantro, lime juice, and salt in a mixing bowl. Pulse several times until the veggies are finely chopped, reaching the ideal consistency. Refrigerate or **Serve:** at room temperature to let flavors mingle

Air Fryer Spinach and Feta Casserole

Prep time: 15 minutes **Cooking time:** 20 minutes
Serve: 1

Ingredients

cooking spray	1 (13.5 ounces) can of
1 cup cottage cheese	spinach
2 eggs, beaten	2 tablespoons butter,
	melted
¼ cup crumbled feta	2 tablespoons all-purpose
cheese	flour
⅛ teaspoon ground	
nutmeg	
1 clove garlic, minced, or	1 ½ teaspoons onion
more to taste	powder

Directions

Preheat an air fryer carefully to 375°F (190 degrees C). Set aside an 8- inch pie tin sprayed with cooking spray.

In a mixing bowl, combine spinach, feta cheese, flour, butter, cottage cheese, eggs, garlic, onion powder, and nutmeg. Stir until all of the Ingredients are properly combined. Pour into the pie pan that has been prepared.
Air fry until the center is set, 15 to 20 minutes.

Flavorful Banana Muffins

Prep time: 10 minutes **Cooking time:** 15 minutes
Serve: 10

Ingredients

1 egg	¾ cup self-rising flour
1 tsp vanilla	½ cup brown sugar
1 tsp cinnamon	1/3 cup olive oil
2 ripe bananas	

Directions

Preheat the air fryer to 320 F. mIn a mixing bowl, add ripe bananas and mash using a fork. Add oil, brown sugar, vanilla, and egg and stir until well combined.

Add cinnamon and flour and mix until just combined. Spoon batter into the silicone muffin molds. Place muffin molds into the air fryer basket and cook for 15 minutes. **Serve:** and enjoy.

Quick & Easy Granola

Prep time: 10 minutes **Cooking time:** 10 minutes
Serve: 4

Ingredients

1 cup rolled oats	2 tbsp butter, melted 3
1 tsp vanilla	tbsp honey
1 tsp cinnamon	½ cup almonds, sliced
	Pinch of salt

Directions

In a mixing bowl, mix together oats, vanilla, butter, honey, cinnamon, almonds, and salt. Add granola mixture into the parchment-lined air fryer basket and cook for 10 minutes. Stir after every 2-3 minutes. **Serve:** and enjoy.

Breakfast Hush Puppies

Prep time: 10 minutes **Cooking time:** 10 minutes
Serve: 4

Ingredients

1 egg	¼ cup onion, chopped
¾ cup milk	½ tsp garlic powder
½ tsp onion powder	¼ tsp sugar
1 ½ tsp baking powder	¾ cup all-purpose flour
½ tsp salt	1 cup yellow cornmeal

Directions

In a mixing bowl, mix together cornmeal, flour, baking powder, sugar, onion, garlic powder, onion powder, and salt Add milk and egg and mix until well combined.

Make small balls from the cornmeal mixture and place into the parchment-lined air fryer basket and cook for 10 minutes. Turn halfway through. **Serve:** and enjoy.

Tasty Breakfast Potatoes

Prep time: 10 minutes **Cooking time:** 25 minutes
Serve: 4

Ingredients

1 ½ lbs. potatoes, diced	¼ tsp fennel seed
¼ tsp garlic powder	¼ cup onion, diced
Salt	Pepper
	2 bell peppers, sliced

Directions

Preheat the air fryer to 360 F. In a mixing bowl, toss potatoes with remaining Ingredients.

Add potato mixture into the air fryer basket and cook for 20-25 minutes. Stir after every 5 minutes. **Serve:** and enjoy.

Blueberry Oatmeal

Prep time: 10 minutes **Cooking time:** 15 minutes
Serve: 2

Ingredients

1 egg	¼ cup blueberries
2 tbsp maple syrup	¼ tsp baking powder
2 tbsp butter, melted	1/3 cup milk
½ tsp vanilla	½ tsp cinnamon
¾ cup rolled oats	¼ tsp salt

Directions

In a mixing bowl, mix together oats, egg, cinnamon, vanilla, baking powder, maple syrup, milk, and salt. Add blueberries and fold well.

Pour oat mixture into the two greased ramekins. Place ramekins into the air fryer basket and cook at 300 F for 12-15 minutes. **Serve:** and enjoy.

Banana Bread

Prep time: 10 minutes **Cooking time:** 15 minutes
Serve: 6

Ingredients

1 egg	¼ cup butter, melted
1/3 cup walnuts, chopped	3 bananas, overripe &
1 cup sugar	mashed
1 ½ cups all-purpose flour	½ tsp salt
1 tsp baking soda	

Directions

In a mixing bowl, mix together flour, baking soda, sugar, walnuts, and salt. Add melted butter, egg, and mashed bananas and mix until well combined.

Pour batter into the greased loaf pan. Place loaf pan into the air fryer basket and cook at 350 F for 12-15 minutes. Slice and **Serve:**.

Air Fryer Celery Root Fries

Prep time: 20 minutes **Cooking time:** 20 minutes
Serve: 1

Ingredients

½ celeriac (celery root), peeled and cut into 1/2-inch sticks
1 tablespoon brown mustard
1 tablespoon olive oil
⅓ cup vegan mayonnaise
1 tablespoon lime juice
3 cups water,
1 teaspoon powdered horseradish
1 pinch salt and ground black pepper

Directions

Place the celery root in a basin. Pour in the lime juice and water. Allow resting for 20 minutes after mixing. Preheat the air fryer carefully to 400°F (200 degrees C). Make the mayonnaise sauce. Combine vegan mayonnaise, mustard, and horseradish powder in a mixing bowl. Store in the refrigerator, covered, until required.

Drain and dry the celery root sticks before reserving them in a basin. Season the fries with salt and pepper after drizzling them with oil. To coat evenly, toss everything together. Place the celery root in the air fryer basket. Cook for about 10 minutes, testing for doneness halfway through. Shake the basket and cook for another 8 minutes, or until the fries are crisp and golden. **Serve:** the fries right away, with vegan mayo on the side.

Air Fryer Fried Okra

Prep time: 15 minutes **Cooking time:** 25 minutes
Serve: 1

Ingredients

1 large egg
1 cup cornmeal
¼ cup all-purpose flour
cooking spray
½ pound okra pods, cut into 1/2-inch slices
salt to taste

Directions

In a shallow bowl, beat the egg; carefully fold in the cut okra. In a gallon-size resealable plastic bag, combine cornmeal and flour. Place 5 okra slices in the cornmeal mixture, seal the bag, and shake. Transfer the breaded okra to a dish. Repeat with the rest of the okra slices.

Preheat the air fryer carefully to 400°F (200 degrees C). Spray half of the breaded okra pieces with cooking spray in the air fryer basket. Cook for 4 minutes. Shake the basket and respray the okra with frying spray.

Cook for another 4 minutes. Cook for 2 minutes after shaking the basket one more. Remove the okra from the basket and season with salt and pepper to taste. Repeat with the rest of the okra slices.

Lumpia in the Air Fryer

Prep time: 15 minutes **Cooking time:** 20 minutes
Serve: 1

Ingredients

1-pound Italian hot sausage links
¼ cup diced onions
½ cup finely chopped water chestnuts
2 cloves garlic, minced
¼ teaspoon ground ginger
½ cup finely sliced green onions
½ cup chopped carrots
2 tablespoons soy sauce
½ teaspoon salt
16 spring roll wrappers
avocado oil cooking spray

Directions

Remove the casing from the sausage and cook it in a pan over medium heat for 4 to 5 minutes, or until slightly browned. Combine the green onions, onions, carrots, and water chestnuts in a mixing bowl. Cook and stir for 5 to 7 minutes, or until the onions are tender and transparent. Cook for 1 to 2 minutes after adding the garlic. Soy sauce, salt, and ginger to taste. Remove from heat after stirring until the filling is fully mixed.

Place a spring roll wrapper at an angle on a plate. Fill the wrapper with a scant 1/4 cup of the filling. Fold the bottom corner over the filling and tuck in the edges to construct a roll. Wet your finger and softly wet the
edges. Rep with the rest of the wrappers and filling. Each roll should be sprayed with avocado oil spray.

Preheat an air fryer carefully to 390°F (198 degrees C). Place the lumpia rolls in the basket, making sure they don't touch; cook in batches as needed. Fry for 4 minutes, then turn and cook for another 4 minutes, or until the crispy skins.

Easy Air Fryer Apple Pies

Prep time: 15 minutes **Cooking time:** 18 minutes
Serve: 1

Ingredients

1 (14.1 ounces) package refrigerated pie crusts (2 pie crusts)
2 tablespoons cinnamon sugar, or to taste
1 (21 ounces) can apple pie filling
1 egg, beaten
1 serving cooking spray

Directions

Roll out 1 pie crust using a rolling pin on a lightly floured board. Cut the pie dough into 10 circles with a 2-1/4-inch round biscuit or cookie cutter. Repeat with the remaining pie dough to make 20 pie crust circles.

Fill approximately half of each circle with apple pie filling. Make a tiny pie by adding a second pie crust circle on top. Don't overfill the container. Crimp the edges of the tiny pies with a fork to seal them.Enjoy.

Vegan Recipes

Air Grilled Tofu

(**Ready in about** 15 minutes | **Servings:** 3)

Ingredients

8 ounces firm tofu, pressed and cut into bite-sized cubes 1 tablespoon tamari sauce
1/2 teaspoon onion powder

1 teaspoon peanut oil
1/2 teaspoon garlic powder

Directions

Toss the tofu cubes in a bowl with the tamari sauce, peanut oil, garlic powder, and onion powder.

Cook your tofu for about 13 minutes in a preheated Air Fryer at 380 degrees F, shaking the basket once or twice to ensure even browning. Good appetite!

Golden Beet Salad with Tahini Sauce

(**Ready in about** 40 minutes | **Servings:** 2)

Ingredients

2 golden beets
Sea salt and ground black pepper, to taste
2 tablespoons soy sauce
1/2 jalapeno pepper, chopped
1 clove garlic, pressed

1 tablespoon sesame oil
2 tablespoons tahini
2 cups baby spinach
1 tablespoon white vinegar
1/4 teaspoon ground cumin

Directions

Toss the golden beets with sesame oil. Cook the golden beets in the preheated Air Fryer at 400 degrees F for 40 minutes, turning them over once or twice to ensure even cooking.

Let your beets cool completely and then, slice them with a sharp knife. Place

the beets in a salad bowl and add in salt, pepper and baby spinach.

In a small mixing dish, whisk the remaining Ingredients until well combined.

Spoon the sauce over your beets, toss to combine and **Serve:** immediately. Bon appétit!

Easy Roasted Fennel

(**Ready in about** 25 minutes | **Servings:** 3)

Ingredients

1 pound fennel bulbs, sliced
1/2 teaspoon dried marjoram
1 tablespoon olive oil

1/2 teaspoon dried basil
1/4 cup vegan mayonnaise
Sea salt and ground black pepper, to taste

Directions

Toss the fennel slices with the olive oil and spices and transfer them to the Air Fryer cooking basket.

Roast the fennel at 370 degrees F for about 20 minutes, shaking the basket once or twice to promote even cooking. **Serve:** the fennel slice with mayonnaise and enjoy!

Asian-Style Brussels Sprouts

(**Ready in about** 20 minutes | **Servings:** 3)

Ingredients

1 pound Brussels sprouts, trimmed and halved
1 tablespoon agave syrup
1 teaspoon rice vinegar
1 clove garlic, minced
1 tbs sesame seeds, toasted

2 tablespoons Shoyu sauce
1 teaspoon coconut oil
1/2 teaspoon Gochujang paste
2 scallion stalks, chopped

Directions

Toss the Brussels sprouts with coconut oil, Shoyu sauce, agave syrup, rice vinegar, Gochujang paste and garlic. Cook the Brussels sprouts in the preheated Air Fryer at 380 degrees F for 15 minutes, shaking the basket halfway through the cooking time.

Place the roasted Brussels sprouts on a serving platter and garnish with scallions and sesame seeds. **Serve:** immediately!

Healthy Jicama & Green Beans

Prep time: 10 minutes **Cooking time:** 45 minutes
Serve: 6

Ingredients
12 oz green beans, sliced in half	1 tsp dried thyme
3 garlic cloves, minced	3 tbsp canola oil
1 tsp dried rosemary	1/2 tsp salt
	1 medium jicama, cubed

Directions

Preheat the air fryer to 400 F. Add green beans, jicama, and remaining ingredients into the mixing bowl and toss well.

Spread green beans and jicama mixture into the air fryer basket and cook for 45 minutes. Stir halfway through. **Serve:** and enjoy.

Crispy Brussels Sprouts

Prep time: 10 minutes **Cooking time:** 15 minutes
Serve: 4

Ingredients
2 cups Brussels sprouts	1/4 cup almonds, crushed
2 tbsp everything bagel seasoning Pepper	Salt
	2 tbsp canola oil

Directions

Preheat the air fryer to 375 F. Add Brussels sprouts into the saucepan with 2 cups of water. Cover and cook for 10 minutes. Drain well and let it cool completely.

Cut each Brussels sprouts in half. Add Brussels sprouts and remaining ingredients into the bowl and toss to coat. Add Brussels sprouts into the air fryer basket and cook for 15 minutes. Stir halfway through. **Serve:** and enjoy.

Flavorful Green Beans

Prep time: 5 minutes **Cooking time:** 10 minutes
Serve: 2

Ingredients
2 cups green beans	1/8 tsp cayenne pepper
1/2 tsp dried oregano	1/8 tsp ground allspice
1/4 tsp ground coriander	1/2 tsp salt
1/4 tsp ground cumin	2 tbsp canola oil
1/4 tsp ground cinnamon	

Directions

Preheat the air fryer to 370 F. Add green beans and remaining ingredients into the mixing bowl and toss well.
Add green beans into the air fryer basket and cook for 8-10 minutes. Stir halfway through. **Serve:** and enjoy.

Easy Ratatouille

Prep time: 10 minutes **Cooking time:** 15 minutes
Serve: 6

Ingredients
1 eggplant, diced	2 bell peppers, diced
2 tbsp herb de Provence	1 onion, diced
1 tbsp vinegar	1 1/2 tbsp olive oil
3 tomatoes, diced	2 garlic cloves, chopped
Pepper	Salt

Directions

Preheat the air fryer to 400 F. Add all ingredients into the bowl and toss well and transfer into the air fryer baking dish. Place baking dish into the air fryer basket and cook for 15 minutes. **Serve:** and enjoy.

Tasty Zucchini Chips

Prep time: 10 minutes **Cooking time:** 12 minutes
Serve: 3

Ingredients
1 large zucchini, cut into slices	3 tbsp roasted pecans, crushed
1 tbsp olive oil	1 tbsp Bagel seasoning
3 tbsp almond flour	

Directions

Preheat the air fryer to 350 F. Add zucchini slices, crushed pecans, almond flour, oil, and bagel seasoning into the mixing bowl and toss until well coated.

Arrange zucchini slices into the air fryer basket and cook for 12 minutes. Turn halfway through. **Serve:** and enjoy.

Crispy Cauliflower Tots

Prep time: 10 minutes **Cooking time:** 12 minutes
Serve: 4

Ingredients
1 large cauliflower head, cut into florets	2 tbsp arrowroot
1/4 cup extra-virgin olive oil	3 tbsp hot sauce
	1 tbsp olive oil Pepper
	Salt

Directions

Preheat the air fryer to 380 F. Toss cauliflower florets with oil and coat with arrowroot. Add cauliflower florets into the air fryer basket and cook for 6 minutes. Meanwhile, in a mixing bowl, mix together hot sauce and extra-virgin olive oil.

Once cauliflower florets are cooked then transfer them into the sauce and toss well. Return cauliflower florets into the air fryer basket and cook for 6 minutes more. Serve and enjoy.

Air Fryer Roasted Garlic

Prep time: 15 minutes **Cooking time:** 20 minutes
Serve: 1

Ingredients

1 head garlic aluminum foil	1 tbsp extra-virgin olive oil
¼ teaspoon salt	¼ tbs ground black pepper

Directions

Preheat the air fryer carefully to 380°F (190 degrees C).
Remove the top of the garlic head and set it on a square piece of aluminum foil. Wrap the foil around the garlic. Season with salt and pepper and drizzle with olive oil. Fold the ends of the foil over the garlic to form a pouch.
16 to 20 minutes in the air fryer until the garlic is tender. Open the foil package with extreme caution, as hot steam will escape.

Air Fryer Latkes

Prep time: 15 minutes **Cooking time:** 25 minutes
Serve: 1

Ingredients

1 (16 ounces) package frozen shredded hash brown potatoes	1 egg
½ cup shredded onion	2 tablespoons matzo meal cooking spray
avocado oil	kosher salt and ground black pepper to taste

Directions

The manufacturer's instructions preheat an air fryer carefully to 375°F (190°C). Next, prepare a piece of parchment or waxed paper.

Place the thawed potatoes and shredded onion between layers of paper towels. Cover with extra paper towels and wring out as much liquid as possible.

Combine the egg, salt, and pepper in a large mixing bowl. With a fork, mix in the potatoes and onion. Stir in the matzo meal until the ingredients are uniformly distributed. Form the mixture into ten 3- to 4- inch broad patties with your hands. Place the patties on a sheet of parchment or waxed paper.

Cooking spray should be sprayed on the air fryer basket. Place half of the patties properly in the basket and coat with cooking spray generously.

Air-fry for 10 to 12 minutes, or until the exterior is crispy and dark golden brown. (If you like a softer latke, check for doneness at 8 minutes.) Transfer the latkes to a plate. In the same manner, cook the remaining patties and coat them with cooking spray before cooking.

Air Fryer Stuffed Mushrooms

Prep time: 15 minutes **Cooking time:** 20 minutes
Serve: 1

Ingredients

1 (16 ounces) package whole white button mushrooms	4 ounces cream cheese, softened
¼ cup finely shredded sharp Cheddar cheese	¼ teaspoon ground paprika
	1 pinch salt
cooking spray	2 scallions

Directions

Gently clean the mushrooms with a moist towel. Remove and discard the stems. Separate the white and green sections of the scallions. Preheat an air fryer carefully to 360°F (182 degrees C).

In a small mixing dish, combine cream cheese, Cheddar cheese, the white sections of the scallions, paprika, and salt. Stuff the filling into the mushrooms, pushing it in with the back of a small spoon to fill the cavity. Cooking sprays the air fryer basket and place the mushrooms inside. You may need to perform two batches depending on the size of your air fryer. Cook for 8 minutes or until the filling is gently browned. Rep with the remaining mushrooms.

Air Fryer Turkey Breast

Prep time: 15 minutes **Cooking time:** 25 minutes
Serve: 1

Ingredients

1 tablespoon finely chopped fresh rosemary	1 teaspoon finely minced fresh garlic
½ teaspoon salt	¼ teaspoon ground black pepper
1 teaspoon finely chopped fresh chives	
2 ¾ pounds skin-on, bone-in split turkey breast	2 tbsp cold unsalted butter

Directions

Preheat the air fryer carefully to 350°F (175 degrees C).
Combine the rosemary, chives, garlic, salt, and pepper on a chopping board. Place thin slices of butter on the herbs and spices and mash until thoroughly combined.

Pat the turkey breast dry and massage it on both sides and beneath the skin with herbed butter.
Place the turkey in the air fryer basket, skin side down, and cook for 20 minutes.

Turn the turkey skin-side up and fry for another 18 minutes, or until an instant-read thermometer placed near the bone registers 165 degrees F (74 degrees C). Transfer to a dish and tent with aluminum foil for 10 minutes to rest. **Serve:** heated, sliced.

Louisiana-Style Eggplant Cutlets

(**Ready in about** 45 minutes | **Servings:** 3)

Ingredients

1 pound eggplant, cut lengthwise into	1/4 cup almond milk
1 cup fresh bread crumbs	1/4 cup plain flour
1/2-inch thick slices	1 teaspoon Cajun seasoning mix
Sea salt and ground black pepper, to taste	1 teaspoon brown mustard 1/2 teaspoon chili powder
1 cup tomato sauce	

Directions

Toss your eggplant with 1 teaspoon of salt and leave it for 30 minutes; drain and rinse the eggplant and set it aside.

In a shallow bowl, mix the flour with almond milk until well combined. In a separate bowl, mix the breadcrumbs with Cajun seasoning mix, salt and black pepper.

Dip your eggplant in the flour mixture, then, coat each slice with the breadcrumb mixture, pressing to adhere.

Cook the breaded eggplant at 400 degrees F for 10 minutes, flipping them halfway through the **Cooking time:**to ensure even browning.

In the meantime, mix the remaining Ingredients for the sauce. Divide the tomato mixture between eggplant cutlets and continue to cook for another 5 minutes or until thoroughly cooked.

Transfer the warm eggplant cutlets to a wire rack to stay crispy. Bon appétit

Fried Green Beans

(**Ready in about** 10 minutes | **Servings:** 2)

Ingredients

1/2 pound green beans, cleaned and trimmed	1/2 teaspoon onion powder
1 tspn extra-virgin olive oil	1/2 tbsp garlic powder
1/2 tbsp shallot powder	1/4 cup pecans,chopped
1/4 tbsp cumin powder	Himalayan salt and freshly ground black pepper, to taste
1/2 teaspoon cayenne pepper	
1 tablespoon soy sauce	1 tablespoon lime juice

Directions

Toss the green beans with olive oil, spices and lime juice.

Cook the green beans in your Air Fryer at 400 degrees F for 5 minutes, shaking the basket halfway through the Cooking tim**e** to promote even cooking.

Toss the green beans with soy sauce and Serve garnished with chopped pecans. Bon appétit!

Portobello Mushroom Schnitzel

(**Ready in about** 10 minutes | **Servings:** 2)

Ingredients

7 ounces Portobello mushrooms	1/4 cup plain flour
1/3 cup beer	1/2 tbsp garlic powder
1/2 teaspoon porcini powder	1 cup breadcrumbs
1/2 teaspoon dried basil	1/4 teaspoon dried oregano 1/4 teaspoon ground cumin 1/4 teaspoon ground bay leaf
1/4 cup chickpea flour ground black pepper, to taste	1/2 teaspoon shallot powder
Kosher salt	

Directions

Set aside the Portobello mushrooms after patting them dry.

Then, in a rimmed plate, combine the flour and beer thoroughly. In a separate bowl, combine the breadcrumbs and spices.

Dip the mushrooms in the flour mixture, then in the breadcrumb mixture.

Cook the breaded mushrooms for 6 to 7 minutes in a preheated Air Fryer at 380 degrees F, flipping halfway through the cooking time. Consume while warm.

Quinoa-Stuffed Winter Squash

(**Ready in about** 30 minutes | **Servings:** 2)

Ingredients

1/2 cup quinoa	1 cup loosely mixed greens, torn into small pieces
1 teaspoon sesame oil	
1 clove garlic, pressed	1 small winter squash, halved lengthwise
1 tablespoon fresh parsley, roughly chopped	Sea salt and ground black pepper, to taste

Directions

Rinse your quinoa, drain it and transfer to a pot with 1 cup of lightly salted water; bring to a boil.

Turn the heat to a simmer and continue to cook, covered, for about 10 minutes; add in the mixed greens and continue to cook for 5 minutes longer.

Stir in the sesame oil and garlic and stir to combine. Divide the quinoa mixture between the winter squash halves and sprinkle it with the salt and pepper.

Cook your squash in the preheated Air Fryer at 400 degrees F for about 12 minutes.

Place the stuffed squash on individual plates, garnish with fresh parsley and **Serve:**. Bon appétit!

Mashed Potatoes with Roasted Peppers

(**Ready in about** 1 hour | **Servings:** 4)

Ingredients

4 potatoes
1 pound bell peppers, seeded and quartered lengthwise
2 Fresno peppers, seeded and halved lengthwise
2 tablespoons cider vinegar
1/2 teaspoon dried dill
1 tbs vegan margarine
4 tablespoons olive oil
1 teaspoon garlic powder
4 garlic cloves, pressed
Kosher salt, to taste
1/2 teaspoon freshly ground black pepper

Directions

Place the potatoes in the Air Fryer basket and cook at 400 degrees F for 40 minutes. Discard the skin and mash the potatoes with the vegan margarine and garlic powder.

Then, roast the peppers at 400 degrees F for 5 minutes. Give the peppers a

half turn; place them back in the cooking basket and roast for another 5 minutes.

Turn them one more time and roast until the skin is charred and soft or 5 more minutes. Peel the peppers and let them cool to room temperature.

Toss your peppers with the remaining Ingredients and **Serve:** with the mashed potatoes. Bon appétit!

Hungarian Mushroom Pilaf

(**Ready in about** 50 minutes | **Servings:** 4)

Ingredients

1 ½ cups white rice
1 pound fresh porcini mushrooms, sliced
2 tablespoons olive oil
1 onion, chopped
1/2 teaspoon dried tarragon
3 cups vegetable broth
2 garlic cloves
2 tablespoons olive oil
1 teaspoon dried thyme
1/4 cup dry vermouth
1 teaspoon sweet Hungarian paprika

Directions

Place the rice and broth in a large saucepan, add water; and bring to a boil. Cover, turn the heat down to low, and continue cooking for 16 to 18 minutes more. Set aside for 5 to 10 minutes.

Now, stir the hot cooked rice with the remaining Ingredients in a lightly greased baking dish.

Cook in the preheated Air Fryer at 370 degrees for 20 minutes, checking periodically to ensure even cooking.

Serve: in individual bowls. Bon appétit!

Rosemary Au Gratin Potatoes

(**Ready in about** 45 minutes | **Servings:** 4)

Ingredients

2 pounds potatoes
1/2 cup almonds, soaked overnight
1 cup unsweetened almond milk
2 tablespoons nutritional yeast
Kosher salt and ground black pepper, to taste
1/4 cup sunflower kernels, soaked overnight
1 teaspoon shallot powder
2 fresh garlic cloves, minced 1/2 cup water
1 tablespoon fresh rosemary
1 teaspoon cayenne pepper

Directions

Bring a large pan of water to a boil. Cook the whole potatoes for about 20 minutes. Drain the potatoes and let sit until cool enough to handle.

Peel your potatoes and slice into 1/8-inch rounds.

Add the sunflower kernels, almonds, almond milk, nutritional yeast, shallot powder, and garlic to your food processor; blend until uniform, smooth, and creamy. Add the water and blend for 30 seconds more.

Place 1/2 of the potatoes overlapping in a single layer in the lightly greased casserole dish. Spoon 1/2 of the sauce on top of the potatoes. Repeat the layers, ending with the sauce.

Top with salt, black pepper, cayenne pepper, and fresh rosemary. Bake in the preheated Air Fryer at 325 degrees F for 20 minutes. Serve warm.

Cinnamon Sugar Tortilla Chips

(**Ready in about** 20 minutes | **Servings:** 4

Ingredients

4 (10-inch) flour tortillas
1 ½ tablespoons ground cinnamon
1/4 cup vegan margarine, melted
1/4 cup caster sugar

Directions

Slice each tortilla into eight slices. Brush the tortilla pieces with the melted margarine.

In a mixing bowl, thoroughly combine the cinnamon and sugar. Toss the cinnamon mixture with the tortillas.

Transfer to the cooking basket and cook at 360 degrees F for 8 minutes or until lightly golden. Work in batches.

They will crisp up as they cool. **Serve:** and enjoy!

Air Fryer French Fries

Prep time: 15 minutes **Cooking time:** 20 minutes
Serve: 1

Ingredients

1 pound russet potatoes, peeled	1 pinch cayenne pepper
½ teaspoon kosher salt	2 teaspoons vegetable oil

Directions

Each potato should be cut lengthwise into 3/8-inch-thick slices. Sections should be cut into 3/8-inch-wide sticks as well.
Cover potatoes with water and soak for 5 minutes to allow extra starches to be released. Drain and cover with a few inches of boiling water (or place in a bowl of boiling water). Allow for a 10-minute resting period.

Drain the potatoes and pat them dry with paper towels. Blot out any excess water and set it aside for at least 10 minutes to cool fully. Drizzle with oil, season with cayenne pepper, and toss to coat in a mixing bowl.

Preheat the air fryer carefully to 375°F (190 degrees C). In the fryer basket, stack potatoes in a double layer. The **Cooking time:** is 15 minutes. Slide the basket out, toss the fries, cook until golden brown, approximately 10 minutes longer. In a mixing dish, toss the fries with salt. **Serve:** right away.

Air-Fryer Fries

Prep time: 20 minutes **Cooking time:** 20 minutes
Serve: 1

Ingredients

1-pound potatoes	¼ teaspoon salt
1 teaspoon vegetable oil	1/4 teaspoon seasoning

Directions

Allow potatoes to soak in water for 30 minutes. Using paper towels, drain and wipe dry. Drizzle oil over the vegetables and toss to coat.

Preheat the air fryer carefully to 400°F (200 degrees C).
Arrange the potatoes in the fryer basket in a double layer. Cook, tossing every 5 minutes, for 15 to 20 minutes, or until golden brown. Season with salt and pepper to taste.

Air Fryer Baba Ghanoush

Prep time: 20 minutes **Cooking time:** 25 minutes
Serve: 1

Ingredients

5 ½ tablespoons olive oil, divided	1 medium eggplant, halved lengthwise
½ teaspoon kosher salt	1 tablespoon chopped fresh parsley
1 bulb garlic	¼ teaspoon ground cumin
¼ cup tahini	2 tablespoons lemon juice, or more to taste
⅛ teaspoon smoked paprika	
2 tbsp crumbled feta cheese	
½ teaspoon lemon zest	

Directions

Season the cut sides of the eggplant with salt. Allow for a 20- to 30- minute resting period. Then, using paper towels, blot dry.

Preheat an air fryer carefully to 400°F (200 degrees C). 1 tablespoon olive oil on the sliced sides of the eggplant. Remove the top 1/4 inch of the garlic bulb to expose the cloves. Wrap the bulb in aluminum foil after brushing it with 1/2 tablespoon olive oil. In the air fryer basket, combine the eggplant and garlic.

Cook in a preheated air fryer for 15 to 20 minutes, or until the eggplant and garlic are soft, and the eggplant is a deep golden-brown color. Allow cooling for about 10 minutes after removing from the oven.

Scoop out the flesh of the eggplant and place it in the bowl of a food processor. Pulse in tahini, lemon juice, 4 cloves, roasted garlic, remaining 4 tablespoons of olive oil, cumin, and paprika until smooth. **Serve:** with feta cheese, parsley, and lemon zest on top.

Air Fryer Roasted Pineapple

Prep time: 15 minutes **Cooking time:** 22 minutes
Serve: 1

Ingredients
1 fresh pineapple

Directions

Preheat the air fryer carefully to 375°F (190 degrees C). Then, using parchment paper, line the air fryer basket.
Using a pineapple core or slicer, core the pineapple and
cut it into rings.

Fill the prepared basket with pineapple rings.
8 to 10 minutes in the air fryer until the slices roast.
Flip the slices over and continue to air fry for 3 to 5 minutes.

Hoisin-Glazed Bok Choy

(**Ready in about** 10 minutes | **Servings:** 4)

Ingredients

1 pound baby Bok choy, bottoms removed, leaves separated
½ teaspoon sage
1 tbsp all-purpose flour
1 teaspoon onion powder
2 garlic cloves, minced
2 tablespoons sesame oil
2 tablespoons hoisin sauce

Directions

Place the Bok choy, garlic, onion powder, and sage in the lightly greased Air Fryer basket.

Cook in the preheated Air Fryer at 350 degrees F for 3 minutes. In a small mixing dish, whisk the hoisin sauce, sesame oil, and flour. Drizzle the sauce over the Bok choy. Cook for a further 3 minutes. Bon appétit!

Herb Roasted Potatoes and Peppers

(**Ready in about** 30 minutes | **Servings:** 4)

Ingredients

1 pound russet potatoes, cut into 1-inch chunks
1 teaspoon dried rosemary
1 teaspoon dried basil
1 teaspoon dried parsley flakes
1/2 teaspoon smoked paprika
2 bell peppers, seeded and cut into 1-inch chunks
1 teaspoon dried oregano
2 tablespoons olive oil
Sea salt and ground black pepper, to taste

Directions

Toss everything into the Air Fryer basket. Roast for 15 minutes at 400°F, tossing the basket halfway through. Working in batches is recommended. **Serve:** immediately and enjoy.

Spicy Roasted Cashew Nuts

(**Ready in about** 20 minutes | **Servings:** 4)

Ingredients

1 cup whole cashews
Salt and ground black pepper, to taste
1 teaspoon olive oil
1/2 teaspoon smoked paprika
1/2 teaspoon ancho chili powder

Directions

In a mixing bowl, combine all of the Ingredients.

Line the Air Fryer basket with parchment paper. In the basket, arrange the spiced cashews in a single layer.

Roast for 6 to 8 minutes at 350°F, shaking the basket once or twice. Working in batches is recommended. Enjoy!

Corn on the Cob with Spicy Avocado Spread

(**Ready in about** 15 minutes | **Servings:** 4)

Ingredients

4 corn cobs
1 clove garlic, pressed
1 tablespoon fresh lime juice
1/2 teaspoon cayenne pepper
1 teaspoon hot sauce
1 tablespoon soy sauce
1/2 teaspoon dried dill
1 avocado, pitted, peeled and mashed
4 teaspoons nutritional yeast
Sea salt and ground black pepper, to taste
2 heaping tablespoons fresh cilantro leaves, roughly chopped

Directions

Spritz the corn with cooking spray. Cook at 390 degrees F for 6 minutes, turning them over halfway through the cooking time.

In the meantime, mix the avocado, lime juice, soy sauce, nutritional yeast, cayenne pepper, dill, salt, black pepper, and hot sauce.

Spread the avocado mixture all over the corn on the cob. Garnish with fresh cilantro leaves. Bon appétit!

Winter Squash and Tomato Bake

(**Ready in about** 30 minutes | **Servings:** 4)

Ingredients

Cashew Cream
1/4 cup lime juice
1 tablespoon tahini
Sea salt, to taste

1/2 cup water Squash
2 ripe tomatoes, crushed
2 tablespoons olive oil
1 cup vegetable broth
2 tablespoons olive oil
1/2 teaspoon dried basil
2 garlic cloves, minced
1/2 cup sunflower seeds, soaked overnight, rinsed and drained
2 teaspoons nutritional yeast
1 pound winter squash, peeled and sliced
Sea salt and ground black pepper, to taste Sauce
6 ounces spinach, torn into small pieces
1/2 teaspoon dried rosemary

Directions

Mix the Ingredients for the cashew cream in your food processor until creamy and uniform. Re**Serve:**.

Place the squash slices in the lightly greased casserole dish. Add the olive oil, salt, and black pepper.

Mix all the Ingredients for the sauce. Pour the sauce over the vegetables. Bake in the preheated Air Fryer at 390 degrees F for 15 minutes.

Top with the cashew cream and bake an additional 5 minutes or until everything is thoroughly heated.

Transfer to a wire rack to cool slightly before sling and serving.

Air Fryer Baked Potatoes

Prep time: 18 minutes **Cooking time:** 20 minutes
Serve: 1

Ingredients

2 large russet potatoes, scrubbed

½ teaspoon coarse sea salt
1 tablespoon peanut oil

Directions

Preheat the air fryer carefully to 400°F (200 degrees C).
Potatoes should be brushed with peanut oil and seasoned with salt. Place them in the air fryer basket, then in the air fryer.

Cook until potatoes are tender, about 1 hour. Prick them with a fork to see whether they're done.

Air Fryer Vegan Buffalo Cauliflower

Prep time: 15 minutes **Cooking time:** 25 minutes
Serve: 1

Ingredients

1 ½ pound cauliflower florets
¾ cup all-purpose flour
1 teaspoon paprika
¼ teaspoon ground black pepper nonstick cooking spray

4 tbsp Egg substitute, liquid
½ teaspoon salt
1 teaspoon garlic powder
½ cup vegan Buffalo wing sauce (such as Frank's®)

Directions

Preheat the air fryer carefully to 400°F (200 degrees C).
In a large mixing basin, combine cauliflower florets. Stir the egg replacement into the florets to coat.

Combine the flour, garlic powder, paprika, salt, and pepper in a large plastic resealable bag. Shake and zip until evenly blended. 1/2 of the florets should be dipped in seasoned flour. Zip it up and shake it to coat. Fill the air fryer basket with florets. Nonstick cooking spray should be sprayed on the tops.

5 minutes in the air fryer. Cook for 5 minutes more after flipping the cauliflower and spraying any powdery places. Repeat with the rest of the cauliflower florets.

Meanwhile, prepare the buffalo wing sauce in a skillet over medium heat. Place the cauliflower in a large mixing basin. Toss the top with the wing sauce until uniformly covered. Serve right away.

Air Fryer Vegan Sweet Potato Fritters

Prep time: 15 minutes **Cooking time:** 20 minutes
Serve: 1

Ingredients

1 ½ cups shredded sweet potato
¼ cup finely diced onions
½ teaspoon salt
¼ teaspoon ground turmeric avocado oil

½ cup almond flour cooking spray
½ tablespoon olive oil
½ tbsp ground black pepper

Directions

Preheat an air fryer carefully to 350°F (175 degrees C).
Combine the shredded sweet potato, almond flour, onions, olive oil, salt, pepper, and turmeric in a mixing bowl. Using a large cookie scoop, divide the mixture into 9 balls and shape it into patties. Place the patties in the air fryer basket, ensuring they don't touch. Coat the tops with cooking spray.

Cook in a preheated air fryer for 10 to 12 minutes, or until the cakes begin to brown on the edges. Flip the patties over, coat with cooking spray, and continue to air fry for 6 to 8 minutes. Allow for a 1-minute rest before removing from the air fryer basket.

Air Fryer Apple Dumplings

Prep time: 10 minutes **Cooking time:** 18 minutes
Serve: 1

Ingredients

2 tablespoons sultana raisins
2 small apples, peeled and cored
2 tablespoons butter, melted

2 sheets puff pastry

1 tablespoon brown sugar

Directions

Preheat an air fryer carefully to 320°F (180 degrees C).
Aluminum foil should be used to line the air fryer basket.
In a mixing dish, combine sultanas and brown sugar.

Place a sheet of puff pastry on a clean work surface. Fill the core of an apple with the sultana mixture and place it on the crust. Fold the dough around the apple to cover it completely. Repeat with the rest of the pastry, apple, and filling.

Brush the dumplings with melted butter and place them in the prepared basket. Cook the dumplings for 25 minutes, or until golden brown and the apples are tender.

Air Fryer Blueberry Chimichangas

Prep time: 15 minutes **Cooking time:** 25 minutes
Serve: 1

Ingredients

½ (8 ounces) package Neufchatel cheese, softened
1 teaspoon vanilla extract
½ tbsp ground cinnamon
5 (7 inches) flour tortillas
avocado oil cooking spray
1 ½ tablespoon white sugar
2 tablespoons sour cream
1 (6 ounces) container blueberries
2 ½ tablespoons white sugar

Directions

Combine Neufchatel cheese, sour cream, sugar, and vanilla extract in a mixing bowl and whisk with an electric hand mixer. Fold in the blueberries with care.

Heat tortillas until soft and malleable in a big pan or directly on the grates of a gas burner. 1/4 cup blueberry mixture should be placed down the center of each tortilla. Fold the top and bottom of the tortillas over the filling, then wrap each tortilla into a burrito form. Mist with avocado oil and set in an air fryer basket.

Cook the chimichangas in the air fryer at 400 degrees F (200 degrees C) for 4 to 6 minutes, or until golden brown. 1 to 2 minutes more, flip each chimichanga over, spritz with cooking spray, and air fry until golden brown. Allow cooling slightly.

In a small dish, combine the sugar and cinnamon. Each chimichangashould be sprayed with avocado oil and rolled with cinnamon sugar.

Air Fryer Polenta Fries

Prep time: 18 minutes **Cooking time:** 20 minutes
Serve: 1

Ingredients

1 (16 ounces) package prepared polenta nonstick olive oil cooking spray
salt and ground black pepper to taste

Directions

Preheat an air fryer carefully to 350°F (175 degrees C). Cut the polenta into long, thin slices that resemble French fries.

Cooking spray should be sprayed on the bottom of the basket. Place half of the polenta fries in the basket and spritz the tops gently with cooking spray. Season with salt and pepper to taste.

Cook for 10 minutes in a preheated air fryer. Flip the fries with a spatula and cook for another 5 minutes, or until crispy. Place the fries on a dish lined with paper towels. Repeat with the other half of the fries.

Air Fryer Falafel

Prep time: 20 minutes **Cooking time:** 25 minutes
Serve: 1

Ingredients

1 cup dry garbanzo beans
¾ cup fresh flat-leafed parsley stems removed
¼ teaspoon baking soda
2 tbsp chickpea flour
1 tbsp ground cumin
salt and ground black pepper to taste
1 ½ cups fresh cilantro, stems removed
1 clove garlic
1 small red onion, quartered
1 tbsp sriracha sauce
1 tbsp ground coriander
½ tbsp baking powder
cooking spray

Directions

Soak chickpeas for 24 hours in a large amount of cold water. Rub your fingers through the wet chickpeas to help loosen and remove the skins. Rinse and drain well. To dry, spread chickpeas on a wide clean dish towel. In a food processor, combine chickpeas, cilantro, parsley, onion, and garlic until rough paste forms. Transfer the mixture to a large mixing basin. Chickpea flour, coriander, cumin, sriracha, salt, and pepper. Allow the mixture to rest for 1 hour, covered.

Preheat an air fryer carefully to 375°F (190 degrees C). To the chickpea mixture, add the baking powder and baking soda. Using your hands, mix until just blended. Create 15 equal-sized balls and softly press them to form patties. Cooking spray should be sprayed on the falafel patties.
Cook for 10 minutes in a preheated air fryer with 7 falafel patties. Cook for 10 to 12 minutes, transfer cooked falafel to a platter and repeat with the remaining 8 falafel.

Air Fryer Roasted Okra

Prep time: 15 minutes **Cooking time:** 20 minutes
Serve: 1

Ingredients

½ pound okra ends trimmed, and pods sliced
⅛ tbsp black pepper
¼ teaspoon salt
1 teaspoon olive oil

Directions

Preheat an air fryer carefully to 350°F (175 degrees C). Combine the okra, olive oil, salt, and pepper in a mixing dish. Place in the air fryer basket in a single layer. Cook for 5 minutes in the air fryer. Cook for 5 minutes more after tossing. Cook for 2 minutes more after tossing. **Serve:** right away In a shallow dish, combine panko breadcrumbs, salt, Italian seasoning, and pepper. Then, in a separate dish, softly beat the remaining egg. Each rice ball should be dipped in egg first, then the panko mixture. Next, spray the air fryer basket with cooking spray and place the rice balls in it.

Beef, Pork & Lamb Recipes

Paprika Porterhouse Steak with Cauliflower

(**Ready in about** 20 minutes | **Servings:** 4)

Ingredients

1 pound Porterhouse
steak, sliced
Coarse sea salt and ground
black pepper, to taste
1/2 teaspoon shallot
powder

1 pound cauliflower, torn
into florets

1 teaspoon butter, room
temperature
1/2 teaspoon porcini
powder 1 teaspoon
granulated garlic
1 teaspoon smoked
paprika

Directions

Brush all sides of the steak with butter and season with
all spices. Season the cauliflower to taste with salt and
pepper.

Place the steak in the cooking basket and roast for 12
minutes at 400 degrees F, turning halfway through.

Remove the cauliflower from the basket and cook your
steak for another 2 to 3 minutes, if necessary. Garnish
the steak with the cauliflower. Consume while warm.

Chuck Roast with Sweet 'n' Sticky Sauce

(**Ready in about** 35 minutes | **Servings:** 3)

Ingredients

1 pound chuck roast
2 tablespoons butter
softened
1 tablespoon coriander,
chopped
1 tablespoon fish sauce
2 tablespoons honey

Sea salt and ground black
pepper, to taste

1 tablespoon fresh
scallions, chopped
1 teaspoon soy sauce

Directions

Season the chuck roast with salt and pepper; spritz a
nonstick cooking oil all over the beef.

Air fry at 400 degrees F for 30 to 35 minutes, flipping
the chuck roast halfway through the cooking time.

While the roast is cooking, heat the other
Ingredients in a sauté pan over medium-high heat.
Bring to a boil and reduce the heat; let it simmer,
partially covered, until the sauce has thickened and
reduced.

Slice the chuck roast into thick cuts and **Serve:**
garnished with sweet 'n' sticky sauce. Bon appétit!

Italian Sausage Peperonata Pomodoro

(**Ready in about** 15 minutes | **Servings:** 2)

Ingredients

2 bell peppers, sliced
1 chili pepper
2 smoked beef sausages
1 teaspoon Italian spice
mix
1 garlic clove, minced

1 yellow onion, sliced
1 teaspoon olive oil
2 medium-sized tomatoes,
peeled and crushed

Directions

Spritz the sides and bottom of the cooking basket with
a nonstick cooking oil. Add the peppers, onion and
sausage to the cooking basket.

Cook at 390 degrees F for 10 minutes, shaking the
basket periodically. Re**Serve:**.

Heat the olive oil in a medium-sized saucepan over
medium-high flame until sizzling; add in the tomatoes
and garlic; let it cook for 2 to 3 minutes.

Stir in the peppers, onion and Italian spice mix.
Continue to cook for 1 minute longer or until heated
through. Fold in the sausages and **Serve:** warm. Bon
appétit!

Flank Steak with Dijon Honey Butter

(**Ready in about** 15 minutes | **Servings:** 3)

Ingredients

1 pound flank steak
1/2 teaspoon olive oil
3 tablespoons butter

Sea salt and red pepper
flakes, to taste
1 teaspoon Dijon mustard
1 teaspoon honey

Directions

Brush the flank steak with olive oil and season with salt
and pepper.

Cook at 400 degrees F for 6 minutes. Then, turn the
steak halfway through the **Cooking time:**and continue
to cook for a further 6 minutes.

In the meantime, prepare the Dijon honey butter by
whisking the remaining Ingredients.

Serve: the warm flank steak dolloped with the Dijon
honey butter. Bon appétit!

Garlic Roasted Beef

Prep time: 15 minutes **Cooking time:** 40 minutes
Servings: 2-4

Ingredients

2 tbsp. of minced garlic	7 oz. of mushrooms
1tsp. of garlic powder	1 tsp. of salt
1 tsp. of black pepper (ground)	1 tbsp. of extra-virgin olive oil
1cups of chicken stock	1 cup of chopped celery stalk
2yellow onions	
1 lb. of beef brisket	

Directions

Merge garlic powder, salt and ground black pepper together in a mixing bowl and stir. Rub the beef brisket with all the spice mixture. Set the pressure cooker to Sauté mode and place the beef brisket in the pressure cooker.

Sauté the meat for about 5 minutes on them, until golden brown. Add celery stalk. Peel the onions, chop vegetables, and slice mushrooms. Detach the beef brisket from the pressure cooker. Put the vegetables into pressure the cooker. Sprinkle the constituents with the organic olive oil and sauté for 10 minutes, stirring frequently. Add the chicken stock, garlic and beef brisket.

Close the pressure cooker lid and cook the dish on Keep Warm mode roughly for about 25 minutes. When the Cooking time ends, release pressure on the cooker and open the lid. Stir the amalgamation and Serve.

Pork Satay

Prep time: 10 minutes **Cooking time:** 25 minutes
Servings: 3-5

Ingredients

12 oz. of pork loin	3 tbsp. of apple cider vinegar treatment
1tbsp. of essential olive oil	
1 tbsp. of sesame oil	1/2 tsp. of red pepper cayenne
1 tsp. of turmeric	
1 tsp. of basil	1 tsp. of Erythritol
1 tsp. of cilantro	1 tsp. of soy sauce
11 tbsp. of fish sauce	

Directions

Chop the pork loin into medium-sized pieces. Place the pork loin in the mixing bowl.

Sprinkle the meat with apple cider vinegar, organic olive oil, sesame oil, turmeric, cayenne, cilantro, basil, Erythritol, soy sauce, and fish sauce, stir well. Thread the meat on the skewers. Set the strain cooker to Sauté mode. Place the skewers in the pressure cooker and Cook the pork satay for about 25 minutes. When cooked, transfer the satays to a wide bowl and allow them to rest before serving.

Beef with Horseradish

Prep time: 10 minutes **Cooking time:** 30 minutes
Servings: 4-6

Ingredients

5 oz. of horseradish	1 lb. of beef brisket
1cup of cream	1 tbsp. of thyme
1 tsp. of coriander	1/2 cup of chicken stock
1 tsp. of oregano	1 tbsp. of fresh dill
1 tsp. of salt	1garlic cloves
1 tbsp. of olive oil	

Directions

Chop the beef rump and sprinkle it with salt. Peel the onions and slice them. Mix the sliced onions with the extra virgin olive oil and stir well.

Mix the burgundy or merlot wine, bay leaves, black-eyed peas, groundginger thyme, red pepper cayenne, freshly squeezed lemon juice, cilantro, oregano, and minced garlic together in a mixing bowl. Set pressure cooker to Sauté mode and add the sliced onion mixture to pressure cooker and sauté for about 10 minutes, stirring frequently.

Add the chopped beef rump and allow it marinate for a handful of minutes. Stir well and close the strain cooker lid. Cook the dish on Sauté mode for about 40 minutes. When the Cooking time ends, open pressure cooker lid and stir again. Transfer the dish to serving bowls. **Serve:** immediately and Enjoy!

Turmeric Meatballs

Prep time: 10 minutes **Cooking time:** 10 minutes
Servings: 5-7

Ingredients

1tbsp. of turmeric	1 tsp. of ground ginger
1/2 tsp. of oregano	1 tsp. of minced garlic
1 tsp. of salt	1 zucchini
10 oz. of ground pork	1 tbsp. of organic olive oil
1 egg yolk	1 tsp. of cilantro

Directions

Mix the turmeric, ground ginger, salt, oregano, and cilantro in a mixing bowl and stir well. Add ground pork into the contents and stir again. Add the egg yolk and minced garlic. Chop the zucchini and transfer it to the blender. Blend the vegetable mixture until smooth. Add zucchini into the meat mixture and stir well. Make medium-sized meatballs from your meat mixture.

Set pressure to succeed cooker to Pressure mode. Pour the organic olive oil into the pressure cooker contents. Place the meatballs in the pressure cooker and close the lid. Cook for about 10 minutes. When the dish is cooked, release pressure and open the load cooker lid. Remove the meatballs and **Serve:**.

Hawaiian Beef Stew

Prep time: 20 minutes **Cooking time:** 25 minutes
Serve: 1

Ingredients

1 tablespoon vegetable oil	4 pounds stew beef
5 stalks celery	10 cups water
5 cloves garlic, minced	½ cup red wine
1 onion, cut into chunks	6 ounces can tomato paste
1 teaspoon ground black pepper	3 potatoes
	4 carrots
2 tablespoons salt, or to taste	3 bay leaves
	2 tablespoons white sugar
¼ cup cornstarch	¼ cup water

Directions

In a medium-high-heat saucepan, heat the oil. Cook and stir the meat for approximately 10 minutes or until browned. Cook for 2 to 3 minutes, or until the garlic is fragrant. Cook until the alcohol has cooked off, about 5 minutes. Cook until the celery and onions are soft, approximately 5 minutes.

Fill the saucepan with 10 glasses of water. Combine tomato paste, salt, sugar, bay leaves, and pepper in a mixing bowl. Bring the water to a boil. Reduce the heat to medium-low. Cook, covered, for 1 hour, or until meat is tender.

Cook until the carrots are slightly soft, about 10 minutes. Cook for 10 to 15 minutes, or until potatoes are soft. Combine the cornstarch and 1/4 cup water; add to the stew. Allow thickening for about 3 minutes.

Greek-Style Beef Pita

Prep time: 15 minutes **Cooking time:** 18 minutes
Serve: 1

Ingredients

1 pound beef sirloin tip steaks, cut 1/8 to 1/4-inch thick	3 teaspoons vegetable oil, divided
¾ cup plain or seasoned hummus	1 tbsp lemon pepper
	4 each whole-wheat pita bread, cut crosswise in half

Directions

Stack beef steaks and cut them half lengthwise, then crosswise into 1- inch broad strips. In a medium mixing dish, combine the beef and lemon pepper.

In a large nonstick pan, heat 2 teaspoons oil over medium-high heat until hot. Stir-fry 1/2 of the meat for 1 to 3 minutes, or until the outer surface of the beef is no longer pink. (Avoid overcooking.) Take out of the skillet. Repeat with the entire meat, adding the remaining 1 teaspoon oil to the skillet as needed.

Fill pita pockets equally with hummus. Fill with equal parts steak and preferred toppings.

Backyard Bourbon Beef Marinade

Prep time: 15 minutes **Cooking time:** 22 minutes
Serve: 1

Ingredients

1 cup Kikkoman Soy Sauce	¾ cup water
3 tablespoons bourbon	2 pounds beef flank steak
1 tbsp crushed garlic clove	2 tablespoons sugar
	1 tablespoon confectioners' sugar

Directions

Except for the beef flank steak, combine all Ingredients in a mixing bowl. Marinate the beef* in the marinade for 12 to 24 hours in the refrigerator. Grill using your preferred manner.

Grilled Beef Fajitas

Prep time: 18 minutes **Cooking time:** 20 minutes
Serve: 1

Ingredients

1 (1 ounces) package fajita seasoning mix	Reynolds Wrap® Heavy Duty Aluminum Foil
1-pound boneless beef top round steak	1 medium red or yellow bell pepper
1 medium green bell pepper, cut into strips	1 tablespoon vegetable oi
1 medium onion	1 8 (8 inches) flour tortillas
Salsa	

Directions

Prepare the fajita spice mix according to the package recommendations and pour over the meat. Marinate the steak for 1 to 2 hours in Reynolds Wrap® Heavy Duty Aluminum Foil.

Form two layers of foil around the outside of a 13x9x2inch baking pan to make a grill pan. Remove the foil and crimp the edges to make a tight rim, resulting in a pan with 1-inch sides. Place on a baking sheet.

Preheat the grill to high heat. Remove the steak from the marinade and discard the marinade. In a foil pan, combine the peppers, onion, and oil. Slide the foil pan from the cookie sheet onto the grill and set the steak next to it.
Grill on high for 8 to 10 minutes in a covered grill. After 5 minutes, stir the veggies and flip the steak. Remove the foil pan from the grill and place it on a cookie sheet. Thinly slice the grilled steak.

Wrap tortillas in foil and place them on the grill while carving meat. Wrap meat, peppers, and onions in warm tortillas and **Serve:** with salsa.

Meatballs Soup

Prep time: 10 minutes **Cooking time:** 15 minutes
Servings: 6- 8

Ingredients

7 oz. of ground pork
2carrot
A tbsp. of minced garlic
1 tsp. of ground black
pepper
1/2 cup of dill
An egg

1 tsp. of oregano
1 onion
6 cups of chicken stock
1 tsp. of paprika
1 tbsp. of flour

Directions

Skin the carrot and onion and chop them. Combine the vegetables together and transfer them into the pressure cooker. Set the load cooker to Pressure mode. Add chicken stock and paprika. Combine the soil pork, oregano, flour, and ground pork in a mixing bowl.

Beat the egg and pour them into the pork mixture. Stir the Ingredients carefully. Make small meatballs using the ground pork mixture place them in the pressure cooker.

Close the cooker lid and cook for about 14 minutes. Wash the dill and chop it. When the dish is cooked, ladle it into serving bowls. Sprinkle the soup with the dill and **Serve:**.

Pork Belly with Peanuts

Prep time: 10 minutes **Cooking time:** 25 minutes
Servings: 4- 6

Ingredients

5 oz. of peanut
1lb. of pork belly
1 tsp. of ground black
pepper
1 tbsp. of cilantro
1garlic cloves

1 cup of chicken stock
1 tbsp. of salt
1 tsp. of onion powder
1 tsp. of paprika
3tbsp. of fresh rosemary

Directions

Rub the pork belly with salt, ground black pepper, onion powder, paprika, and cilantro. Set pressure cooker to Pressure mode. Put the pork belly into the cooker followed by rosemary and chicken stock.

Close pressure cooker lid and cook for about 25 minutes. Crush the peanuts. When the **Cooking time:**ends, open pressure cooker lid and remove the pork belly. Dry the pork belly with a paper towel. After that, slice it and sprinkle crushed peanuts before serving.

Pork with Every One of the Almonds and Sage

Prep time: 15 minutes **Cooking time:** 40 minutes
Servings: 5-7

Ingredients

3 lb. of pork loin
3 tbsp. of sage
3 garlic cloves
1 tsp. of lemon zest
1 tbsp. of almond flakes
A cup of almond milk

3 carrots
5 tbsp. of chicken stock
5tbsp. of extra-virgin olive
oil
1 tbsp. of salt

Directions

Pat the pork loin with the sage and leave them to chill for about 10 minutes. Peel the garlic cloves and carrots. Cut the carrots into halves. Place the garlic cloves, halved carrots, and lemon zest into the pressure cooker.

Add the fundamental organic olive oil, almond milk, salt, and almond flakes. Set pressure cooker to Sauté mode.
Put the pork into pressure cooker and close its lid. Cook the dish on meat mode for about 40 minutes.

When the **Cooking time:**elapses, open the cooker and remove the pork. Allow the pork-meal to cool a bit. Slice it and **Serve:** while warm.

Rack of Lamb

Prep time: 15 minutes **Cooking time:** 25 minutes
Servings: 4-6

Ingredients

13 oz. of lamb rack
1tbsp. of Erythritol
A tsp. of ground black
pepper
3tbsp. of butter
1 tsp. of curry
1 tsp. of fresh rosemary

A cup of burgundy or
merlot wine
1 cup of chicken stock
1 onion
1 tbsp. of extra virgin
organic olive oil
1 tsp. of cilantro

Directions

Combine Erythritol, ground black pepper, cilantro, chicken stock, curry, and rosemary in a mixing bowl and stir.

Peel the onion and chop it. Add the chopped onion in the mixture and stir. Place the lamb rack chicken stock mixture and allow it to marinate for about 10 minutes Set pressure cooker to Pressure mode. Add the butter into pressure cooker and melt it. Add the marinated lamb rack and sprinkle it with curry.

Secure the lid and cook for about 25 minutes. When the **Cooking time:**elapses, remove your rack of lamb meal from the cooker. Allow it to cool before serving.

Pork Chili

Prep time: 15 minutes **Cooking time:** 45 minutes
Servings: 6-8

Ingredients

1cup of black soybeans	1 cup of chicken stock
10 oz. of ground pork	1 tbsp. of butter
A tsp. of cilantro	1 cup of chopped bok
1 tsp. of oregano	choy 1/4 cup of green
1 tsp. of tomato paste	beans 3**Servings:** of water
3carrots	2red onions
	A tbsp. of salt

Directions

Combine the ground pork with tomato paste, butter, cilantro, and oregano, and salt, stirs well.
Set pressure cooker to Sauté mode and add the ground pork mixture.

Sauté the mixture for about 2 minutes while stirring frequently. Add the green beans and water; peel the carrots and red onions. Chop the vegetables and add them in to the pressure cooker.

Sprinkle the stew mixture with bok choy, and stir. Close pressure cooker lid and cook the dish on Pressure mode for about 40 minutes.

When the **Cooking time:**elapses, open the pressure cooker lid and mix the chili well. Transfer the pork chili to serving bowls.

Marinated Pork Steak

Prep time: 20 minutes **Cooking time:** 25 minutes
Servings: 4-6

Ingredients

1/4 cup of beer	¼ cup of virgin olive oil
1tsp. of cayenne pepper	1 onion
1 tsp. of cilantro	1 tsp. of ground black
1 tsp. of oregano	pepper
1 tbsp. of salt	1 lb. of pork tenderloin

Directions

Combine the red pepper cayenne, extra virgin organic olive oil, cilantro, oregano, salt, and ground black pepper together in a mixing bowl.

Peel the onion and grind it. Add the onion to the spice contents and mix it until smooth, add beer and stir well. Dip the pork tenderloin in the beer mixture and allow it to marinate for at least 10 minutes. Set pressure cooker to Pressure mode.

Transfer the marinated meat to the pressure cooker and cook for about 25 minutes. When the Cooking time ends, release the cooker's pressure and open its lid. Remove the cooked meat from the cooker and **Serve:**.

Lamb Estrada's

Prep time: 15 minutes **Cooking time:** 25 minutes
Servings: 3-5

Ingredients

2 onions	1 tbsp. of paprika
1 tbsp. of extra virgin essential olive oil	1 tbsp. of cilantro
	1/2 tsp. of bay leaf
1 tsp. of oregano	1 tbsp. of sea salt
1lb. of lamb	1/4 chili
1/4 cup of burgundy or merlot wine	1 tsp. of black-eyed peas
1 tsp. of apple cider vinegar	

Directions

Chop the lamb roughly and combine the chopped lamb with oregano, cilantro, sea salt, chili, red, apple cider vinegar treatment, and black- eyed peas in a mixing bowl and stir well. Let the mixture sit. Peel the onions and blend well using a blender.

Take the chopped meat and hang with wooden skewers. Spread the meat with the blended onion. Preheat pressure cooker on Sauté mode for about 3 minutes. Place the lamb skewers in the pressure cooker and sprinkle the meat with olive oil.

Secure the lid and cook for about 25 minutes. When your lamp espetadas is cooked, remove it from the pressure cooker and allow it to cool before serving.

Onion Lamb Kebabs

Prep time: 10 minutes **Cooking time:** 20 minutes
Serving 4

Ingredients

18 oz. lamb kebab	1 teaspoon cumin powder
1teaspoon chili powder	1 egg
2oz. onion, chopped	2teaspoon sesame oil

Directions

Whisk onion with egg, chili powder, oil, cumin powder, and salt in a bowl. Add lamb to coat well then thread it on the skewers. Place these lamb skewers in the Air fryer basket.

Choose "Power Button" of Air Fry Oven and turn the dial to select the "Air Fry" mode. Choose the Time button and again turn the dial to set the **Cooking time:**to 20 minutes.

Now press the Temp button and rotate the dial to set the temperature at 395 degrees F. Once preheated, place the Air fryer basket in the oven and close its lid. Slice and **Serve:** warm.

Glazed Sausage

Prep time: 10 minutes **Cooking time:** 15 minutes
Servings: 4-6

Ingredients

1tbsp. of Erythritol
1 tbsp. of butter
1 lb. of ground pork
1tbsp. of liquid stevia
1 tsp. of oregano
1 tsp. of water
1 tbsp. of coconut flour
6 oz. of ground chicken
1 tbsp. of salt
1 tsp. of cilantro
1 onion
1 tbsp. of ground black pepper

Directions

Peel the onion and grate it. Pour the grated onion, ground pork, ground chicken, salt, oregano, cilantro, and ground black pepper in a mixing bowl. Add the coconut flour and mix well. Combine liquid stevia, Erythritol, and water in another bowl.

Stir the mixture well to dissolve Erythritol, make medium-sized sausages patties from the meat mixture. Set the pressure cooker to Sauté mode. Add the butter into the cooker and allow it melt. Pour the sausage patties into the pressure cooker and sauté the patties for about 4 minutes.

Sprinkle the sausage patties with liquid stevia mixture and close the lid. Cook the dish for another 10 minutes on Sauté mode. When the **Cooking time:**ends, remove the cooked sausage patties from pressure cooker and **Serve:**.

Roast Lamb Shoulder

Prep time: 10 minutes **Cooking time:** 60 minutes
Serving 2

Ingredients

1lb. boneless lamb shoulder roast
4 cloves garlic, minced
3tablespoon olive oil, divided Salt
2 lb. baby potatoes halved
1 tablespoon rosemary, chopped
2teaspoon thyme leaves
Black pepper

Directions

Toss potatoes with all the herbs, seasonings, and oil in a baking tray. Choose "Power Button" of Air Fry Oven and turn the dial to select the "Air Roast" mode.

Choose the Time button and again turn the dial to set the Cooking time to 60 minutes.

Now rest the Temp button and rotate the dial to set the temperature at 370 degrees F. Once preheated, set the lamb baking tray in the oven and close its lid. Slice and **Serve:** warm.

Ginger Pork Chops

Prep time: 10 minutes **Cooking time:** 35 minutes
Servings: 3-5

Ingredients

2 tbsp. of ground ginger
1lb. of pork chop
1 tsp. of ground black pepper
1 tsp. of garlic powder
1 cup of soy sauce
1 tsp. of parsley
1 tbsp. of freshly-squeezed lemon juice
1 cup of water

Directions

Combine the soy sauce and water in a mixing bowl. Add fresh lemon juice and mix.

Sprinkle the mixture with ground ginger, parsley, ground black pepper, and garlic powder. Add freshly squeezed lemon juice and stir well.

Cut the pork chop roughly using a sharp object. Put the pork on the soy sauce mixture and allow it to sit for about 15 minutes.

Set pressure cooker to Sauté mode. Place the amalgamation into the cooker and close its lid. Cook the dish for about 35 minutes. When cooked, open pressure cooker lid and **Serve:** the ginger pork chops while hot.

Salisbury Steak

Prep time: 10 minutes **Cooking time:** 15 minutes
Servings: 3-5

Ingredients

1/2 cup of onion soup mix
A cup of water
1lb. of ground beef
A tsp. of ground white pepper
2eggs
1 tsp. of tomato paste
A tbsp. of mustard
1 tsp. of salt
1 tbsp. of extra virgin organic olive oil

Directions

Whisk the eggs in the mixing bowl and whisk them. Add the mustard, salt, and ground white pepper, stir well until smooth. Dip the beef in the egg mixture and ensure it mixes well. Make mid-sized balls from the meat mixture and flatten them.

Set the pressure cooker to Sauté mode and pour the olive oil into pressure and preheat it in sauté mode. Add the steaks and sauté the dish for 2 minutes on both sides. Combine the tomato paste and onion soup together and stir well.

Pour the soup mixture to the pressure cooker and close the lid. Cook the dish on Pressure mode for about 5 minutes. When the **Cooking time:**elapses, remove Salisbury steak from the pressure cooker and **Serve:** with gravy.

Pork Tenders with Bell Peppers

Prep time: 5 minutes **Cooking time:** 15 minutes
Servings: 4

Ingredients

11 Oz Pork Tenderloin	1 tbsp. Olive Oil
1Bell Pepper, in thin strips	1 Red Onion, sliced
Pepper to taste	1Tsps. Provencal Herbs
1/2 tbsp. Mustard	Black

Directions

Preparing the Ingredients. Preheat the Pro Breeze air fryer to 390 degrees. In the oven dish, mix the bell pepper strips with the onion, herbs, and some salt and pepper to taste.

Attach half a tablespoon of olive oil Divide the pork tenderloin into four pieces and rub it with salt, pepper, and mustard.
Thinly coat the pieces with remaining olive oil and place them upright in the oven dish on top of the pepper mixture

Air Frying. Place the bowl into the Air fryer. Set the timer to 20 minutes and roast the meat and the vegetables
Turn the meat and mix the peppers halfway through
Serve: with a fresh salad

Wonton Meatballs

Prep time: 15 minutes **Cooking time:** 10 minutes
Servings: 4

Ingredients

1-pound ground pork	1/4 cup chopped green
2 large eggs	onions
fresh ginger cloves garlic,	1/4 cup chopped fresh
minced	cilantro tablespoon
1teaspoons soy sauce	minced
	1teaspoon oyster sauce
1/2 teaspoon kosher salt	1 teaspoon black pepper

Directions

Preparing the Ingredients, merge the pork, eggs, green onions, cilantro, ginger, garlic, soy sauce, oyster sauce, salt, and pepper.

Merge on low speed until all of the ingredients are incorporated, 2 to 3 minutes. Form the mixture into 12 meatballs and arrange in a single layer in the air fryer basket.

Air Frying. Set the Pro Breeze air fryer to 350F for 10 minutes. Use a meat thermometer to ensure the meatballs have reached an internal temperature of 145F. Set the meatballs to a bowl and **Serve**

Easy Air Fryer Marinated Pork Tenderloin

Prep time: 1 hour and 10 minutes **Cooking time:** 30 minutes
Servings: 4 to 6

Ingredients

1/4 cup olive oil	1/4 cup of soy sauce
1/4 cup freshly squeezed	1 tablespoon Dijon
lemon juice	mustard
	1 teaspoon salt
1/2 teaspoon freshly	1pounds pork tenderloin
ground black pepper	1garlic clove, minced

Directions

Preparing the Ingredients. In a mixing bowl, make the marinade. Mix the olive oil, soy sauce, lemon juice, minced garlic, Dijon mustard, salt, and pepper. Re**Serve:** 1/4 cup of the marinade.

Place the tenderloin in a large bowl and pour the remaining marinade over the meat. Cover and marinate in the refrigerator for about 1 hour. Place the marinated pork tenderloin into the air fryer basket.

Air Frying. Set the temperature of your Pro Breeze AF to 400F. Set the timer and roast for 10 minutes. Using tongs flip the pork and baste it with half of the re**Serve:**d marinade. Reset the timer and roast for 10 minutes more.
Using tongs, flip the pork, and then baste with the remaining marinade.

Reset the timer and roast for another 10 minutes, for a total Cooking time of 30 minutes.

Barbecue Flavored Pork Ribs

Prep time: 5 minutes **Cooking time:** 15 minutes
Servings: 6

Ingredients

1/4 cup honey, divided	2 tablespoons tomato
3/4 cup BBQ sauce	ketchup
1 tablespoon soy sauce	1tablespoon
13/4 pound pork ribs	Worcestershire sauce
1/2 teaspoon garlic	Freshly ground white
powder	pepper, to taste

Directions

Preparing the Ingredients. In a large bowl, merge 3 tablespoons of honey and the remaining ingredients except for the pork ribs. Refrigerate to marinate for about 20 minutes.

Preheat the Pro Breeze air fryer to 355 degrees F. Place the ribs in an Air fryer basket.

Air Frying. Cook for about 13 minutes. Detach the ribs from the Air fryer and coat with remaining honey.
Serve: hot.

Bacon Cheeseburger Casserole

Prep time: 10 Minutes **Cooking time:** 35 minutes
Servings: 6

Ingredients

1small onion, chopped
1 tablespoon
Worcestershire sauce
1/2 can (15 ounces)
tomato sauce
1/4 cup sliced dill pickles
6 bacon strips, cooked and
crumbled
8-ounces frozen Tater Tots

1 tbsp ground mustard
1-pound ground beef
1/2 cup grape tomatoes,
chopped
1/2 cup shredded cheddar
cheese
4-ounces process cheese
(Velveeta)

Directions

Lightly grease baking pan of air fryer with cooking
spray. Add beef and half of onions. For 10 minutes,
cook on 390F. Halfway through cooking time, stir and
crumble beef.

Stir in Worcestershire, mustard, Velveeta, and tomato
sauce. Mix well. Cook for 4 minutes until melted.
Mix well and evenly spread in pan. Top with cheddar
cheese and then bacon strips.

Evenly top with tater tots. Cover pan with foil.
Cook for 15 minutes at 390F. Uncover and bake for
10 minutes more until tops are lightly browned. **Serve:**
and enjoy topped with pickles and tomatoes and
remaining onion.

Baked Cheese 'n Pepperoni Calzone

Prep time: 10 Minutes **Cooking time:** 25 minutes
Servings: 4

Ingredients

1cup chopped pepperoni
1 to 2 tablespoons 2%
milk
1 tablespoon grated
Parmesan cheese
1/4 cup shredded part-
skim mozzarella cheese

1 loaf frozen bread dough,
thawed

1/2 teaspoon Italian
seasoning, optional
1/2 cup pasta sauce with
meat

Directions

In a bowl mix well mozzarella cheese, pizza sauce, and
pepperoni. On a lightly floured surface, divide dough
into four portions. Set each into a 6-in. circle; top each
with a scant 1/3 cup pepperoni mixture. Fold dough
over filling; pinch edges to seal.

Lightly grease baking pan of air fryer with cooking
spray. Place dough in a single layer and if needed, cook
in batches. For 25 minutes, cook on 330F preheated
air fryer or until dough is lightly browned. **Serve:** and
enjoy.

Beef Recipe Texas-Rodeo Style

Prep time: 10 Minutes **Cooking time:** 1 hour **Servings:**
6

Ingredients

1/2 cup honey
1/2 teaspoon dry mustard
1clove of garlic, minced
Salt and pepper to taste

1/2 cup ketchup
3pounds beef steak sliced
1 tablespoon chili powder
2onion, chopped

Directions

Stick all Ingredients in a Ziploc bag and allow
marinating in the fridge for at least 2 hours. Preheat
the air fryer to 390F. Place the grill pan accessory in
the air fryer.

Grill the beef for 15 minutes per batch making sure
that you flip it every 8 minutes for even grilling.
Meanwhile, pour the marinade on a saucepan and
allow simmering over medium heat until the sauce
thickens. Baste the beef with the sauce before serving.

Beef Roast in Worcestershire-Rosemary

Prep time: 10 Minutes **Cooking time:** 2 hours **Servings:**
6

Ingredients

1onion, chopped
1 tbs Worcestershire sauce
3 stalks of celery, sliced
1-pound beef chuck roast
2cloves of garlic, minced

1 tablespoon butter
1 teaspoon thyme
1 teaspoon rosemary
2cups water
3tablespoons olive oil

Directions

Preheat the air fryer for 5 minutes. Set all Ingredients in a
deep baking dish that will fit in the air fryer. Bake for 2 hours
at 350F. Braise the meat with its sauce every 30 minutes until
cooked.

Beefy Bell Pepper 'n Egg Scramble

Prep time: 10 Minutes **Cooking time:** 30 minutes
Servings: 4

Ingredients

1green bell pepper, seeded
and chopped
3tablespoons olive oil
6 cups eggs, beaten

1-pound ground beef
2cloves of garlic, minced
Salt and pepper to taste
1 onion, chopped

Directions

Preheat the air fryer for 5 minutes with baking pan
insert.
In a baking dish mix the ground beef, onion, garlic,
olive oil, and bell pepper. Season with salt and pepper
to taste.
Pour in the beaten eggs and give a good stir. Place the
dish with the beef and egg mixture in the air fryer.
Bake for 30 minutes at 330F.

Almond Flour 'n Egg Crusted Beef

Prep time: 10 Minutes **Cooking time:** 15 minutes
Servings: 1

Ingredients
1/2 cup almond flour	1/2-pound beef schnitzel
1egg beaten	2tablespoons vegetable oil
1 slice of lemon to **Serve:**	

Directions

Preheat the air fryer for 5 minutes. Mix the oil and almond flour together. Dip the schnitzel into the egg and dredge in the almond flour mixture.

Press the almond flour so that it sticks on to the beef. Set in the air fryer and cook for 15 minutes at 3500F. **Serve:** with a slice of lemon.

Easy Teriyaki BBQ Recipe

Prep time: 10 Minutes **Cooking time:** 15 minutes
Servings: 2

Ingredients
1tablespoon honey	1 tablespoon soy sauce
1 tablespoon mirin	1 thumb-sized piece of
14 oz. lean diced steak,	fresh
with fat trimmed	ginger, grated

Directions

Merge all Ingredients in a bowl and marinate for at least an hour. Turning over halfway through marinating time.
Thread mead into skewers. Place on skewer rack.
Cook for 5 minutes at 390oF or to desired doneness.
Serve: and enjoy.

Apricot Glazed Pork Tenderloins

Prep time: 10 Minutes **Cooking time:** 30 minutes
Servings: 3
Ingredients
1/2teaspoon salt	1/2 teaspoon pepper
2tablespoons minced fresh	2tablespoons olive oil,
rosemary or 1 tablespoon	divided
dried rosemary, crushed	4garlic cloves, minced
3 tablespoons lemon juice	Apricot Glaze Ingredients
1 cup apricot	2 garlic cloves, minced
	1-lb pork tenderloin

Directions

Mix well pepper, salt, garlic, oil, and rosemary. Brush all over pork. If needed cut pork crosswise in half to fit in air fryer. Lightly grease baking pan of air fryer with cooking spray. Add pork. For 3 minutes per side, brown pork in a preheated 390F air fryer. Meanwhile, mix well all glaze Ingredients in a small bowl. Baste pork every 5 minutes. Cook for 20 minutes at 330F.
Serve: and enjoy.

Baby Back Rib Recipe from Kansas City

Prep time: 10 Minutes **Cooking time:** 50 minutes
Servings: 2

Ingredients
1/4 cup apple cider vinegar 1/4 cup molasses	1/4 teaspoon cayenne pepper
1 tablespoon brown sugar	1 tablespoon liquid smoke
1 tbsp Worcestershire sauce	seasoning, hickory
1 teaspoon dry mustard	Salt and pepper to taste
1-pound pork ribs, small	1cup ketchup
2cloves of garlic	

Directions

Bring all ingredients in a Ziploc bag and allow marinating in the fridge for at least 2 hours. Preheat the air fryer to 390F. Place the grill pan accessory in the air fryer.

Grill meat for 25 minutes per batch. Flip the meat halfway through the cooking time.

Bacon, Spinach and Feta Quiche

Prep time: 10 Minutes **Cooking time:** 30 minutes
Servings: 3

Ingredients
6 EGGS	salt and freshly ground
1/2-pound fresh spinach	pepper to taste
3 slices bacon, chopped	1/2 pinch cayenne pepper
11/2 teaspoons butter	1/2 pinch salt
1-1 /2 ounces crumbled feta cheese	1/4 onion, diced

Directions

Lightly grease baking pan of air fryer with butter. Add spinach and for 2 minutes, cook on 360F.
Drain well the spinach and squeeze dry. Chop and set aside.

Add bacon in air fryer pan and cook for 6 minutes or until crisped. Discard excess fat.
Stir in onion and season with salt. Cook for another 5 minutes. Stir in chopped spinach and cook for another 5 minutes to heat through.

Meanwhile, in a bowl whisk well eggs, cayenne pepper, black pepper, and salt. Remove basket, evenly spread mixture in pan, and pour in eggs. Sprinkle feta cheese on top.

Cook for another 15 minutes, until eggs are cooked to desired doneness. **Serve:** and enjoy.

Lamb Cutlets

Prep time: 10 minutes **Cooking time:** 12 minutes
Servings: 3-5

Ingredients

14 oz. of ground lamb	1tsp. of ground black
2 white onions	pepper
1 tbsp. of salt	1 tsp. of cilantro
1/2 tsp. of ground	1 tsp. of organic essential
rosemary	olive oil
1 cup of fresh basil	1 tsp. of minced garlic
1/4 tsp. of sage	1 tsp. of paprika
1 egg	

Directions

Combine the ground lamb, ground black pepper, egg, salt, cilantro, ground rosemary, minced garlic, and paprika in a mixing bowl and stir well.

Peel the onions and dice them. Add the diced onion on the ground lamb mixture and stir well. Chop the basil and pour sage over it. Set pressure cooker to Sauté mode. Pour the virgin organic olive oil in to the pressure cooker and add basil mixture.

Sauté the amalgamation for about 2 minutes while stirring frequently. Remove the basil mixture from the cooker. Make medium-sized cutlets from the lamb mixture and hang them in the pressure cooker. Cook the cutlets for about 10 minutes or until golden brown on both sides. Remove the lamb cutlets from the cooker and allow it to cool before serving.

Lamb with Thyme

Prep time: 10 minutes **Cooking time:** 45 minutes
Servings: 6-8

Ingredients

1cup of fresh thyme	1 tbsp. of essential olive
1 tbsp. of turmeric	oil
1 tsp. of oregano	1 tbsp. of ground black
1lb. of lamb	pepper
1/4 cup of rice wine	4tbsp. of butter
1 tsp. of Erythritol	1 tsp. of paprika
1/4 cup of chicken stock	

Directions

Chop the fresh thyme and mix it with oregano, ground black pepper, paprika, rice wine, Erythritol, chicken stock, and turmeric.

Sprinkle the lamb with the spice mixture and stir it carefully. Transfer the lamb mixture to a pressure cooker and add olive oil.

Close the pressure cooker lid and cook the dish on meat mode for about 45 minutes. When the lamb meal is cooked remove it from the pressure cooker. Allow it to rest and slice it. Enjoy!

Lamb Chops with Rosemary Sauce

Prep time: 10 minutes **Cooking time:** 52 minutes
Serving 8

Ingredients

8 lamb loin chops	1small onion, peeled and
Salt & black pepper to	chopped
taste	
For the sauce	1 onion, peeled and
1 tablespoon rosemary	chopped
leaves	1 oz. butter
1 oz. plain flour	6 fl. oz. milk
6 fl. oz. vegetable stock	Salt and black pepper, to
2tablespoons cream,	taste
whipping	

Directions

Place the lamb loin chops, and onion in a baking tray, then drizzle salt and black pepper on top. Choose "Power Button" of Air Fry Oven and turn the dial to select the "Bake" mode. Choose the Time button and again turn the dial to set the **Cooking time:**to 45 minutes.

Now press the Temp button and rotate the dial to set the temperature at 350 degrees F. Once preheated, set the lamb baking tray in the oven and close its lid.

Set the white sauce by melting butter in a saucepan the sti in onions Sauté for 5 minutes, then stir flour and stir cook for 2 minutes. Stir in the rest of the ingredients and mix well. Pour the sauce over baked chops and **Serve:**.

Garlicky Lamb Chops

Prep time: 10 minutes **Cooking time:** 45 minutes
Serving 8

Ingredients

8 medium lamb chops	3 thin lemon slices
2 garlic cloves, crushed	1/2 teaspoon black
1teaspoon dried oregano	pepper
1 teaspoon salt	1/4 cup olive oil

Directions

Set the medium lamb chops in a baking tray and rub them with olive oil. Attach lemon slices, garlic, oregano, salt, and black pepper on top of the lamb chops.

Choose "Power Button" of Air Fry Oven and turn the dial to select the "Air Roast" mode. Choose the Time button and again turn the dial to set the **Cooking time:**to 45 minutes.

Now press the Temp button and rotate the dial to set the temperature at 400 degrees F. Once preheated, set the lamb baking tray in the oven and close its lid. Slice and **Serve:** warm.

Moist & Tender Ham

Prep time: 10 minutes **Cooking time:** 35 minutes
Serve: 4

Ingredients
3 lbs. cooked ham For glaze	1 tsp dry mustard
1 tbsp pineapple juice	1 tbsp honey
	2 tbsp brown sugar

Directions

Preheat the air fryer to 320 F. Wrap ham in aluminum foil and place into the air fryer basket and cook for 25 minutes. In a small bowl, mix together pineapple juice, brown sugar, honey, and mustard.

After 25 minutes brush ham with glaze and cook for 10-15 minutes more. Slice and **Serve:**.

Juicy Pork Tenderloin

Prep time: 10 minutes **Cooking time:** 18 minutes
Serve: 4

Ingredients
1 ½ lbs. pork tenderloin	½ tsp Italian seasoning
1 tbsp balsamic vinegar	Salt
1 tsp Dijon mustard	1 tsp olive oil
Pepper	

Directions

Preheat the air fryer to 400 F. In a small bowl, mix together mustard, vinegar, Italian seasoning, pepper, and salt.

Brush pork tenderloin with oil and rub with mustard mixture. Place pork tenderloin into the air fryer basket and cook for 16-18 minutes. Slice and **Serve:**.

Steak Kebab

Prep time: 10 minutes **Cooking time:** 10 minutes
Serve: 4

Ingredients
1 lb. sirloin steak, cut into 1-inch pieces	1 bell pepper, cut into 1-inch pieces
For marinade	2 tbsp vinegar
1 tsp ginger garlic paste	1/4 cup soy sauce
2 tbsp olive oil	1 onion, cut 1-inch pieces
1 tsp pepper	

Directions

Preheat the air fryer to 350 F. Add meat pieces and remaining Ingredients into the zip-lock bag. Seal bag and place in the refrigerator overnight. Thread marinated meat pieces, onion, and bell pepper onto the skewers.

Place skewers into the air fryer basket and cook for 10 minutes. Turn halfway through. **Serve:** and enjoy.

Onion Garlic Pork Chops

Prep time: 10 minutes **Cooking time:** 12 minutes
Serve: 4

Ingredients
4 pork chops, boneless	1/2 tsp celery seeds, crushed
1/2 tsp granulated onion	
2 tsp canola oil	1/2 tsp salt
1/2 tsp parsley	1/2 tsp granulated garlic

Directions

Preheat the air fryer to 350 F. In a small bowl, mix together garlic, celery seeds, onion, parsley, and salt. Brush pork chops with oil and rub with spice mixture. Place pork chops into the air fryer basket and cook for 12 minutes. Turn halfway through. **Serve:** and enjoy.

Easy Beef Roast

Prep time: 10 minutes **Cooking time:** 45 minutes
Serve: 8

Ingredients
2 1/2 lbs. beef roast	1 tsp rosemary
1/2 tsp onion powder	1 tsp dill
2 tbsp canola oil	1/2 tsp garlic powder
1/2 tsp pepper Salt	

Directions

Preheat the air fryer to 360 F. In a small bowl, mix together rosemary, pepper, garlic powder, onion powder, dill, and oil and rub all over the beef roast.

Place beef roast into the air fryer basket and cook for 45 minutes. **Serve:** and enjoy.

Flavorful Pork Patties

Prep time: 10 minutes **Cooking time:** 35 minutes
Serve: 6

Ingredients
1 egg, lightly beaten	1 tsp garlic powder
1 tsp smoked paprika	1 carrot, minced
1 onion, minced	2 lbs. ground pork
1/2 cup almond flour	Salt
Pepper	

Directions

Preheat the air fryer to 375 F. Add meat and remaining Ingredients into the large bowl and mix until well combined.

Make patties from the meat mixture and place into the air fryer basket and cook for 35 minutes. Turn patties after 20 minutes. **Serve:** and enjoy.

Beef Taco Fried Egg Rolls

Prep time: 10 minutes **Cooking time:** 15 minutes
Serving 8

Ingredients

1tsp. cilantro	1chopped garlic cloves
1 C. shredded Mexican cheese	1/2 can cilantro lime rote
1/2 packet taco seasoning	1/2 chopped onion
16 egg roll wrappers	1 tbsp. olive oil
	1 pound lean ground beef

Directions

Ensure that your air fryer is preheated to 400 degrees. Add onions and garlic to a skillet, cooking till fragrant. Then add taco seasoning, pepper, salt, and beef, cooking till beef is broke up into tiny pieces and cooked thoroughly. Add rotel and stir well.

Lay out egg wrappers and brush with water to soften a bit.
Load wrappers with beef filling and add cheese to each.
Fold diagonally to close and use water to secure edges. Brush filled egg wrappers with olive oil and add to the air fryer. Cook 8 minutes, flip, and cook another 4 minutes.
Serve:d sprinkled with cilantro.

Lamb Baked with Tomato Topping

Prep time: 10 minutes **Cooking time:** 1hr 40 minutes
Serving 8

Ingredients

8 lamb shoulder chops, trimmed	1tablespoon olive oil
1 large brown onion, chopped	1/4 cup plain flour
2garlic cloves, crushed	2medium carrots, peeled and diced
2 1/2 cups beef stock	2 tablespoons tomato paste
2cups potato gems	1 cup frozen peas
	2 dried bay leaves

Directions

Dust the lamb chops with flour and sear it in a pan layered with olive oil. Sear the lamb chops for 4 minutes per side. Transfer the chops to a baking tray.

Add onion, garlic, and carrot to the same pan. Sauté for 5 minutes, then stir in tomato paste, stock and all other Ingredients. Stir cook for 4 minutes then pour this sauce over the chops.

Choose "Power Button" of Air Fry Oven and turn the dial to select the "Bake" mode. Choose the Time button and again turn the dial to set the **Cooking time:**to 1 hr. 30 minutes. Now press the Temp button and rotate the dial to set the temperature at 350 degrees F. Once preheated, place the baking pan in the oven and close its lid. **Serve:** warm.

Pub Style Corned Beef Egg Rolls

Prep time: 10 minutes **Cooking time:** 5 minutes
Serving 10

Ingredients

Olive oil	1/2 C. orange marmalade
4 C. corned beef and cabbage	10 egg roll wrappers
1egg	Brandy Mustard Sauce
1tbsp. whole grain mustard 1 tsp. dry mustard powder	1/16th tsp. pepper
	1/2 C. chicken stock
1 C. heavy cream	1/4 C. brandy
1/4 tsp. curry powder	5 slices of Swiss cheese
1/2 tbsp. cilantro	1 minced shallot
2tbsp. ghee	3/4 C. dry white wine

Directions

To make mustard sauce, add shallots and ghee to skillet, cooking until softened. Then add brandy and wine, heating to a low boil. Cook 5 minutes for liquids to reduce. Add stock and seasonings. Simmer 5 minutes.
Turn down heat and add heavy cream. Cook on low till sauce reduces and it covers the back of a spoon. Place sauce in the fridge to chill.

Crack the egg in a bowl and set to the side. Lay out an egg wrapper with the corner towards you. Brush the edges with egg wash. Place 1/3 cup of corned beef mixture into the center along with 2 tablespoons of marmalade and 1/2 a slice of Swiss cheese.

Fold the bottom corner over filling. As you are folding the sides, make sure they are stick well to the first flap you made. Place filled rolls into prepared air fryer basket. Spritz rolls with olive oil. Cook 10 minutes at 390 degrees, shaking halfway through cooking. **Serve:** rolls with Brandy Mustard sauce and devour!

Roasted Stuffed Peppers

Prep time: 10 minutes **Cooking time:** 5 minutes
Serving 4

Ingredients

4 ounces shredded cheddar cheese	1/2 tsp. salt
1tsp. Worcestershire sauce	1/2 tsp. pepper
8 ounces lean ground beef	1/2 C. tomato sauce
1 minced garlic clove	1 tsp. olive oil
2green peppers	1/2 chopped onion

Directions

Ensure your air fryer is preheated to 390 degrees. Spray with olive oil. Cut stems off bell peppers and remove seeds. Cook in boiling salted water for 3 minutes.
Sauté garlic and onion together in a skillet until golden in color. Take skillet off the heat. Mix pepper, salt,

Tim's Smoked Pork Butt

Prep time: 15 minutes **Cooking time:** 22 minutes
Serve: 1

Ingredients

1 tablespoon garlic powder
8 pounds boneless pork butt
3 tablespoons applewood rub seasoning (such as McCormick® Grill Mates®)
2 tbsp smoked paprika
1 tablespoon ground black pepper

⅔ cup brown sugar substitute (such as Sukrin® Gold)
2 tablespoons onion powder
2 (12 fluid ounces) bottles of hard apple cider
1 tablespoon salt
2 (12 fluid ounces) cans or bottles of stout beer, divided

Directions

Season with brown sugar replacement, applewood rub, onion powder, smoked paprika, garlic powder, salt, and pepper in a mixing bowl.

Trim the butt of the pig but leave a layer of fat on one side. 1/2 cup seasoning blend should be applied to the entire pork butt. Refrigerate for three days, covered with plastic wrap. Set aside any leftover spice blend for another use.

Preheat, the smoker to 230°F (110 degrees C). Fill the smoker with your preferred wood chips or pellets. Place the pork butt onto the center rack, fat side up. In a drip pan, combine 12 ounces of stout and 12 ounces of cider.

Pork should be smoked for 4 hours. Add the rest of the stout and cider to the drip pan, along with more wood chips or pellets. Continue to smoke for another 3 hours. Remove the drip pan and save the drippings in a basin.
Continue to smoke the pork for 1 to 3 hours more, or until a meat thermometer reads 196 degrees F (91 degrees C). Then, allow for an hour of relaxation.

Using two forks, pull the pork apart. Pour as much of the con**Serve**d drippings as you like over the pulled pork. Serve

Simply the Easiest Beef Brisket

Prep time: 10 minutes **Cooking time:** 18 minutes
Serve: 1

Ingredients

1 (3 pounds) beef brisket, trimmed of fat

1 (12 fluid ounces) can of beer
¾ cup packed brown sugar

salt and pepper to taste
1 medium onion, thinly slice
1 (12 ounces) bottle tomato-based chili sauce

Directions

Preheat the oven carefully to 325 degrees Fahrenheit (165 degrees C).

Season the brisket with salt and pepper on all sides and set it in a glass baking dish. Add a layer of sliced onions on top. Combine the beer, chili sauce, and brown sugar in a medium mixing bowl. Pour the sauce over the roast. Wrap the dish in aluminum foil securely.

In a preheated oven, bake for 3 hours. Bake for a further 30 minutes after removing the aluminum foil. Allow the brisket to rest for a few minutes before slicing and returning to the dish. Reheat in the oven, spooning the sauce over the cut meat.

Best Ever Beef Marinade

Prep time: 18 minutes **Cooking time:** 20 minutes
Serve: 1

Ingredients

1 cup vegetable oil
½ cup lemon juice

¼ cup Dijon mustard
1 clove garlic, minced

¾ cup soy sauce
¼ cup Worcestershire sauce
salt and ground black pepper to taste

Directions

Combine the vegetable oil, soy sauce, lemon juice, Worcestershire sauce, Dijon mustard, and garlic in a mixing bowl. Season with salt and pepper to taste.

Poultry Recipes

Festive Turkey with Chili Mayo

(**Ready in about** 45 minutes | **Servings:** 4)

Ingredients

3 teaspoons olive oil
1/2 teaspoon marjoram
Coarse salt and ground black pepper, to taste
1/4 cup mayonnaise
1 tablespoon chili sauce
1 teaspoon basil
1/2 tbsp garlic powder
1 teaspoon shallot powder
2 pounds turkey breast, boneless Chili mayo
1/4 cup sour cream
1/2 teaspoon stone-ground mustard

Directions

Start by preheating your Air Fryer to 360 degrees F.

In a mixing bowl, thoroughly combine the olive oil with spices. Rub the turkey breast with the spice mixture until it is well coated on all sides. Air fry for 40 minutes, turning them over halfway through the cooking time.

Your instant-read thermometer should read 165 degrees.

Meanwhile, mix all of the Ingredients for the chili mayo. Place in your refrigerator until ready to **Serve:**.

Place the turkey breast skin-side up on a cutting board and slice it against the grain; **Serve:** with chili mayo and enjoy!

Garlic Butter Chicken Wings

(**Ready in about** 20 minutes | **Servings:** 3)

Ingredients

1 pound chicken wings
1 teaspoon garlic paste
1 lemon, cut into slices
Salt black pepper, to taste
2 tablespoons butter

Directions

Pat dry the chicken wings with a kitchen towel and season all over with salt and black pepper. In a bowl, mix together butter and garlic paste. Rub the mixture all over the wings.

Cook in the preheated Air Fryer at 380 degrees F for 18 minutes. **Serve:** garnished with lemon slices. Bon appétit!

Homemade Chicken Burgers

(**Ready in about** 20 minutes | **Servings:** 4)

Ingredients

1 ¼ pounds chicken white meat, ground
1/2 white onion, finely chopped
Sea salt and ground black pepper, to taste
1 ½ cups breadcrumbs
2 small pickles, sliced
1 teaspoon fresh garlic, finely chopped
1 teaspoon paprika
4 burger buns
1/2 cup cornmeal
2 tablespoons ketchup
4 lettuce leaves
1 teaspoon yellow mustard

Directions

Thoroughly combine the chicken, onion, garlic, salt and black pepper in a mixing dish. Form the mixture into 4 equal patties. In a shallow bowl, mix paprika with cornmeal and breadcrumbs. Dip each patty in this mixture, pressing to coat well on both sides.

Spritz a cooking basket with a nonstick cooking spray. Air fry the burgers at 370 degrees F for about 11 minutes or to your desired degree of doneness.

Place your burgers on burger buns and **Serve:** with toppings. Bon appétit!

Italian-Style Turkey Meatballs

(**Ready in about** 20 minutes | **Servings:** 5)

Ingredients

1 ½ pounds ground turkey
1/2 cup tortilla chips, crumbled
1 egg, beaten
2 tablespoons Italian parsley, finely chopped
1 teaspoon Italian seasoning mix
1/2 cup parmesan cheese, grated
1 yellow onion, finely chopped
2 cloves garlic, minced
1 tablespoon soy sauce
1 teaspoon olive oil

Directions

Combine all of the Ingredients listed above until thoroughly combined. Form the mixture into 10 meatballs.

Spritz a nonstick cooking spray into a cooking basket. Cook at 360°F for about 10 minutes, or until done to your liking. Good appetite!

Spanish Chicken with Golden Potatoes

(**Ready in about** 25 minutes | **Servings:** 4)

Ingredients

2 tablespoons butter, melted	4 chicken drumsticks bonein
1 pound Yukon Gold potatoes, peeled and diced	1 teaspoon fresh garlic, minced
1 teaspoon dried rosemary, crushed	1 teaspoon cayenne pepper
1 teaspoon dried thyme, crushed	1 lemon, 1/2 juiced, 1/2 cut into wedges
1/3 teaspoon freshly ground black pepper	2 tablespoons sherry Kosher salt, to taste

Directions

Start by preheating your Air Fryer to 370 degrees F. Then, grease a baking pan with the melted butter. Arrange the chicken drumsticks in the baking pan. Bake in the preheated Air Fryer for 8 minutes. Add the diced potatoes.

Drizzle chicken and potatoes with lemon juice. Sprinkle with garlic, rosemary, thyme, cayenne pepper, black pepper, and salt. Turn the temperature to 400 degrees F and cook for a further 12 minutes. Make sure to shake the basket once or twice. Remove from the Air Fryer basket and sprinkle sherry on top. **Serve:** with the lemon wedges. Enjoy

Pizza Spaghetti Casserole

(**Ready in about** 30 minutes | **Servings:** 4)

Ingredients

8 ounces spaghetti	1 pound smoked chicken sausage, sliced
2 tomatoes, pureed	1 tablespoon Italian seasoning mix
1/2 cup Asiago cheese, shredded	1 tablespoon fresh basil leaves, chiffonade
3 tablespoons Romano cheese, grated	

Directions

Bring a large pot of lightly salted water to a boil. Cook your spaghetti for 10 minutes or until al dente; drain and re**Serve:**, keeping warm.

Stir in the chicken sausage, tomato puree, Asiago cheese, and Italian seasoning mix.

Then, spritz a baking pan with cooking spray; add the spaghetti mixture to the pan. Bake in the preheated Air Fryer at 325 degrees F for 11 minutes.

Top with the grated Romano cheese. Turn the temperature to 390 degrees F and cook an additional 5 minutes or until everything is thoroughly heated and the cheese is melted.

Garnish with fresh basil leaves. Bon appétit!

Turkey Breakfast Frittata

(**Ready in about** 50 minutes | **Servings:** 4)

Ingredients

1 tablespoon olive oil	1 pound turkey breasts, slices
3 tablespoons Greek yogurt	3 tablespoons Cottage cheese, crumbled
1/4 teaspoon red pepper flakes, crushed Himalayan salt, to taste	1 red bell pepper, seeded and sliced
1 green bell pepper, seeded and sliced	1/4 teaspoon ground black pepper
	6 large-sized eggs

Directions

Grease the cooking basket with olive oil. Add the turkey and cook in the preheated Air Fryer at 350 degrees F for 30 minutes, flipping them over halfway through. Cut into bite-sized strips and re**Serve:**.

Now, beat the eggs with Greek yogurt, cheese, black pepper, red pepper, and salt. Add the bell peppers to a baking pan that is previously lightly greased with a cooking spray. Add the turkey strips; pour the egg mixture over all Ingredients. Bake in the preheated Air Fryer at 360 degrees F for 15 minutes. **Serve:** right away!

Nana's Turkey Chili

(**Ready in about** 1 hour | **Servings:** 4)

Ingredients

1/2 medium-sized leek, chopped	2 garlic cloves, minced
1 jalapeno pepper, seeded and minced	1/2 red onion, chopped
2 cups tomato puree	2 tablespoons olive oil
1 pound ground turkey, 85% lean 15% fat	1 bell pepper, seeded and chopped
1/2 teaspoon black peppercorns	2 cups chicken stock
1 teaspoon mustard seeds	Salt, to taste
	1 teaspoon chili powder
	1 teaspoon ground cumin
	1 (12-ounce) can kidney beans, rinsed and drained

Directions

Start by preheating your Air Fryer to 365 degrees F.

Place the leeks, onion, garlic and peppers in a baking pan; drizzle olive oil evenly over the top. Cook for 4 to 6 minutes. Add the ground turkey. Cook for 6 minutes more or until the meat is no longer pink.

Now, add the tomato puree, 1 cup of chicken stock, black peppercorns, salt, chili powder, mustard seeds, and cumin to the baking pan. Cook for 24 minutes, stirring every 7 to 10 minutes. Stir in the canned beans and the remaining 1 cup of stock; let it cook for a further 9 minutes; make sure to stir halfway through. Bon appétit!

Asian Chicken Filets with Cheese

(**Ready in about** 50 minutes | **Servings:** 2)

Ingredients

4 rashers smoked bacon
1 teaspoon garlic, minced
1/4 tbsp black pepper, preferably freshly ground
1 tbsp mild curry powder
1 tbsp black mustard seeds
1/2 cup Pecorino Romano cheese, freshly grated
1/2 tbsp coarse sea salt
1/2 cup coconut milk
1 (2-inch) piece ginger, peeled and minced
2 chicken filets
1/3 cup tortilla chips, crushed

Directions

Start by preheating your Air Fryer to 400 degrees F. Add the smoked bacon and cook in the preheated Air Fryer for 5 to 7 minutes. Re**Serve:**.

In a mixing bowl, place the chicken fillets, salt, black pepper, garlic, ginger, mustard seeds, curry powder, and milk. Let it marinate in your refrigerator about 30 minutes.

In another bowl, mix the crushed chips and grated Pecorino Romano cheese.

Dredge the chicken fillets through the chips mixture and transfer them to the cooking basket. Reduce the temperature to 380 degrees F and cook the chicken for 6 minutes.

Turn them over and cook for a further 6 minutes. Repeat the process until you have run out of Ingredients.

Serve: with re**Serve:**d bacon. Enjoy!

Roasted Citrus Turkey Drumsticks

(**Ready in about** 55 minutes | **Servings:** 3)

Ingredients

3 medium turkey drumsticks, bone-in
1 teaspoon cayenne pepper
1 teaspoon dried parsley flakes
Zest of one orange
1/4 cup orange juice
Sea salt and ground black pepper, to taste
1 teaspoon fresh garlic, minced
1 teaspoon onion powder
1/2 butter stick, melted

Directions

Rub all Ingredients onto the turkey drumsticks.

Preheat your Air Fryer to 400 degrees F. Cook the turkey drumsticks for 16 minutes in the preheated Air Fryer.

Loosely cover with foil and cook an additional 24 minutes.

Once cooked, let it rest for 10 minutes before slicing and serving. Bon appétit!

Turkey Bacon with Scrambled Eggs

(**Ready in about** 25 minutes | **Servings:** 4)

Ingredients

1/2 pound turkey bacon
2 tablespoons yogurt
1/2 teaspoon sea salt
2 green onions, finely chopped
4 eggs
1/3 cup milk
1 bell pepper, finely chopped
1/2 cup Colby cheese, shredded

Directions

Place the turkey bacon in the cooking basket.

Cook at 360 degrees F for 9 to 11 minutes. Work in batches. Re**Serve:** the fried bacon.

In a mixing bowl, thoroughly whisk the eggs with milk and yogurt. Add salt, bell pepper, and green onions.

Brush the sides and bottom of the baking pan with the re**Serve:**d 1 teaspoon of bacon grease.

Pour the egg mixture into the baking pan. Cook at 355 degrees F about 5 minutes. Top with shredded Colby cheese and cook for 5 to 6 minutes more. **Serve:** the scrambled eggs with the re**Serve:**d bacon and enjoy!

Chinese Duck (Xiang Su Ya)

(**Ready in about** 30 minutes + marinating time | **Servings:** 6)

Ingredients

2 pounds duck breast, boneless
1 teaspoon Chinese 5-spice powder
1 teaspoon Szechuan peppercorns
1 teaspoon coarse salt
1/4 cup molasses
1 tbsp light soy sauce
2 green onions, chopped
1/2 teaspoon ground black pepper Glaze
3 tablespoons Shaoxing rice wine
1 tablespoon soy sauce
3 tablespoons orange juice

Directions

In a ceramic bowl, place the duck breasts, green onions, light soy sauce, Chinese 5-spice powder, Szechuan peppercorns, and Shaoxing rice wine. Let it marinate for 1 hour in your refrigerator.

Preheat your Air Fryer to 400 degrees F for 5 minutes.

Now, discard the marinade and season the duck breasts with salt and pepper. Cook the duck breasts for 12 to 15 minutes or until they are golden brown.

Repeat with the other Ingredients.In the meantime, add the re**Serve:**d marinade to the saucepan that is preheated over medium-high heat. Add the molasses, orange juice, and 1 tablespoon of soy sauce. Bring to a simmer and then, whisk constantly until it gets syrupy. Brush the surface of duck breasts with glaze so they are completely covered. Place duck breasts back in the Air Fryer basket; cook an additional 5 minutes. Enjoy!

Chicken Kebab

Prep time: 10 minutes **Cooking time:** 6 minutes
Servings: 3

Ingredients

1lb. ground chicken	1 tbsp. fresh lemon juice
1green onion, chopped	1/4 cup almond flour
3garlic cloves	1 egg, lightly beaten
1/3 cup fresh parsley, chopped	4oz. onion, chopped
	1/2 tsp. pepper
1/4 tsp. turmeric powder	

Directions

Attach all ingredients into the food processor and process until well combined. Transfer chicken mixture to the bowl and place in the refrigerator for 1 hour.

Divide mixture into the 6 equal portions and roll around the soaked wooden skewers. Spray air fryer basket with cooking spray. Place skewers into the air fryer basket and cooks at 400 F for 6 minutes. **Serve:** and enjoy.

Mediterranean Chicken

Prep time: 10 minutes **Cooking time:** 35 minutes
Servings: 6

Ingredients

4 lbs. whole chicken, cut into pieces	2 garlic cloves, minced
2 tbsp. olive oil	2 lemons, sliced
1tsp. lemon zest	2tsp. kosher salt
	2 tsp. ground sumac

Directions

Rub chicken with oil, sumac, lemon zest, and salt. Place in the refrigerator for 2-3 hours. Add lemon sliced into the air fryer basket top with marinated chicken. Cook at 350 for 35 minutes. **Serve:** and enjoy.

Asian Chicken Wings

Prep time: 10 minutes **Cooking time:** 30 minutes
Servings: 2

Ingredients

4 chicken wings	3/4 tbsp. Chinese spice
1 tsp. mixed spice Pepper	Salt
1tbsp. soy sauce	

Directions

Add chicken wings into the bowl. Add remaining ingredients and toss to coat. Set chicken wings into the air fryer basket. Cook at 350 f for 15 minutes.

Turn chicken to another side and cook for 15 minutes more. **Serve:** and enjoy.

Delicious Chicken Fajitas

Prep time: 10 minutes **Cooking time:** 15 minutes
Servings: 4

Ingredients

4 chicken breasts	1 bell pepper, sliced
1 1/2 tbsp. fajita seasoning	3/4 cup cheddar cheese, shredded
2tbsp olive oil	
1onion, sliced	

Directions

Preheat the air fryer at 380 F. Coat chicken with oil and rub with seasoning. Place chicken into the air fryer baking dish and top with bell peppers and onion.

Cook for 15 minutes. Top with shredded cheese and cook for 1-2 minutes until cheese is melted. **Serve:** and enjoy.

Juicy and Spicy Chicken Wings

Prep time: 10 minutes **Cooking time:** 25 minutes
Servings: 4

Ingredients

2 lbs. chicken wings	1tsp. Worcestershire sauce
12 oz. hot sauce	1 tsp. Tabasco
6 tbsp. butter, melted	

Directions

Spray air fryer basket with cooking spray. Add chicken wings into the air fryer basket and cook at 380 F for 25 minutes. Shake basket after every 5 minutes.

Meanwhile, in a bowl, mix together hot sauce, Worcestershire sauce, and butter. Set aside. Add chicken wings into the sauce and toss well. **Serve:** and enjoy.

Curried Drumsticks

Prep time: 10 minutes **Cooking time:** 22 minutes
Servings: 2

Ingredients

2 turkey drumsticks	11/2 tbsp. ginger, minced
1/4 tsp. cayenne pepper	1 tsp. kosher salt
2 tbsp red curry paste	1/3 cup coconut milk
1/4 tsp. pepper	

Directions

Add all ingredients into the bowl and stir to coat. Place in refrigerator for overnight. Spray air fryer basket with cooking spray. Place marinated drumsticks into the air fryer basket and cook at 390 F for 22 minutes. **Serve:** and enjoy.

Keto Lemon-Garlic Chicken Thighs in the Air Fryer

Prep time: 15 minutes **Cooking time:** 18 minutes
Serve: 1

Ingredients

¼ cup lemon juice
1 teaspoon Dijon mustard
⅛ teaspoon ground black pepper
4 skin-on, bone-in chicken thighs

2 tablespoons olive oil
¼ teaspoon salt
2 cloves garlic, minced
4 lemon wedges

Directions

Combine the lemon juice, olive oil, Dijon mustard, garlic, salt, and pepper in a mixing bowl. Set aside the marinade.

Fill a large resealable plastic bag halfway with chicken thighs. Pour marinade over chicken and close bag, ensuring that all chicken portions are covered. Refrigerate for at least 2 hours before serving. Preheat the air fryer carefully to 360°F (175 degrees C). Take the chicken out of the marinade and blot it dry with paper towels. Cook the chicken in batches if required in the air fryer basket.

Fry for 22 to 24 minutes, or until the chicken is no longer pink at the bone and the juices flow clear. A thermometer near the bone should read 165 degrees F. (74 degrees C). When serving, squeeze a lemon slice over each piece.

Air Fryer Bacon-Wrapped Chicken Thighs

Prep time: 15 minutes **Cooking time:** 22 minutes
Serve: 1

Ingredients

½ stick butter softened
¼ teaspoon dried thyme,
¼ teaspoon dried basil
⅓ pound thick-cut bacon
2 teaspoons minced garlic

½ clove minced garlic
⅛ teaspoon coarse salt
freshly black pepper
1 ½ pounds boneless skinless chicken thighs

Directions

Combine melted butter, garlic, thyme, basil, salt, and pepper in a mixing bowl. Place the butter on wax paper and roll it up tightly to produce a butter log. Refrigerate for 2 hours, or until firm.
One bacon strip should be placed flat on a sheet of wax paper. Sprinkle with garlic and place the chicken thigh on top of the bacon. Remove the chicken thigh. Place 1-2 tablespoons of the cool finishing butter in the center of each chicken thigh. Insert one end of the bacon into the center of the chicken thigh. Fold the bacon over the chicken thigh and wrap it around it. Repeat with the rest of the thighs and bacon.

Asian Style Salt and Pepper Chops

Prep time: 10 minutes **Cooking time:** 20 minutes
Servings: 2

Ingredients

1egg white
1/4 teaspoon ground black pepper
2to 3 boneless pork chops
3tablespoons peanut oil
2 jalapeno peppers, stems removed, seeded and sliced 1 teaspoon sea salt

1/2 teaspoon sea salt
3/4 cup potato starch (can use cornstarch) Oil in an oil mist bottle (I used peanut)
2 green onions,
1/4 teaspoon ground black pepper

Directions

Whisk the egg white, salt and pepper in a bowl until it is foamy. Cut the pork chops in pieces and place in the bowl making sure to coat each piece well.

Cover and refrigerate 20 minutes. Remove the chop pieces from the egg white bowl and drop into the potato starch. Coat evenly.Warmth the air fryer to 390 degrees F.
Spray the air fryer basket with the oil in the mist bottle and place the chop pieces in the basket. Spray them liberally with the oil as well.

Cook for 9 minutes shaking the basket frequently. Turn the chop pieces, spray with oil and put in for another 4 to 6 minutes or until brown and crispy. Heat up a wok on the stove and spray some oil into it. Sauté the onions, jalapenos, salt and pepper for about 1 minute.
Add the pork and sauté 2 to 3 minutes. **Serve:** with rice.

Paprika Pork Ribs

Prep time: 30 minutes **Cooking time:** 15 minutes
Servings: 2

Ingredients

1pound ribs, cut apart so they fit in the air fryer
1 1/2 tablespoons paprika

21/2 tablespoons olive oil
1 teaspoon salt

Directions

Place the ribs in a large bowl. Pour in the paprika, olive oil and salt and stir around or mix with your hands to make sure the ribs are all coated.

Set the basket of the air fryer with cooking spray and place the coated ribs in. Cook at 360 degrees F – Do not preheat the air fryer! Cook for 20 minutes, removing the basket and shaking the ribs around 2 times during those 20 minutes. They should be done and the meat should pull away from the bone.

Chicken with Golden Roasted Cauliflower

(**Ready in about** 30 minutes | **Servings:** 4)

Ingredients

2 pounds chicken legs
2 tablespoons olive oil
1 teaspoon sea salt
1 teaspoon dried
marjoram
2 garlic cloves
minced
1/3 cup Pecorino Romano
cheese, freshly grated

1/2 teaspoon ground
black pepper
1 tbsp smoked paprika
1 (1-pound) head
cauliflower, broken into
small florets
1/2 teaspoon dried thyme
Salt, to taste

Directions

Toss the chicken legs with the olive oil, salt, black pepper, paprika, and marjoram.

Cook in the preheated Air Fryer at 380 degrees F for 11 minutes. Flip the chicken legs and cook for a further 5 minutes.

Toss the cauliflower florets with garlic, cheese, thyme, and salt.

Increase the temperature to 400 degrees F; add the cauliflower florets and cook for 12 more minutes. **Serve:** warm.

Adobo Seasoned Chicken with Veggies

(**Ready in about** 1 hour 30 minutes | **Servings:** 4)

Ingredients

2 pounds chicken wings,
rinsed and patted dry
1/2 teaspoon red pepper
flakes, crushed
1 teaspoon granulated
onion 1 teaspoon ground
turmeric
2 cloves garlic, peeled but
not chopped
2 tbsp tomato powder
2 bell peppers, seeded and
sliced
4 carrots, trimmed and
halved

1/4 teaspoon ground
black pepper
1 teaspoon paprika
1 teaspoon coarse sea salt
1 tablespoon dry Madeira
wine
2 stalks celery, diced
1 large Spanish onion,
diced
1 teaspoon ground cumin
2 tablespoons olive oil

Directions

In a large mixing bowl, combine all of the Ingredients. Cover and place in the refrigerator for 1 hour.

Place the chicken wings in a baking dish.

Cook the chicken wings for 7 minutes in a preheated Air Fryer at 380 degrees F.

Cook for 15 minutes more after adding the vegetables, shaking the basket once or twice. **Serve:** hot.

Chicken and Brown Rice Bake

(**Ready in about** 50 minutes | **Servings:** 3)

Ingredients

1 cup brown rice
1 tablespoon butter,
melted
Kosher salt and ground
black pepper, to taste
1 onion, chopped
1 cup tomato puree

2 cups vegetable broth
2 garlic cloves, minced
1/2 cup water
3 chicken fillets
1 tbsp cayenne pepper
1 tablespoon fresh chives,
chopped

Directions

Heat the brown rice, vegetable broth and water in a pot over high heat. Bring it to a boil; turn the stove down to simmer and cook for 35 minutes.

Grease a baking pan with butter.

Spoon the prepared rice mixture into the baking pan. Add the onion, garlic, salt, black pepper, cayenne pepper, and chicken. Spoon the tomato puree over the chicken.

Cook in the preheated Air Fryer at 380 degrees F for 12 minutes. **Serve:** garnished with fresh chives. Enjoy!

Sticky Exotic Chicken Drumettes

(**Ready in about** 25 minutes | **Servings:** 4)

Ingredients

2 tablespoons peanut oil
1 tablespoon yellow
mustard
2 tablespoons honey
1/2 teaspoon sambal oelek
1/4 cup chicken broth
1 ½ pounds chicken
drumettes, bone-in
Salt and ground white
pepper, to taste

1 tablespoon tamari sauce
1 clove garlic, peeled and
minced
2 tablespoons fresh orange
juice

1/2 cup raw onion rings,
for garnish

Directions

Start by preheating your Air Fryer to 380 degrees F.

Line the cooking basket with parchment paper. Lightly grease the parchment paper with 1 tablespoon of peanut oil. In a mixing bowl, thoroughly combine the remaining 1 tablespoon of oil honey, tamari sauce, mustard, garlic, orange juice, and sambal oelek. Whisk to combine well.

Arrange the chicken drumettes in the prepared cooking basket. Season with salt and white pepper.

Spread 1/2 of the honey mixture evenly all over each breast. Pour in the chicken broth. Cook for 12 minutes.

Turn them over, add the remaining 1/2 of the honey mixture, and cook an additional 10 minutes. Garnish with onion rings and **Serve:** immediately.

Barbeque Pork Ribs-Finger Licking' Good

Prep time: 5 minutes **Cooking time:** 15 minutes
Servings: 2

Ingredients

1 tablespoon dark brown sugar
1 tablespoon paprika (sweet) 1 teaspoon poultry seasoning
1/2 teaspoon ground black pepper

1 teaspoon garlic powder
1 teaspoon onion powder
1/2 teaspoon prepared mustard powder
1 tablespoon kosher salt
2 1/4-pounds St Louis-style pork spareribs

Directions

In a bowl, whisk the brown sugar, onion powder, garlic powder, paprika, poultry seasoning, mustard powder, salt and pepper. Rub this mixture into the ribs on both sides until it is completely covered.

Set the basket of the air fryer with cooking spray and place the ribs in on end leaning against the basket crossing each other.

Set the heat to 350 degrees F and cook 35 minutes. The ribs come out brown and crispy.

Garlic Butter Pork Chops

Prep time: 10 minutes **Cooking time:** 15 minutes
Servings: 4

Ingredients

2 teaspoons parsley
1/4 teaspoon pepper
1 tablespoon coconut butter
1 tablespoon coconut oil

1/2 teaspoon kosher salt
2 teaspoons grated garlic pork chops

Directions

Mix the parsley, salt, pepper, garlic, coconut oil and coconut butter and mix with a rubber spatula squishing everything together so it is well mixed. Take your hands and rub the mixture in all pork chops on both sides.

Fold into aluminum foil and refrigerate at least 2 hours or overnight. When ready to cook, preheat the air fryer to 350 degrees F for 5 minutes. Unwrap the chops from the aluminum and place 2 of them in a pan that
fits inside of the air fryer that has been sprayed with cooking spray. Spread them out as well as possible. Cook 7 minutes, turn and cook another 8 minutes. Remove and repeat with the other two chops

Air Fryer Chicken Fajitas

Prep time: 20 minutes **Cooking time:** 25 minutes
Serve: 1

Ingredients

1 medium red bell pepper
1 large onion, slice petals
3 teaspoons olive oil, divided salt and pepper to taste
8 (6 inches) flour tortillas, warmed

1 medium green bell pepper, cut into thin strips
1 pound chicken tenders, cut into strips
2 teaspoons fajita seasoning

Directions

Combine the bell pepper strips and onion petals in a large mixing basin. Drizzle with 2 tablespoons olive oil and season with salt and pepper. Stir until everything is well blended. In a separate dish, toss the chicken strips with the fajita spice. Drizzle with the remaining 1 teaspoon olive oil and stir with your fingertips until evenly incorporated.

Preheat the air fryer carefully to 350 degrees Fahrenheit (175 degrees C). Cook for 12 minutes, shaking halfway through, with the chicken in the basket. Transfer to a platter and set aside while you prepare the veggies. Cook for 14 minutes, shaking halfway through, in the air fryer basket with the vegetable mixture. Distribute the chicken and veggie mixture among the tortillas.

Air Fryer Chimichangas

Prep time: 15 minutes **Cooking time:** 20 minutes
Serve: 1

Ingredients

1 tablespoon vegetable oil
2 cups shredded cooked chicken
1/4 cup chicken broth
1 (4 ounces) can hot fire-roasted diced green chiles
1/2 teaspoon salt
1 cup shredded Mexican cheese blend

1/2 cup diced onion
1/2 (8 ounces) package Neufchatel cheese,
1 1/2 tablespoons chicken taco seasoning mix
6 (10 inches) flour tortillas
1/4 tbsp black pepper
avocado oil cooking spray

Directions

In a medium skillet, heat the oil. Cook until the onion is tender and transparent, 4 to 6 minutes. Combine the chicken, Neufchatel cheese, diced chiles, chicken broth, taco seasoning, salt, and pepper in a mixing bowl. Cook and stir until the mixture is fully mixed and the Neufchatel has softened.

Heat tortillas until soft and malleable in a big pan or directly on the grates of a gas burner. Fill each tortilla with a third of the chicken mixture and a heaping spoonful of Mexican cheese

Crispy Ranch Air Fryer Nuggets

Prep time: 10 minutes **Cooking time:** 18 minutes
Serve: 1

Ingredients

1 pound chicken tenders, cut into 1.5 to 2-inch pieces 1 package dry ranch salad dressing mix
1 cup panko breadcrumbs

2 tablespoons flour
1 egg, lightly beaten
1 serving olive oil cooking spray

Directions

Toss the chicken in a bowl with the ranch seasoning to mix. Allow for 5-10 minutes of resting time. Fill a resealable bag halfway with flour. Place the panko breadcrumbs on a dish and the egg in a small bowl. Preheat the air fryer carefully to 390°F (200 degrees C). Toss the chicken in the bag to coat. Dip the chicken in the egg mixture lightly, allowing excess to drain off. Roll the chicken in panko, pushing the crumbs into the meat.

Spray the air fryer basket with oil and arrange the chicken pieces inside, ensuring no overlap. Depending on the size of your air fryer, you may need to prepare two batches. Next, spray the chicken lightly with cooking spray. 4 minutes in the oven. Cook for 4 minutes more, or until the chicken is no longer pink on the inside. **Serve:** right away.

Air Fryer Bang-Bang Chicken

Prep time: 18 minutes **Cooking time:** 20 minutes **Serve:** 1

Ingredients

1 cup mayonnaise
2 tbsp Sriracha sauce
1 pound chicken breast tenderloins, cut into bite-size pieces

½ cup sweet chili sauce
⅓ cup flour
1 ½ cups panko breadcrumbs
2 green onions, chopped

Directions

Combine the mayonnaise, sweet chili sauce, and Sriracha in a large mixing bowl. Set aside a third of a cup of the mixture. Fill a big resealable plastic bag halfway with flour. Close the bag and shake to coat the chicken. Stir the coated chicken pieces into the large mixing bowl with the mayonnaise mixture. In a separate big plastic resealable bag, place the panko breadcrumbs. Drop chicken pieces into breadcrumbs in batches, close, and shake to coat.

Preheat the air fryer carefully to 400°F (200 degrees C). Fill the air fryer basket with as many chicken pieces as you can without overflowing it. Cook for 10 minutes in a hot air fryer. Cook for 5 minutes more on the other side. Rep with the remaining chicken. Pour the saved sauce over the fried chicken in a large mixing bowl. Stir in the green onions and toss to coat. **Serve:** right away.

Air Fryer Chicken Strips

Prep time: 15 minutes **Cooking time:** 20 minutes
Serve: 1

Ingredients

1 cup all-purpose flour
1 tablespoon paprika
½ teaspoon ground black pepper
1 large egg
cooking spray

1 tablespoon parsley flakes
1 teaspoon seasoned salt
1 ½ pounds chicken tenderloins

Directions

Preheat the air fryer carefully to 400°F (200°C) according to the manufacturer's instructions. Combine the flour, paprika, parsley, seasoned salt, and pepper in a large mixing bowl. In a separate dish, beat the egg.

Dredge each chicken strip in seasoned flour, then in beaten egg, and last in seasoned flour.
Fill the basket with as many strips as you can without overflowing it. Spray the tops of the strips lightly with cooking spray. 8 minutes in the oven, turn the strips over, and sprinkle the tops gently with additional cooking spray. Cook for an additional 8 minutes. Rep with the rest of the strips.

Air Fryer Cornflake-Crusted Chicken Tenders

Prep time: 18 minutes **Cooking time:** 20 minutes
Serve: 1

Ingredients

1 egg
1 pinch salt
1 ounce finely shredded Parmesan cheese
½ teaspoon granulated garlic
1 pinch salt

1 tablespoon pesto
1 cup crushed cornflakes
½ teaspoon Catanzaro herbs
1 pound chicken tenders

Directions

Preheat the air fryer carefully to 400°F (200 degrees C). In a shallow bowl, combine the egg, pesto, and salt. Separately, combine cornflake crumbs, Parmesan cheese, Catanzaro herbs, garlic, and salt in a separate dish.

Dip each piece of chicken in the egg wash first, then in the cornflake mixture, brushing off excess breading. Finally, place the chicken in the air fryer basket.

After 5 minutes, rotate the chicken pieces and air fry until the center is no longer pink and the juices run clear, about 5 minutes more.

Brown Sugar Ham Steak

Prep time: 10 minutes **Cooking time:** 15 minutes
Servings: 8

Ingredients

1-8ounce bone in fully cooked ham steak	5 tablespoons brown sugar
	5 tbsp butter, in slices

Directions

Lay a piece of foil big enough to completely fold the ham steak in on a flat surface and place the steak in the middle.
Melt the butter (I do it in the microwave) and add the brown sugar. Stir until combined.

Spread half the thick butter/brown sugar spread on the ham steak and turn it over.

Spread the rest on the side of the ham steak.
Pre heat the air fryer to 380 degrees F for 4 minutes.
Fold the foil up and over the ham steak creating an envelope that will not leak over the steak.
Place the folded ham steak in the basket of the air fryer and cook for 8 minutes.

Remove from the air fryer and carefully unfold the foil watching for steam. The ham steak should be done and coated with the rich brown sugar and butter sauce.
If you are making more than one ham steak, be careful. It might not take as long to cook subsequent steaks because the air fryer will be hot.

Pepperoni and Chicken Pizza Bake

Prep time: 10 minutes **Cooking time:** 15 minutes
Servings: 4

Ingredients

2 cups cubed cooked chicken	1cup low-carb, sugar-free pizza sauce
20 slices pepperoni	1 cup shredded mozzarella cheese
1/4 cup grated Parmesan cheese	

Directions

In a 4-cup round baking dish add chicken, pepperoni, and pizza sauce. Stir so meat is completely covered with sauce.
Top with mozzarella and grated Parmesan. Place dish into the air fryer basket.

Adjust the temperature to 375F and set the timer for 15 minutes. Dish will be brown and bubbling when cooked. **Serve:** immediately.

Crispy Boneless Pork Chops

Prep time: 10 minutes **Cooking time:** 15 minutes
Servings: 4

Ingredients

6 pork chops with fat trimmed 1teaspoon kosher salt, divided	1/2 teaspoon garlic powder 1/2 teaspoon onion powder 1 1/4 teaspoon paprika
1/2 cup panko bread crumbs	1/3 cup crushed cornflake crumbs
1/4 teaspoon chili powder tablespoons grated Parmesan cheese	1 egg, beaten
Olive oil in a mist bottle	1/8 teaspoon black pepper

Directions

Rub the chops with 1/2 teaspoon of the salt and set them aside. In a shallow bowl, combine the cornflakes, panko crumbs, garlic powder, onion powder, paprika, chili powder, Parmesan cheese, pepper and the remaining salt.

Mix well and set the bowl aside. Whisk the egg in another bowl and set it aside. Warmth the air fryer to 400 degrees F Soak the chops in the egg and then in the crumb mixture pressing it in on both sides.

Place three of the chops in and spray liberally with oil. Cook for 6 minutes, turn and spray with oil again and cook another 6 minutes. Repeat with other chops.

Mexican Taco Chicken Fingers

Prep time: 10 minutes **Cooking time:** 10 minutes
Servings: 4

Ingredients

1egg, whisked	1/2 cup parmesan cheese, preferably freshly grated
1/2 cup tortilla chips crushed	
1/2 teaspoon onion powder 1/2 teaspoon garlic powder 1 teaspoon red chili powder	1 1/2 pounds chicken breasts, boneless skinless cut into strips

Directions

Whisk the egg in a shallow bowl. In a separate bowl, whisk the parmesan cheese, tortilla chips, onion powder, garlic powder, and red chili powder.

Dip the chicken pieces into the egg mixture. Then, roll the chicken pieces over the breadcrumb mixture.
Cook the chicken at 380 degrees F for 12 minutes, turning them over halfway through the cooking time.
Bon appétit!

Ranch Chicken Wings

Prep time: 1 hour 15 minutes **Cooking time:** 25 minutes
Servings: 3

Ingredients

1pound chicken wings, boneless	1 teaspoon Ranch seasoning mix
2tablespoons olive oil	
Kosher salt and ground pepper, to taste	

Directions

Pat the chicken dry with kitchen towels. Toss the chicken with the remaining ingredients. Cook the chicken wings at 380 degrees F for 22 minutes, turning them over halfway through the cooking time. Bon appétit!

Roasted Turkey Legs with Scallions

Prep time: 5 minutes **Cooking time:** 45 minutes
Servings: 4

Ingredients

11/2 pounds turkey legs	1 tablespoon butter, melted
1 teaspoon garlic, pressed	Sea salt and ground black pepper, to taste
1 teaspoon hot paprika	2tablespoons scallions, chopped

Directions

Toss the turkey legs with the remaining ingredients, except for the scallions. Cook the turkey legs at 400 degrees F for 40 minutes, turning them

over halfway through the cooking time. Garnish the roasted turkey legs with the fresh scallions and enjoy!

Turkey and Avocado Sliders

Prep time: 15 minutes **Cooking time:** 25 minutes
Servings: 4

Ingredients

1pound turkey, ground	1 avocado, peeled, pitted and chopped
1 tablespoon olive oil	Kosher salt and ground pepper, to taste
1garlic cloves, minced	
1/2 cup breadcrumbs	
8 small rolls	

Directions

Mix the turkey, olive oil, avocado, garlic, breadcrumbs, salt, and black pepper until everything is well combined. Form the mixture into eight small patties.

Cook the patties at 380 degrees F for about 20 minutes or until cooked through; make sure to turn them over halfway through the cooking time. **Serve:** your patties in the prepared rolls and enjoy!

Chicken Salad Sandwich

Prep time: 15 minutes **Cooking time:** 20 minutes
Servings: 4

Ingredients

1pound chicken breasts, boneless and skinless	1 carrot, chopped
1 small onion, chopped	1 stalks celery, chopped
1 cup mayonnaise	Sea salt and ground black pepper, to taste
4 sandwich buns	

Directions

Pat the chicken dry with paper towels. Place the chicken in a lightly oiled cooking basket. Cook the chicken breasts at 380 degrees F for 12 minutes, turning them over halfway through the cooking time.

Shred the chicken breasts using two forks; transfer it to a salad bowl and add in the celery, carrot, onion, mayo, salt, and pepper. Toss to combine and **Serve:** in sandwich buns. Enjoy!

Italian-Style Chicken Drumsticks

Prep time: 15 minutes **Cooking time:** 25 minutes
Servings: 4

Ingredients

4 chicken drumsticks, bone-in 1 tablespoon butter	1/2 teaspoon cayenne pepper
Sea salt and ground pepper, to taste	1 teaspoon Italian herb mix

Directions

Rub the chicken drumsticks dry with paper towels. Toss the chicken drumsticks with the remaining ingredients.
Cook the chicken drumsticks at 370 degrees F for 20 minutes, turning them over halfway through the cooking time. Bon appétit!

Thai Hot Chicken Drumettes

Prep time: 5 minutes **Cooking time:** 25 minutes
Servings: 3

Ingredients

1pound chicken drumettes, bone-in	2tablespoons sesame oil
1/4 cup Thai hot sauces	1teaspoon tamari sauce
	salt and freshly ground pepper, to taste

Directions

Toss the chicken drumettes with the remaining ingredients. Cook the chicken drumettes at 380 degrees F for 22 minutes, turning them over halfway through the cooking time. Bon appétit!

Air Fryer Buffalo Chicken Wings

Prep time: 15 minutes **Cooking time:** 18 minutes
Serve: 1

Ingredients

2 ½ pounds chicken wings	⅔ cup cayenne pepper sauce
½ cup butter	2 tablespoons vinegar
1 teaspoon garlic powder	¼ teaspoon cayenne pepper
1 tablespoon olive oil	

Directions

Preheat the air fryer carefully to 360°F (182 degrees C). Place the wings in a large mixing basin. Drizzle oil over the wings and massage until evenly covered. Cook for 25 minutes with half of the wings in the air fryer basket. Flip the wings with tongs and cook for another 5 minutes. Place the cooked wings in a large mixing dish. Rep with the remaining wings.

In a small saucepan over medium heat, mix hot pepper sauce, butter, vinegar, garlic powder, and cayenne pepper while the second batch is cooking. Keep stirring and heating until the wings are done. Toss cooked wings with sauce to coat.

Air Fryer Chicken Nuggets

Prep time: 15 minutes **Cooking time:** 22 minutes
Serve: 1

Ingredients

1 cup buttermilk	2 pounds chicken tenderloins, cut into nugget size
1 cup flour	
1 tablespoon paprika	1 tablespoon parsley flakes
3 tablespoons grated Parmesan cheese	1 teaspoon salt
1 teaspoon ground black pepper	2 cups panko breadcrumbs cooking spray
2 eggs	

Directions

In a large mixing basin, combine the buttermilk and chicken and set aside while you make the seasoned flour.
Combine the flour, Parmesan cheese, paprika, parsley, salt, and pepper
in a large mixing bowl. Separately, beat the eggs. On a flat dish, spread out the breadcrumbs. Each chicken nugget should be dredged in flour, then in beaten egg, and finally in breadcrumbs.
Preheat the air fryer carefully to 400°F (200 degrees C). Cooking spray should be sprayed on the basket. Fill the basket with as many nuggets as you can without overflowing it. Spray the tops of the nuggets lightly with cooking spray.
The **Cooking time:**is 10 minutes. Cook for a further 2 minutes after flipping the chicken nuggets. Repeat with the remaining nuggets.

Bacon Wrapped Pork Tenderloin

Prep time: 10 minutes **Cooking time:** 20 minutes
Servings: 4-6

Ingredients

1 to 2 tablespoons Dijon mustard	3 to 4 strips bacon
	1 pork tenderloin
2 tablespoons butter, divided	1 small onion, peeled and chopped
2 to 3 Granny Smith apples, peeled, cored and cut in slices	1 tablespoon flour
	Garnish with fresh chopped rosemary
1 cup vegetable broth	salt and pepper to taste

Directions

Preheat the air fryer to 360 for about 5 minutes. Spread the mustard onto the pork loin and wrap it with uncooked bacon.

Place it in the air fryer basket that has been treated with cooking spray and cook 15 minutes. Turn the roast and cook another 10 to 15 minutes until brown and crisp on the outside. Check that internal temperature is around 145 degrees F.

Heat 1 teaspoon of the butter in a saucepan and sauté the onions 1 to 2 minutes. Add the apple slices and sauté 3 to 5 minutes or until soft. Pour the onions and apples into a bowl and set it aside. Use the same pan and add the remaining butter, melting it. Stir in the flour to make a roux

Slowly add the broth while stirring until it is well combined and not lumpy. Let it come to a simmer with bubbles forming around the edges. It will thicken. Add the apple and onion mixture and stir in well. Slice the roast after it rests about 5 to 8 minutes and pour the gravy over top.

Almond-Crusted Chicken

Prep time: 15 minutes **Cooking time:** 25 minutes
Servings: 4

Ingredients

1/4 cup slivered almonds	2 (6-ounce) boneless, skinless chicken breasts
2 tablespoons full-fat mayonnaise	1 tablespoon Dijon mustard

Directions

Pulse the almonds in a food processor or chop until finely chopped. Place almonds evenly on a plate and set aside. Completely slice each chicken breast in half lengthwise. Mix the mayonnaise and mustard in a small bowl and then coat chicken with the mixture.

Lay each piece of chicken in the chopped almonds to fully coat. Carefully move the pieces into the device.

Flavors Chicken Thighs

Prep time: 10 minutes **Cooking time:** 20 minutes
Serve: 4

Ingredients

4 chicken thighs, bone-in & skin-on	1/2 tsp oregano
3/4 tsp onion powder	1 tsp smoked paprika
1/2 tsp kosher salt	3/4 tsp garlic powder
	1 tbsp canola oil

Directions

Preheat the air fryer to 380 F. Add chicken thighs and remaining ingredients into the large zip-lock bag. Seal bag and shake well. Add marinated chicken into the air fryer basket and cook for 20 minutes. Turn halfway through.
Serve: and enjoy.

Chicken Masala

Prep time: 15 minutes **Cooking time:** 36 minutes
Servings: 4

Ingredients

Rosemary (finely chopped) 1 tbsp. Oil 2 tbsp.	Corn starch 3 tsp.
Brown champignons (sliced) 250g Chicken stock 1 pot	Chicken breasts 4
	Baby potatoes (halved) 500g Masala wine 200ml
Shallots (finely chopped) 2 Water 400ml	Salt and pepper

Directions

Set the temp to HIGH and pick SEAR/SAUTÉ. Click the START/STOP key and allow 5 minutes to preheat.
Put the potatoes, 1 tablespoon of oil, rosemary, pepper and salt and in a big dish. Toss until evenly flavored with the potatoes.

After preheating, put 1 tablespoon of oil and breasts of chicken in the pot, season with pepper and salt, and brown on both sides for around 2 to 3 minutes on either side. Detach the chicken from the pot and set it aside.
In the oven, put the mushrooms and shallots and sauté for 2 min. Then add the Masala wine and plan for a reduction time of 5 minutes.

Add the water, chicken stock and corn starch to the mixture. Once again, in the oven, put the chicken. To retain the higher position of the rack, place the rack that is reversible in the jar. Place it with potatoes that are seasoned.

Gather the pressure lid to pre**Serve:** the pressure release mechanism's SEAL position. Set to LOW and PRESSURE to pick. Use 10 minutes for clock scheduling. Select START/STOP to start. **Serve:** sweet.

Chicken Wings

Prep time: 20 minutes **Cooking time:** 30 minutes
Servings: 6

Ingredients

Ginger crushed 1 inch	Ground Cardamom 1/2 tbsp. Paprika 2 tsp.
Plain Yoghurt 200g	
Garlic cloves crushed 3	Chili Powder 1/2 tbsp.
Ground Cumin 1 tbsp.	Salt 1 tbsp.
Garam masala Powder1 tbsp.	Lemon Juice 2 tbsp.
	Ground Black Pepper 2 tbsp.
Ground Coriander 1 tbsp.	

Directions

Put the basket of air fryer in and close the machine's door.
At 200 C, select an Air Fry. Set a timer of 20 minutes. Insert chicken wings to guarantee they don't really smoke and turn after 5 minutes.

Mix all ingredients in a bowl for marinade and whisk them together. Toss the wings into the marinade. Put the wings again to the air fryer on the grill set at 260 C for a minute or two.

Chicken, Mushroom, Leek, and Pie of Puff Pastry

Prep time: 25 minutes **Cooking time:** 65 minutes
Servings: 4

Ingredients

Light olive oil 2 tbsp. Egg yolk 1	Skinless, boneless chicken thighs 300g, cut into of 2cm
Chopped tarragon 1 1/2 tbsp. Chestnut mushrooms 300g	Large leek 1, cut into 1 1/2cm slices Chopped flat parsley 1 1/2 tbsp.
Sprigs thyme 4, leaves picked	Ready-made béchamel/white sauce 275ml
Chunky smoked bacon pancetta lardoons 60g	Dijon mustard 2 tbsp.
Chopped chives 1 1/2 tbsp.	All-butter puff pastry 200g (preferably in a block), kept fridge cold
To taste, salt and pepper	

Directions

Put the basket of air fryer in and close the machine's door.
At 200 C, select an Air Fry. Set a timer of 20 minutes. Insert chicken wings to guarantee they don't really smoke and turn after 5 minutes. Mix all ingredients in a bowl for marinade and whisk the together. Toss the wings into the marinade. Put the wings again to the air fryer on the grill setting at 260 C for a minute or two.

Air Fryer Stuffing Balls

Prep time: 15 minutes **Cooking time:** 20 minutes
Serve: 1

Ingredients

1 tablespoon butter	¼ cup finely chopped onion
½ cup finely chopped celery	5 cups stale bread, cut into cubes
1 teaspoon dried parsley	
½ teaspoon poultry seasoning	½ teaspoon salt
¼ tbs ground black pepper	1 egg, well beaten
cooking spray	¼ cup no-salt-added chicken broth

Directions

In a small pan over medium heat, melt the butter. Cook until the celery and onion are cooked, about 5 minutes.

Combine the bread, parsley, poultry seasoning, salt, and pepper in a mixing bowl. Incorporate the sautéed onion and celery. With one hand, slowly pour the egg into the bowl while mixing to ensure that the mixture is equally covered. Repeat with the chicken broth and stir everything together until fully blended. Divide the filling mixture into 8 equal amounts and roll it into balls on a platter. Refrigerate for at least 15 minutes before serving.

Preheat the air fryer carefully to 350°F (180 degrees C). Remove the stuffing balls from the refrigerator and gently coat them with cooking spray. Place the stuffing balls in the air fryer, sprayed side down, without touching. Lightly spray the opposite side. Cook for 5 minutes in a hot air fryer, then turn and cook for 2 minutes.

Air-Fried Buffalo Chicken

Prep time: 18 minutes **Cooking time:** 20 minutes
Serve: 1

Ingredients

½ cup plain fat-free Greek yogurt	¼ cup egg substitute
1 tablespoon hot sauce	1 tbsp cayenne pepper
1tbs garlic pepper seasoning	1 tbsp sweet paprika
1 cup panko breadcrumbs	1 teaspoon hot sauce
	1-pound skinless, boneless chicken breasts

Directions

Combine Greek yogurt, egg replacement, and 1 tablespoon + 1 teaspoon spicy sauce in a mixing dish. Combine the panko breadcrumbs, paprika, garlic pepper, and cayenne pepper in a separate bowl. Coat chicken strips with panko bread crumb mixture after dipping them in the yogurt mixture. In an air fryer, arrange coated chicken strips in a single layer. Cook for 10 minutes per side or until uniformly browned

Honey-Sriracha Air Fryer Wings

Prep time: 15 minutes **Cooking time:** 20 minutes
Serve: 1

Ingredients

12 fresh chicken wing drumettes	½ teaspoon salt
½ teaspoon garlic powder	1 tablespoon butter
2 teaspoons rice vinegar	¼ cup honey
	1 tablespoon sriracha sauce

Directions

Preheat the air fryer carefully to 360°F (182 degrees C). Toss the chicken wings in a basin with the salt and garlic powder to coat. Fill the air fryer basket halfway with wings. Cook the wings for 25 minutes, shaking the basket every 7 to 8 minutes. When the timer goes off, switch off the air fryer and leave the wings in the basket for another 5 minutes. Meanwhile, in a small saucepan over medium heat, melt the butter. Bring butter, honey, rice vinegar, and sriracha sauce to a boil. Reduce the heat to medium-low and cook the sauce for 8 to 10 minutes, stirring regularly. Remove from fire and set aside; the sauce will thicken as it cools. In a mixing dish, combine the cooked wings and the sauce. Next, make the extra sauce to **Serve:** with the wings.

Healthier Bang Bang Chicken in the Air Fryer

Prep time: 15 minutes **Cooking time:** 25 minutes
Serve: 1

Ingredients

1 egg	½ cup milk
1 tbsp hot pepper sauce	½ cup flour
½ cup tapioca starch	1 ½ teaspoon seasoned salt
½ teaspoon cumin	1-pound boneless, skinless chicken breasts
1 teaspoon garlic granules	3 tablespoons sweet chili sauce
¼ cup plain Greek yogurt	
cooking spray	1 teaspoon hot sauce

Directions

Preheat the air fryer carefully to 380°F (190 degrees C).

Whisk together the egg, milk, and spicy sauce in a small bowl. Combine the flour, tapioca starch, salt, garlic, and cumin in a separate bowl. Dredge the chicken pieces in the dry mix first, then in the egg mixture, brushing off excess. Place the chicken in the air fryer basket in batches, be careful not to overcrowd it, and lightly spritz with oil.

Cook for about 10 minutes per batch, shaking the basket every 5 minutes until the chicken is no longer pink in the middle and the juices flow clear. Combine Greek yogurt, sweet chili sauce, and spicy sauce in a small bowl. **Serve:** the sauce beside the chicken.

Air Fryer Sweet and Sour Chicken Wings

Prep time: 15 minutes **Cooking time:** 25 minutes
Serve: 1

Ingredients

1 ½ pounds chicken wings, tips discarded
1 teaspoon ground black pepper
¼ cup pineapple juice
1 tablespoon brown sugar
1 teaspoon paprika
1 teaspoon sesame oil
1 tablespoon cornstarch
¾ teaspoon sesame seeds
1 stalk green onion, sliced

2 tablespoons baking powder
½ cup white vinegar
1 teaspoon salt
¼ cup ketchup
1 tablespoon reduced-sodium soy sauce
1 tablespoon water
1 teaspoon Sriracha sauce

Directions

Preheat the air fryer carefully to 380°F (190 degrees C). Coat the basket with cooking spray. Using a paper towel, pat dries the chicken wings. Combine baking powder, salt, pepper, and paprika in a resealable plastic bag. Place some chicken wings in the bag and shake vigorously until the wings are fully covered. Shake off any extra baking powder mixture, then repeat with the remaining wings until all of them are covered.

Cook the chicken wings in the air fryer basket for 22 to 23 minutes, turning halfway through. Meanwhile, add vinegar, pineapple juice, ketchup, brown sugar, soy sauce, Sriracha, and sesame oil in a small saucepan over medium heat. Bring to a boil, stirring constantly. For around 2 minutes, bring the water to a boil. Then, reduce the heat to a low simmer. In a small bowl, mix the cornstarch and water. Pour into the pot and stir vigorously until the sauce thickens about 1 minute. Thin the sauce with a little water if it's too thick.

Increase the temperature of the air fryer to 400 degrees F (200 degrees C) and cook the wings for another 2 minutes, or until they are cooked through and crispy brown.

Pour the sauce into a large mixing dish and toss in the cooked wings. Toss well to coat. **Serve:** immediately, garnished with sesame seeds and green onion.

Vegetables & Side Dishes Recipes

Roasted Broccoli and Cauliflower with Tahini Sauce

(**Ready in about** 15 minutes | **Servings:** 3)

Ingredients

1/2 pound broccoli, broken into florets
1/2 pound cauliflower, broken into florets
1 teaspoon onion powder
1 tablespoons tahini
Salt and chili flakes, to taste

1/2 teaspoon porcini powder 1/4 teaspoon cumin powder 1/2 teaspoon granulated garlic
1 teaspoon olive oil
2 tablespoons soy sauce
1 teaspoon white vinegar

Directions

Start by preheating your Air Fryer to 400 degrees F.

Now, toss the vegetables with the onion powder, porcini powder cumin powder, garlic and olive oil. Transfer your vegetables to the lightly greased cooking basket.

Air Fry your veggies in the preheated Air Fryer at 400 degrees F for 6 minutes. Remove the broccoli florets from the cooking basket. Continue to cook the cauliflower for 5 to 6 minutes more.

Meanwhile, make the tahini sauce by simply whisking the remaining Ingredients in a small bowl. Spoon the sauce over the warm vegetables and **Serve:** immediately. Bon appétit!

Sweet & Sticky Baby Carrots

(**Ready in about** 45 minutes | **Servings:** 3)

Ingredients

1 tablespoon coconut oil
1 pound baby carrots
2 lemongrasses, finely chopped
3 tablespoons honey

1 teaspoon fresh ginger, peeled and grated
1 teaspoon lemon thyme

Directions

Toss all Ingredients in a mixing bowl and let it stand for 30 minutes. Transfer the baby carrots to the cooking basket.

Cook the baby carrots at 380 degrees F for 15 minutes, shaking the basket halfway through the **Cooking time:** to ensure even cooking.

Serve: warm and enjoy!

Green Bean Salad with Goat Cheese and Almonds

(**Ready in about** 15 minutes | **Servings:** 3)

Ingredients

1 ½ pounds green beans, trimmed and cut into small chunks
1 teaspoon deli mustard
2 bell peppers, deseeded and sliced
1 tablespoon Shoyu sauce Dressing
2 tbs extra-virgin olive oil

1 small-sized red onion, sliced
Sea salt black pepper to taste
1/4 cup almonds
1/2 cup goat cheese, crumbled
1 tbsp champagne vinegar
1 clove garlic, pressed

Directions

Season the green beans with salt and black pepper to your liking. Brush them with a nonstick cooking oil.

Place the green beans in the Air Fryer cooking basket. Cook the green beans at 400 degrees F for 5 minutes and transfer to a salad bowl. Stir in the onion and bell peppers.

Then, add the raw almonds to the cooking basket. Roast the almonds at 350 degrees F for 5 minutes, shaking the basket periodically to ensure even cooking.

In the meantime, make the dressing by blending all Ingredients until well incorporated. Dress your salad and top with goat cheese and roasted almonds. Enjoy!

Roasted Asparagus with Pecorino Romano Cheese

(**Ready in about** 10 minutes | **Servings:** 3)

Ingredients

1 pound asparagus spears, trimmed
1/2 tbsp shallot powder
1/4 tsp cumin powder
1/2 tsp dried rosemary
1 tbs sesame seeds, toasted

1/2 tbsp garlic powder
1 teaspoon sesame oil
Coarse sea salt and ground black pepper, to taste 4 tablespoons Pecorino Romano cheese, grated

Directions

Begin by preheating your Air Fryer to 400°F.

Toss the asparagus with the sesame oil, spices, and cheese before placing it in the Air Fryer cooking basket.

Cook the asparagus for 5 to 6 minutes in a preheated Air Fryer, shaking the basket halfway through to ensure even browning. **Serve:** warm, garnished with toasted sesame seeds. Good appetite!

Rainbow Vegetable and Parmesan Croquettes

(**Ready in about** 40 minutes | **Servings:** 4)

Ingredients

1 pound potatoes, peeled	2 tablespoons butter
Salt and black pepper, to taste	1 carrot, grated
1/2 cup mushrooms, chopped	4 tablespoons milk
1 clove garlic, minced	1/2 teaspoon cayenne pepper
1/2 cup panko bread crumbs	3 tablespoons scallions, minced
1/2 cup all-purpose flour	1/2 cup parmesan cheese, grated
2 eggs	2 tablespoons olive oil
1/4 cup broccoli, chopped	

Directions

In a large saucepan, boil the potatoes for 17 to 20 minutes. Drain the potatoes and mash with the milk, butter, salt, black pepper, and cayenne pepper.

Add the mushrooms, broccoli, carrots, garlic, scallions, and olive oil; stir to combine well. Shape the mixture into patties. In a shallow bowl, place the flour; beat the eggs in another bowl; in a third bowl, combine the breadcrumbs with the parmesan cheese.

Dip each patty into the flour, followed by the eggs, and then the breadcrumb mixture; press to adhere.

Cook in the preheated Air Fryer at 375 degrees F for 16 minutes, shaking halfway through the cooking time. Bon appétit!

Fried Asparagus with Goat Cheese

(**Ready in about** 15 minutes | **Servings:** 3)

Ingredients

1 bunch of asparagus, trimmed	1/2 teaspoon kosher salt
1/4 teaspoon cracked black pepper, to taste	1 tablespoon olive oil
1/2 teaspoon dried dill weed	1/2 cup goat cheese, crumbled

Directions

Place the asparagus spears in the lightly greased cooking basket. Toss the asparagus with the olive oil, salt, black pepper, and dill.

Cook in the preheated Air Fryer at 400 degrees F for 9 minutes. **Serve:** garnished with goat cheese. Bon appétit!

Tater Tot Vegetable Casserole

(**Ready in about** 40 minutes | **Servings:** 6)

Ingredients

1 tablespoon olive oil	2 cloves garlic, minced
1 red bell pepper, seeded and sliced	1 yellow bell pepper, seeded and sliced
1 shallot, sliced	1 ½ cups kale
1 (28-ounce) bag frozen tater tots	1 cup milk
Sea salt and ground black pepper, to your liking	6 eggs
	4 tablespoons seasoned breadcrumbs
1 cup Swiss cheese, shredded	

Directions

Heat the olive oil in a saucepan over medium-high heat. Sauté the shallot, garlic, and peppers for 2 to 3 minutes. Add the kale and cook until wilted.

Arrange the tater tots evenly over the bottom of a lightly greased casserole dish. Spread the sautéed mixture over the top.

In a mixing bowl, thoroughly combine the eggs, milk, salt, pepper, and shredded cheese. Pour the mixture into the casserole dish. Lastly, top with the seasoned breadcrumbs. Bake at 330 degrees F for 30 minutes or until top is golden brown. Bon appétit!

Roasted Brussels Sprout Salad

(**Ready in about** 35 minutes + chilling time | **Servings:** 2)

Ingredients

1/2 pound Brussels sprouts	Coarse sea salt and ground black pepper, to taste
1 tablespoon olive oil	
2 ounces baby arugula	2 ounces pancetta, chopped
Lemon Vinaigrette	2 tablespoons extra virgin olive oil
1 shallot, thinly sliced	
1 teaspoon Dijon mustard	2 tbsp fresh lemon juice
1 tablespoon honey	

Directions

Start by preheating your Air Fryer to 380 degrees F.

Add the Brussels sprouts to the cooking basket. Brush with olive oil and cook for 15 minutes. Let it cool to room temperature about 15 minutes.

Toss the Brussels sprouts with the salt, black pepper, baby arugula, and shallot.

Mix all Ingredients for the dressing. Then, dress your salad, garnish with pancetta, and **Serve:** well chilled. Bon appétit!

Spanish Patatas Bravas

(**Ready in about** 15 minutes | **Servings:** 3)

Ingredients

1 pound russet potatoes, cut into 1-inch cubes
1 cup tomatoes, crushed
1/2 teaspoon paprika
2 garlic cloves, crushed
A pinch of brown sugar
Salt and ground black pepper, to taste
1/2 teaspoon chili powder
2 teaspoons canola oil

Directions

Toss the potatoes with 1 teaspoon of oil, salt and black pepper. Transfer the potato chunks to the lightly oiled Air Fryer cooking basket.

Cook the potatoes in your Air Fryer at 400 degrees F for 12 minutes total, shaking the basket halfway through the cooking time.

In the meantime, heat the remaining teaspoon of oil in a saucepan over medium-high heat. Once hot, stir in the other Ingredients cook for 8 to 10 minutes until cooked through.

Spoon the sauce over roasted potatoes and **Serve:** immediately. Enjoy!

Vegetable Oatmeal Fritters

(**Ready in about** 20 minutes | **Servings:** 3)

Ingredients

1 cup rolled oats
1/2 teaspoon shallot powder 1/2 teaspoon porcini powder 1/2 teaspoon garlic powder
1/2 cup celery, grated
1/2 teaspoon mustard seeds
1 ½ cups water
2 tablespoons soy sauce
1 cup white mushrooms, chopped
1 carrot, grated

1/2 teaspoon cumin
2 tablespoons tomato ketchup

Directions

Start by preheating your Air Fryer to 380 degrees F.

Thoroughly combine all Ingredients. Shape the batter into equal patties and place them in the cooking basket. Spritz your patties with a nonstick cooking spray.

Cook the fritters in the preheated Air Fryer for 15 minutes, turning them over halfway through the cooking time.

Serve: with your favorite dipping sauce. Bon appétit!

Favorite Winter Bliss Bowl

(**Ready in about** 25 minutes | **Servings:** 3)

Ingredients

1 pound cauliflower florets
9 ounces frozen crab cakes
1 cup iceberg lettuce
1 red bell pepper, deseeded and sliced
2 tbsp fresh lemon juice
2 tbsp cilantro leaves, chopped
Sea salt and freshly ground black pepper, to taste
1 cup quinoa
1 cup baby spinach
1 tablespoon extra-virgin olive oil
1 teaspoon yellow mustard
1 teaspoon olive oil

Directions

Brush the cauliflower and crab cakes with olive oil; season them with salt and black pepper and transfer them to the cooking basket.
Cook the cauliflower at 400 degrees F for about 12 minutes total, shaking the basket halfway through the cooking time.
Then, cook the crab cakes at 400 degrees F for about 12 minutes total, flipping them halfway through the cooking time.
In the meantime, rinse your quinoa, drain it and transfer to a soup pot with 2 cups of lightly salted water; bring to a boil.
Turn heat to a simmer and continue to cook, covered, for about 20 minutes; fluff with a fork and transfer to a serving bowl.
Add the cauliflower and crab cakes to the bowl. Add your greens and bell pepper to the bowl. In a small mixing dish, whisk the lemon juice, extra- virgin olive oil and yellow mustard.
Drizzle the dressing over all Ingredients, garnish with fresh cilantro and **Serve:** immediately. Bon appétit!

Mexican-Style Roasted Corn Salad

(**Ready in about** 15 minutes | **Servings:** 2)

Ingredients

2 ears of corn, husked
4 ounces Cotija cheese crumbled
1/2 red onion, chopped
1/2 teaspoon Mexican oregano
1 cup Mexican Escabeche
2 tablespoons extra-virgin olive oil
Fresh juice of 1 lime
Kosher salt and freshly ground black pepper, to taste

Directions

Start by preheating your Air Fryer to 390 degrees F.

Place the corn on the cob in the lightly greased cooking basket; cook the corn on the cob for 10 minutes, turning over halfway through the cooking time.

Once the corn has cooled, use a sharp knife to cut off the kernels into a salad bowl. Toss the corn kernels with the remaining Ingredients and **Serve:** immediately. Enjoy!

Winter Bliss Bowl

(**Ready in about** 45 minutes | **Servings:** 3)

Ingredients

1 cup pearled barley
sea salt and ground black pepper, to taste
2 tablespoons champagne vinegar
4 tablespoons olive oil, divided
2 tablespoons cilantro leaves, chopped

1 (1-pound) head cauliflower, broken into small florets Coarse
1 teaspoon yellow mustard
4 tablespoons mayonnaise
10 ounces ounce canned sweet corn, drained

Directions

Cook the barley in a saucepan with salted water. Bring to a boil and cook approximately 28 minutes. Drain and re**Serve:**.

Start by preheating the Air Fryer to 400 degrees F.

Place the cauliflower florets in the lightly greased Air Fryer basket. Season with salt and black pepper; cook for 12 minutes, tossing halfway through the cooking time.

Toss with the re**Serve:**d barley. Add the champagne vinegar, mayonnaise, mustard, olive oil, and corn. Garnish with fresh cilantro. Bon appétit!

Fish & Seafood Recipes

Colorful Salmon and Fennel Salad

(**Ready in about** 20 minutes | **Servings:** 3)

Ingredients

1 pound salmon
Sea salt and ground black pepper, to taste
1/2 teaspoon paprika
1 tablespoon lime juice
1 tablespoon sesame seeds, lightly toasted
1 cucumber, sliced
1 fennel, quartered
1 tablespoon balsamic vinegar
1 teaspoon olive oil
1 tablespoon extra-virgin olive oil
1 tomato, sliced

Directions

Toss the salmon and fennel with 1 teaspoon olive oil, salt, black pepper, and paprika in a mixing bowl.

Cook for 12 minutes in a preheated Air Fryer at 380 degrees F, shaking the basket once or twice.

Transfer the salmon to a salad bowl and cut it into bite-sized strips.

Combine the fennel, balsamic vinegar, lime juice, 1 tablespoon extra-virgin olive oil, tomato, and cucumber in a mixing bowl.

Toss well to combine and **Serve:** topped with lightly toasted sesame seeds. Enjoy!

Parmesan Chip-Crusted Tilapia

(**Ready in about** 15 minutes | **Servings:** 3)

Ingredients

1 ½ pounds tilapia, slice into 4 portions Sea salt and ground black pepper, to taste
1/4 cup parmesan cheese, preferably freshly grated
2 tablespoons buttermilk
1 teaspoon granulated garlic
1/4 cup almond flour
1/2 tbsp cayenne pepper
1 egg, beaten
1 cup tortilla chips, crushed

Directions

Generously season your tilapia with salt, black pepper and cayenne pepper.
Prepare a bread station. Add the granulated garlic, almond flour and parmesan cheese to a rimmed plate.
Whisk the egg and buttermilk in another bowl and place crushed tortilla chips in the third bowl.
Dip the tilapia pieces in the flour mixture, then in the egg/buttermilk mixture and finally roll them in the crushed chips, pressing to adhere well.
Cook in your Air Fryer at 400 degrees F for 10 minutes, flipping halfway through the cooking time. **Serve:** with chips if desired. Bon appétit!

Keto Cod Fillets

(**Ready in about** 15 minutes | **Servings:** 2)

Ingredients

2 cod fish fillets
1 teaspoon Old Bay seasoning 1 egg, beaten
1 teaspoon butter, melted
2 tablespoons coconut milk, unsweetened
1/3 cup coconut flour, unsweetened

Directions

Place the cod fish fillets, butter and Old Bay seasoning in a Ziplock bag; shake until the fish is well coated on all sides.

In a shallow bowl, whisk the egg and coconut milk until frothy.

In another bowl, place the coconut flour. Dip the fish fillets in the egg mixture, then, coat them with coconut flour, pressing to adhere.

Cook the fish at 390 degrees F for 6 minutes; flip them over and cook an additional 6 minutes until your fish flakes easily when tested with a fork. Bon appétit!

Easiest Lobster Tails Ever

(**Ready in about** 10 minutes | **Servings:** 2)

Ingredients

2 (6-ounce) lobster tails
1/2 teaspoon dried rosemary
1/2 teaspoon garlic, pressed
1 teaspoon deli mustard
1 teaspoon olive oil
1 teaspoon fresh cilantro, minced

Sea salt and ground black pepper, to taste

Directions

Toss the lobster tails with the other Ingredients until they are well coated on all sides.

Cook the lobster tails at 370 degrees F for 3 minutes. Then, turn them and cook on the other side for 3 to 4 minutes more until they are opaque.

Serve: warm and enjoy!

Salmon Parcel

Prep time: 15 minutes **Cooking time:** 23 minutes
Servings: 2

Ingredients

2 (4-oz.) salmon fillets	1/4 cup white sauce
6 asparagus stalks	1 teaspoon oil
1/4 cup champagne	Salt and ground black pepper, as required

Directions

In a bowl, merge together all the Ingredients. Divide the salmon mixture over 2 pieces of foil evenly. Seal the foil around the salmon mixture to form the packet.

Choose "Power Button" of Air Fry Oven and turn the dial to select the "Air Fry" mode. Choose the Time button and again turn the dial to set the **Cooking time:** to 13 minutes.

Now press the Temp button and rotate the dial to set the temperature at 355 degrees F. Press "Start/Pause" button to start.

When the unit beeps to show that it is preheated, open the lid. Arrange the salmon parcels in "Air Fry Basket" and insert in the oven. **Serve:** hot.

Ranch Tilapia

Prep time: 15 minutes **Cooking time:** 13 minutes
Servings: 4

Ingredients

3/4 cup cornflakes, crushed	1 (1-oz.) packet dry ranch-style dressing mix
2 1/2 tbsp vegetable oil	
2 eggs	4 (6-oz.) tilapia fillets

Directions

In a shallow bowl, beat the eggs. In another bowl, add the cornflakes, ranch dressing, and oil and mix until a crumbly mixture form.

Dip the fish fillets into egg and then, coat with the breadcrumb's mixture.

Choose "Power Button" of Air Fry Oven and turn the dial to select the "Air Fry" mode. Choose the Time button and again turn the dial to set the cooking time to 13 minutes.

Now press the Temp button and rotate the dial to set the temperature at 356 degrees F. Press "Start/Pause" button to start. When the unit beeps to show that it is preheated, open the lid.

Arrange the tilapia fillets in greased "Air Fry Basket" and insert in the oven. **Serve:** hot.

Salmon with Broccoli

Prep time: 15 minutes **Cooking time:** 12 minutes
Servings: 2

Ingredients

11/2 cups small broccoli florets	2 tablespoons vegetable oil, divided
Salt and ground black pepper, as required	1 tablespoon soy sauce
1 teaspoon light brown sugar	1 teaspoon rice vinegar
1 scallion, thinly sliced	2 (6-oz.) skin-on salmon fillets
1/4 teaspoon cornstarch	1 (1/2-inch) piece fresh ginger, grated

Directions

In a bowl, merge together the broccoli, 1 tablespoon of oil, salt, and black pepper. In another bowl, mix well the ginger, soy sauce, vinegar, sugar, and cornstarch.

Coat the salmon fillets with remaining oil and then with the ginger mixture. Choose "Power Button" of Air Fry Oven and turn the dial to select the "Air Fry" mode.

Choose the Time button and again turn the dial to set the **Cooking time:** to 12 minutes. Now press the Temp button and rotate the dial to set the temperature at 375 degrees F.
Press "Start/Pause" button to start.

When the unit beeps to show that it is preheated, open the lid. Arrange the broccoli florets in greased "Air Fry Basket" and top with the salmon fillets. Insert the basket in the oven. **Serve:** hot.

Sesame-Crusted Tuna Steak

Prep time: 5 minutes **Cooking time:** 8 minutes **Servings:** 2

Ingredients

2 (6-ounce) tuna steaks	1 tablespoon coconut oil, melted
1/2 teaspoon garlic powder	
2 teaspoons white sesame seeds	2 teaspoons black sesame seeds

Directions

Brush each tuna steak with coconut oil and sprinkle with garlic powder. In a large bowl, mix sesame seeds and then press each tuna steak into them, covering the steak as completely as possible. Place tuna steaks into the air fryer basket.

Adjust the temperature to 400F and set the timer for 8 minutes. Flip the steaks halfway through the cooking time. Steaks will be well-done at 145F internal temperature. **Serve:** warm.

Salmon with Prawns and Pasta

Prep time: 20 minutes **Cooking time:** 18 minutes
Servings: 4

Ingredients

14 oz. pasta (of your choice) 4 (4-oz.) salmon steaks
1/2 lb. cherry tomatoes, chopped
2 tablespoons fresh thyme, chopped

2 tablespoons olive oil
4 tablespoons pesto, divided
8 large prawns, peeled and deveined
2 tablespoons fresh lemon juice

Directions

Set a large pan of salted boiling water, add the pasta and cook for about 8-10 minutes or until desired doneness. Meanwhile, in the bottom of a baking pan, spread 1 tablespoon of pesto.

Place salmon steaks and tomatoes over pesto in a single layer and drizzle with the oil. Arrange the prawns on top in a single layer. Drizzle with lemon juice and sprinkle with thyme.

Choose "Power Button" of Air Fry Oven and turn the dial to select the "Air Fry" mode. Choose the Time button and again turn the dial to set the **Cooking time:** to 8 minutes. Now press the Temp button and rotate the dial to set the temperature at 390 degrees F.

Press "Start/Pause" button to start. When the unit beeps to show that it is preheated, open the lid. Arrange the baking pan in "Air Fry Basket" and insert in the oven. Rinse the pasta and transfer into a large bowl. Add the remaining pesto and toss to coat well. Divide the pasta onto serving plate and top with salmon mixture. **Serve:** immediately.

Salmon in Papillote with Orange

Prep time: 20 Minutes **Cooking time:** 30 Minutes
Servings: 4

Ingredients

600g salmon fillet
4 oranges
1 lemon

2 cloves of garlic
Chives to taste

Directions

Pour the freshly squeezed orange juice, the lemon juice, the zest of the two oranges into a bowl. Add two tablespoons of oil, salt, and garlic. Dip the previously washed salmon fillet and leave it in the marinade for one hour, preferably in the refrigerator Place the steak and part of your marinade on a sheet of foil. Salt and sprinkle with chives and a few slices of orange.

Set to 160C. Simmer for 30 minutes. Open the sheet let it evaporate, and **Serve:** with a nice garnish of fresh orange.

Salmon Burgers

Prep time: 20 minutes **Cooking time:** 22 minutes
Servings: 6

Ingredients

3 large russet potatoes, peeled and cubed
3/4 cup frozen vegetables (of your choice), parboiled and drained
Salt and ground black pepper, as required
1/4 cup olive oil

1 egg
6-oz. cooked salmon fillet
1 teaspoon fresh dill, chopped
2 tbsp parsley, chopped
1 cup breadcrumbs

Directions

In a pan of the boiling water, cook the potatoes for about 10 minutes. Drain the potatoes well. Set the potatoes into a bowl and mash with a potato masher.

Set aside to cool completely. In another bowl, add the salmon and flake with a fork. Add the cooked potatoes, egg, parboiled vegetables, parsley, dill, salt and black pepper and mix until well combined.

Make 6 equal-sized patties from the mixture. Coat patties with breadcrumb evenly and then drizzle with the oil evenly. Choose "Power Button" of Air Fry Oven and turn the dial to select the "Air Fry" mode.

Choose the Time button and again turn the dial to set the **Cooking time:** to 12 minutes. Now press the Temp button and rotate the dial to set the temperature at 355 degrees F.

Press "Start/Pause" button to start. When the unit beeps to show that it is preheated, open the lid. Arrange the patties in greased "Air Fry Basket" and insert in the oven.
Flip the patties once halfway through. **Serve:** hot.

Shrimp, Zucchini and Cherry Tomato Sauce

Prep time: 10 Minutes **Cooking time:** 30 Minutes
Servings: 4

Ingredients

2 zucchinis
7 cherry tomatoes
Salt to taste

300 shrimp
1 clove garlic

Directions

Pour the oil, add the garlic clove, and diced zucchini. Cook for 15 minutes at 150C.

Add the shrimp and the pieces of tomato, salt, and spices.
Cook for another 5 to 10 minutes or until the shrimp water evaporates.

Grilled Tilapia with Portobello Mushrooms

(**Ready in about** 20 minutes | **Servings:** 2)

Ingredients
2 tilapia fillets
1/2 teaspoon red pepper flakes, crushed
1/2 teaspoon dried sage, crushed
1 tsp dried parsley flakes

1 tablespoon avocado oil
1/4 teaspoon lemon pepper 1/2 teaspoon sea salt
A few drizzles of liquid smoke
4 medium-sized Portobello mushrooms

Directions

Toss all Ingredients in a mixing bowl; except for the mushrooms.

Transfer the tilapia fillets to a lightly greased grill pan. Preheat your Air Fryer to 400 degrees F and cook the tilapia fillets for 5 minutes.

Now, turn the fillets over and add the Portobello mushrooms. Continue to cook for 5 minutes longer or until mushrooms are tender and the fish is opaque. **Serve:** immediately.

Authentic Mediterranean Calamari Salad

(**Ready in about** 15 minutes | **Servings:** 3)

1 pound squid, cleaned, sliced into rings
2 tablespoons sherry wine
1/2 teaspoon ground black pepper
1 cup grape tomatoes
1 teaspoon yellow mustard
1/3 cup Kalamata olives, pitted and sliced
1/2 cup mayonnaise

1/2 teaspoon granulated garlic Salt, to taste
1/2 teaspoon basil
1/2 teaspoon dried rosemary
1 small red onion, thinly sliced
1/2 cup fresh flat-leaf parsley leaves, coarsely chopped

Directions

Start by preheating the Air Fryer to 400 degrees F. Spritz the Air Fryer basket with cooking oil.

Toss the squid rings with the sherry wine, garlic, salt, pepper, basil, and rosemary. Cook in the preheated Air Fryer for 5 minutes, shaking the basket halfway through the cooking time.

Work in batches and let it cool to room temperature. When the squid is cool enough, add the remaining **Ingredients**.

Gently stir to combine and **Serve:** well chilled. Bon appétit!

Filet of Flounder Cutlets

(**Ready in about** 15 minutes | **Servings:** 2)

Ingredients
1 egg
1/2 cup Pecorino Romano cheese, grated
2 flounder fillets
1 teaspoon dried parsley flakes

1/2 cup cracker crumbs
1/2 teaspoon cayenne pepper
Sea salt and white pepper, to taste

Directions

To make a breading station, whisk the egg until frothy.

In another bowl, mix the cracker crumbs, Pecorino Romano cheese, and spices.

Dip the fish in the egg mixture and turn to coat evenly; then, dredge in the cracker crumb mixture, turning a couple of times to coat evenly.

Cook in the preheated Air Fryer at 390 degrees F for 5 minutes; turn them over and cook another 5 minutes. Enjoy!

King Prawns with Lemon Butter Sauce

(**Ready in about** 15 minutes | **Servings:** 4)

Ingredients
King Prawns
2 cloves garlic, minced
1/2 cup Pecorino Romano cheese, grated
1 teaspoon garlic powder
1 teaspoon mustard seeds
2 tablespoons olive oil

2 tbs fresh lemon juice
1/2 teaspoon Worcestershire sauce

1 ½ pounds king prawns, peeled and deveined
Sea salt and ground white pepper, to your
2 tablespoons butter liking
1/2 teaspoon onion powder
1/4 teaspoon ground black pepper
Sauce

Directions

All Ingredients for the king prawns should be thoroughly combined in a plastic closeable bag; shake to combine well.

Place the coated king prawns in the Air Fryer basket that has been lightly greased.

Cook for 6 minutes at 390°F in a preheated Air Fryer, shaking the basket halfway through. Working in batches is recommended.

Meanwhile, melt the butter in a small saucepan over medium heat and add the remaining Ingredients.

Reduce the heat to low and whisk for 2 to 3 minutes, or until thoroughly heated. Pour the sauce over the hot king prawns. Good appetite!

Spicy Salmon

Prep time: 10 minutes **Cooking time:** 11 minutes
Servings: 2

Ingredients

1 teaspoon smoked paprika
1 teaspoon onion powder
Salt and ground black pepper, as required
2 teaspoons olive oil

1 teaspoon garlic powder
1 teaspoon cayenne pepper
2 (6-oz.) (11/2-inch thick) salmon fillets

Directions

Add the spices in a bowl and mix well. Drizzle the salmon fillets with oil and then, rub with the spice mixture. Choose "Power Button" of Air Fry Oven and turn the dial to select the "Air Fry" mode.

Choose the Time button and again turn the dial to set the **Cooking time:**to 11 minutes. Now press the Temp button and rotate the dial to set the temperature at 390 degrees F.
Press "Start/Pause" button to start.

When the unit beeps to show that it is preheated, open the lid. Arrange the salmon fillets in greased "Air Fry Basket" and insert in the oven. **Serve:** hot.

Lemony Salmon

Prep time: 10 minutes **Cooking time:** 8 minutes
Servings: 3

Ingredients

11/2 lbs. salmon
1 lemon, cut into slices
Salt and ground black pepper, as required

1/2 teaspoon red chili powder
1 tablespoon fresh dill, chopped

Directions

Season the salmon with chili powder, salt, and black pepper. Choose "Power Button" of Air Fry Oven and turn the dial to select the "Air Fry" mode.

Choose the Time button and again turn the dial to set the **Cooking time:**to 8 minutes. Now press the Temp button and rotate the dial to set the temperature at 375 degrees F.

Press "Start/Pause" button to start. When the unit beeps to show that it is preheated, open the lid. Arrange the salmon fillets in greased "Air Fry Basket" and insert in the oven. Garnish with fresh dill and **Serve:** hot.

Honey Glazed Salmon

Prep time: 10 minutes **Cooking time:** 8 minutes
Servings: 2

Ingredients

2 (6-oz.) salmon fillets
Salt, as required

2 tablespoons honey

Directions

Sprinkle the salmon fillets with salt and then, coat with honey. Choose "Power Button" of Air Fry Oven and turn the dial to select the "Air Fry" mode.

Choose the Time button and again turn the dial to set the **Cooking time:**to 8 minutes. Now press the Temp button and rotate the dial to set the temperature at 355 degrees F.

Press "Start/Pause" button to start. When the unit beeps to show that it is preheated, open the lid. Arrange the salmon fillets in greased "Air Fry Basket" and insert in the oven. **Serve:** hot.

Sweet and Sour Glazed Salmon

Prep time: 12 minutes **Cooking time:** 20 minutes
Servings: 2

Ingredients

1/3 cup soy sauce
3 teaspoons rice wine vinegar
1 teaspoon water

1/3 cup honey
4 (31/2-oz.) salmon fillets

Directions

In a small bowl, merge together the soy sauce, honey, vinegar, and water. In another small bowl, re**Serve:** about half of the mixture.

Add salmon fillets in the remaining mixture and coat well.
Cover the bowl and refrigerate to marinate for about 2 hours.

Choose "Power Button" of Air Fry Oven and turn the dial to select the "Air Fry" mode. Choose the Time button and again turn the dial to set the cooking time to 12 minutes.

Now press the Temp button and rotate the dial to set the temperature at 355 degrees F. Press "Start/Pause" button to start. When the unit beeps to show that it is preheated, open the lid.

Arrange the salmon fillets in greased "Air Fry Basket" and insert in the oven. Flip the salmon fillets once halfway through and coat with the re**Serve:**d marinade after every 3 minutes. **Serve:** hot.

Shrimp Skewers with Vermouth

Prep time: 10 Minutes **Cooking time:** 5 Minutes
Servings: 4

Ingredients
11/2 pounds (680 g) shrimp	2 cloves garlic, crushed
1 lemon, cut into wedges	1/4 cup vermouth

Directions

Warm the air fryer to 400F (205C).
Toss the shrimp with the vermouth, olive oil, garlic, salt, and pepper in a bowl and then set it in the fridge to marinate for 1 hour.

Remove the shrimp from the refrigerator and discard the marinade. Skewer the shrimp by piercing through the center and transfer to the basket.

Cook in the warmed air fryer for 5 minutes, flipping the shrimp halfway through. Relish with the lemon wedges and **Serve:** hot.

Fish Sticks

Prep time: 15 minutes **Cooking time:** 12 minutes
Servings: 4

Ingredients
4 (4 ounces) fillets of frozen cod or tilapia thawed	1/4 cup of whole wheat flour
1 tsp. of garlic powder	1 tsp. of salt plus more for sprinkling after air frying
1/2 tsp. of pepper	1 large lemon juiced, plus more for serving after air frying
2 large eggs	
1 cup of panko breadcrumbs	
2 tsp. of old bay	1 tsp. of paprika
	Tarter sauce (recommended for serving)

Directions

Firstly, on your Air-fryer. Then preheat at 400F and set the timer to 10 to 12 minutes.

Then press "Start", the Air-fryer will notify at you when it's finished preheating.
Once warmth set the basket with cooking spray and place in approximately 6 pieces of fish and make sure they aren't touching.

After 5 minutes, carefully flip each piece of fish, and then continue cooking for the remaining 5 minutes.

Remove from Air-fryer, sprinkle with more salt (if necessary) and a generous squeeze of lemon. Repeat with remaining fish. **Serve:** and enjoy with tarter sauce!

Zesty Ranch Fish Fillets

Prep time: 5 minutes **Cooking time:** 12 minutes
Servings: 2 - 4

Ingredients
3/4 cup of bread crumbs or panko	130g packet of dry ranch-style dressing mix
2 eggs beaten	4 tilapia salmon or other fish fillets
2 1/2 tbsp. of vegetable oil	Lemon wedges to garnish

Directions

Preheat your Air-fryer at 180C. Merge the panko/breadcrumbs and the ranch dressing mix together. Attach in the oil and keep stirring until the mixture becomes loose and crumbly.

After that, soak the fish fillets into the egg, letting the excess drip off, dip the fish fillets into the crumb mixture, making sure they are coated evenly and thoroughly. Now place fish fillets into your Air-fryer carefully and cook for 12 to 13 minutes, depending on the thickness of the fillets. Remove and **Serve:** immediately. Press the lemon wedges over the fish if desired.

Fish and Chips

Prep time: 5 minutes **Cooking time:** 10 minutes
Servings: 2 - 4

Ingredients
1 lb. of cod fillet cut into strips	2 tsp. paprika
	1/2 cup of all-purpose flour
1/2 tsp. of garlic powder	1/4 tsp. of black pepper
1/4 tsp. of salt	Large egg beaten
2 cups of panko breadcrumbs Tartar sauce for serving	Lemon wedges for serving

Directions

Mix-up flour with the paprika, garlic powder and salt in a small bowl. Set the egg in another bowl and the panko breadcrumbs in a third bowl.

Set the fish dry using a paper towel. After that, dredge the fish in the flour mixture, then the egg and finally the panko breadcrumbs.

Press it down lightly until the crumbs sticks. Then spray both sides with oil. Now Air-fry at 400F for about for 10 to 12 minutes, turning halfway through cooking until it's crispy and lightly golden. **Serve:** immediately with fries and tartar sauce, and enjoy!

Cornmeal Coated Catfish

Prep time: 15 minutes **Cooking time:** 14 minutes
Servings: 4

Ingredients

2 tablespoons cornmeal	2 teaspoons Cajun seasoning
1/2 tbs garlic powder Salt	2 (6-oz.) catfish fillets
1 tablespoon olive oil	1/2 teaspoon paprika

Directions

In a bowl, mix together the cornmeal, Cajun seasoning, paprika, garlic powder, and salt. Add the catfish fillets and coat with the mixture. Now, coat each fillet with oil.

Choose "Power Button" of Air Fry Oven and turn the dial to select the "Air Fry" mode. Choose the Time button and again turn the dial to set the cooking time to 14 minutes. Now press the Temp button and rotate the dial to set the temperature at 400 degrees F.

Press "Start/Pause" button to start. When the unit beeps to show that it is preheated, open the lid. Arrange the catfish fillets in greased "Air Fry Basket" and insert in the oven. After 10 minutes of cooking, flip the fillets and spray with the cooking spray. **Serve:** hot

Breaded Flounder

Prep time: 15 minutes **Cooking time:** 12 minutes
Servings: 3

Ingredients

1 egg	1 cup dry breadcrumbs
3 (6-oz.) flounder fillets	1 lemon, sliced
1/4 cup vegetable oil	

Directions

In a bowl, beat the egg In another bowl, attach the breadcrumbs and oil and merge until crumbly mixture is formed. Dip flounder fillets into the beaten egg and then, coat with the breadcrumb mixture.

Choose "Power Button" of Air Fry Oven and turn the dial to select the "Air Fry" mode. Choose the Time button and again turn the dial to set the **Cooking time:**to 12 minutes. Now press the Temp button and rotate the dial to set the temperature at 356 degrees F. Press "Start/Pause" button to start.

When the unit beeps to show that it is preheated, open the lid. Arrange the flounder fillets in greased "Air Fry Basket" and insert in the oven. Season with the lemon slices and **Serve:** hot.

Roasted Salmon with Vegetables

Prep time: 15 Minutes **Cooking time:** 14 Minutes
Servings: 2

Ingredients

1 large carrot, peeled and sliced	1 small onion, thinly sliced
	1/4 cup low-fat sour cream
2 (5-ounce / 142-g) salmon fillets	1 fennel bulb, thinly sliced

Directions

Preheat the air fryer to 400F (205C).
In a bowl, mix the carrot, fennel bulb, and onion. Toss well.
Transfer the vegetable mixture to a 6-inch metal pan, and then put the pan in the air fryer basket.

Roast in the preheated air fryer for 4 minutes, or until the vegetables are fork-tender. Remove the pan from the air fryer. Add the sour cream to the pan and season with ground pepper, and then spread the salmon fillets on top.

Set the pan to the air fryer and roast for an additional 10 minutes or until the fish flakes easily when tested with a fork.
Let the salmon and vegetables cool for 5 minutes before serving.

Quick Coconut Shrimp

Prep time: 10 Minutes **Cooking time:** 8 Minutes
Servings: 4

Ingredients

1/4 cup all-purpose flour	1/3 cup shredded unsweetened coconut
1 egg	
1 pound (454 g) raw shrimp, peeled, deveined, and patted dry	1/4 cup panko bread crumbs

Directions

Heat the air fryer to 400F (20°C). On a plate, place the flour. In a small bowl, toss the egg until frothy.

In a separate bowl, mix the coconut, bread crumbs, salt, and pepper. Dredge the shrimp in the flour, shake off any excess, dip them in the egg, and finally coat them in the coconut-bread mixture.

Set the air fryer basket with cooking spray. Put the breaded shrimp in the basket and spray with cooking spray.

Cook in the warmed air fryer for 8 minutes, flipping the shrimp once during cooking, or until the shrimp are opaque and crisp. Remove from the basket and **Serve:** on a plate.

Cod Parcel

Prep time: 20 minutes **Cooking time:** 15 minutes
Servings: 2

Ingredients

2 tablespoons butter, melted	1 tablespoon fresh lemon juice
1/2 teaspoon dried tarragon	
Salt and ground black pepper, as required	1/2 cup carrots, peeled and julienned
1/2 cup red bell peppers,	1/2 cup fennel bulbs, julienned
2 (5-oz.) frozen cod fillets, thawed	1 tablespoon olive oil

Directions

In a large bowl, merge together the butter, lemon juice, tarragon, salt, and black pepper. Add the bell pepper, carrot, and fennel bulb and generously coat with
the mixture. Arrange 2 large parchment squares onto a smooth surface.

Coat the cod fillets with oil and then, sprinkle evenly with salt and black pepper. Arrange 1 cod fillet onto each parchment square and top each evenly with the vegetables.

Top with any remaining sauce from the bowl.
Fold the parchment paper and crimp the sides to secure fish and vegetables. Choose "Power Button" of Air Fry Oven and turn the dial to select the "Air Fry" mode.

Choose the Time button and again turn the dial to set the **Cooking time:**to 15 minutes. Now press the Temp button and rotate the dial to set the temperature at 350 degrees F. Press "Start/Pause" button to start.

When the unit beeps to show that it is preheated, open the lid. Arrange the cod parcels in "Air Fry Basket" and insert in the oven. **Serve:** hot.

Salted Marinated Salmon

Prep time: 10 Minutes **Cooking time:** 30 Minutes
Servings: 2

Ingredients

500g salmon fillet	1 kg of coarse salt

Directions

Place the baking paper on the basket and the salmon on top (skin side up) covered with coarse salt.

Set the air fryer to 150C. Cook everything for 25 to 30 minutes. At the end of cooking, remove the salt from the fish and **Serve:** with a drizzle of oil.

Cod Burgers

Prep time: 15 minutes **Cooking time:** 7 minutes
Servings: 6

Ingredients

1/2 lb. cod fillets	1/2 teaspoon fresh lime zest, grated finely
1/2 egg	
1/2 teaspoon red chili paste Salt, to taste	1/2 tablespoon fresh lime juice
3 tablespoons coconut, grated and divided	1 tablespoon fresh parsley, chopped
	1 small scallion, chopped

Directions

In a food processor, add cod filets, lime zest, egg, chili paste, salt and lime juice and pulse until smooth. Transfer the cod mixture into a bowl.

Add 11/2 tablespoons coconut, scallion and parsley and mix until well combined. Make 6 equal-sized patties from the mixture.

In a shallow dish, place the remaining coconut. Coat the patties in coconut evenly. Choose "Power Button" of Air Fry Oven and turn the dial to select the "Air Fry" mode.

Choose the Time button and again turn the dial to set the **Cooking time:**to 7 minutes. Now press the Temp button and rotate the dial to set the temperature at 375 degrees F.

Press "Start/Pause" button to start. When the unit beeps to show that it is preheated, open the lid. Arrange the patties in greased "Air Fry Basket" and insert in the oven. **Serve:** hot.

Stuffed Cuttlefish

Prep time: 20 Minutes **Cooking time:** 30 Minutes
Servings: 4

Ingredients

small cuttlefish	50g of breadcrumbs
Garlic to taste	Parsley to taste
1 egg	

Directions

Clean the cuttlefish, cut, and separate the tentacles. In a blender, pour the breadcrumbs, the parsley (without the branches), the egg, the salt, a drizzle of olive oil, and the sepia tentacles. Blend until you get a dense mixture. Fill the sepia with the mixture obtained. Place the cuttlefish in the bowl.

Beer Battered Fish

Prep time: 10 minutes **Cooking time:** 12 minutes
Servings: 5

Ingredients

1 cup of all-purpose flour
2 tbsp. of cornstarch
1 egg beaten
1 tsp. of salt
1/2 tsp. of paprika
11/2 lb. of cod cut into 4 or 5 pieces

1/2 tsp. of baking soda 6 oz. of beer
3/4 cup of all flour
1/4 tsp. of ground black pepper
Vegetable oil
Pinch of cayenne pepper

Directions

Merge the 1 cup of flour, cornstarch and baking soda in a large bowl and add the beer and egg, stir until it's smooth. Seal the bowl of batter with plastic wrap and refrigerate for at least 20 minutes. Combine the 3/4 cup of flour, paprika, salt, black pepper and cayenne pepper in a shallow dredging pan.

Set the cod fish fillets dry with a paper towel. Now dip the fish into the batter, coating all sides and allow the excess batter to drip off and then coat each fillet with the seasoned flour.

Whisk any leftover flour on the fish fillets and pat gently to adhere the flour to the batter. After that, pre-heat your air fryer at 390F. Air-fry for 12 minutes at 390F. **Serve:** with lemon wedges, malt vinegar and tartar sauce.

Breaded Sea Scallops

Prep time: 10 minutes **Cooking time:** 5 minutes
Servings: 2 - 4

Ingredients

1/2 cup of finely crushed buttery crackers
1 lb. of sea scallops, patted dry
2 tbsp. of butter, melted

1/2 tsp. of seafood seasoning
1 serving cooking spray
1/2 tsp. of garlic powder

Directions

Preheat the Air-fryer to 390F. Merge cracker crumbs, garlic powder, and seafood seasoning together in a bowl.
Place dissolved butter in a second bowl. Then start to dip each scallop in the melted butter and roll in the breading until it's completely coated.

Bring on a plate and repeat with the remaining scallops. Set the air fryer basket with cooking spray. Set scallops in the prepared basket so that they don't touching each other. You may require working in batches. Cook in the preheated air-fryer. Turn scallops over gently with a small spatula and cook.

Crab Cakes

Prep time: 15 minutes **Cooking time:** 10 minutes
Servings: 4 - 5

Ingredients

1 large egg, beaten
1 tsp. of Worcestershire sauce

2 tbsp. of finely chopped green onion
1 pinch of salt and black pepper to taste
11 crackers saltine crackers, crushed
1 tsp. of baking powder

2 tbsp. of mayonnaise
1 tsp. of seafood seasoning 1/2 tsp. of hot pepper sauce
1 lb. of lump crabmeat, drained and picked over
3 tbsp. of milk
4 wedges lemon
1 serving olive oil cooking spray
1 tsp. of Dijon mustard

Directions

Mix-up egg, mayonnaise, Worcestershire sauce, mustard, seafood seasoning, and hot pepper sauce in a small mixing bowl and stir in green onion and set aside.

Set crab meat in a medium bowl and break up with a fork. Then add milk, salt, and pepper and toss to coat. Attach crushed saltines and baking powder and toss lightly to combine. Attach to the egg mixture, stirring gently and being careful not to break apart the crab lumps.
Spoon crab with a 1/3-cup measure and form into 8 patties. Set patties on a plate, cover, and refrigerate for about 1 hour or until its firm.

Preheat your Air-fryer at 400F then spray crab cakes on both sides with cooking spray and place them in the air fryer basket. Cook and then gently turn the cakes over, and cook 5 minutes longer until it turns crispy brown. **Serve:** immediately!

Lemon Pepper Shrimp

Prep time: 5 minutes **Cooking time:** 10 minutes
Servings: 2 -4

Ingredients

1 tbsp. of olive oil
1 lemon, juiced
1/4 tsp. of garlic powder

1 tsp. of lemon pepper
1/4 tsp. of paprika
12 oz. of uncooked medium shrimp, peeled and deveined 1 Lemon, sliced

Directions

Preheat your Air-fryer to 400F. Then mix olive oil, lemon juice, lemon pepper, paprika, and garlic powder in a bowl. Add shrimp and toss until it's coated.

Set shrimp in the air fryer and cook until it turns pink and firm for about 6 to 10 minutes. **Serve:** with lemon slices.

Crispy Fish Tacos with Slaw

Prep time: 15 minutes **Cooking time:** 18 minutes
Servings: 2 - 4

Ingredients

1 serving nonstick of cooking spray
4 cups of cabbage slaw mix
1 tbsp. of olive oil
1/4 cup of all-purpose flour
1/4 tsp. of ground black pepper
1/4 tsp. of ground cayenne pepper
1 pound of cod fillets, cut into bite-sized pieces

1 tbsp. of chopped fresh jalapeno pepper
1 tbsp. of lime juice
1 tbsp. of apple cider vinegar
1/4 cup of yellow cornmeal
2 tbsp. of taco seasoning mix
8 (6 inch) corn tortillas
1/2 tsp. of salt

Directions

Preheat an air fryer to 400 F and spray the basket of the Air-fryer with cooking spray. Merge cabbage slaw, jalapeno pepper, lime juice, olive oil, vinegar, salt, pepper, and cayenne pepper in a large bowl. Then mix until evenly combined and set it aside.

Merge together flour, cornmeal, and taco seasoning in a separate bowl. Attach fish pieces and toss until evenly coated, discarding any remaining seasoning mix. Set in the prepared Air-fryer basket and mist lightly with cooking spray.

Cook fish in the preheated air fryer and shake the basket, then cook until fish is crispy and flakes easily with a fork, for about 5 minutes more.

Crumbed Fish

Preparation 10 minutes **Cooking time:** 12 minutes
Servings: 2 - 4

Ingredients

1 cup of dry bread crumbs
1/4 cup of vegetable oil
1 sliced lemon

4 each of flounder fillets
1 egg, beaten

Directions

Preheat your Air-fryer at 350F in a bowl, mix bread crumbs and oil together and stir until mixture. Soak fish fillets into the egg; shake off any excess. Dip fillets into the

bread crumb mixture; coat evenly and fully.
Set coated fillets gently in the preheated air fryer and cook for about 12 minutes until fish flakes easily with a fork. Garnish with lemon slices. **Serve:** and enjoy!

Healthy White Fish with Garlic and Lemon

Prep time: 5 minutes **Cooking time:** 12 minutes
Servings: 2 - 4

Ingredients

12 oz. of tilapia filets or 2 filets (6 oz. each)
1/2 tsp. of garlic powder (2.5 ml)
Kosher salt or sea salt , to taste
Fresh chopped parsley

1/2 tsp. of lemon pepper seasoning (2.5 ml)
1/2 tsp. of onion powder (optional)
Lemon wedges
Fresh cracked black pepper , to taste

Directions

Pre-heat your Air-fryer at 360F for 5 minutes. Wash and pat dry the fish filets. Cover or coat with olive oil spray and season with garlic powder,

lemon pepper, and/or onion powder, salt and pepper. Lay perforated Air-fryer baking paper inside base of air fryer and lightly spray the paper. If you are not using a liner, spray enough olive oil spray at the base of the Air-fryer basket to make sure fish does not stick.

Set the fish on top of the paper and add a few lemon wedges next to fish. Line with Parchment Paper.

After that, Air-Fry at 360F for about 6 to12 minutes. Sprinkle with chopped parsley and **Serve:** warm with the toasted lemon wedges.

Southern Fried Catfish Nuggets

Prep time: 5 minutes **Cooking time:** 17 minutes
Servings: 2

Ingredients

2 pounds of catfish nuggets 1/4 cup of oil

10 ounces box of fish fry mix

Directions

Firstly, wash fish and set aside. Whisk half the box of fish fry mix into a large Ziploc bag.

Attach the Catfish Nuggets into the bag with the fish fry mix. Secure the bag and shake well to coat. Using the tongs, detach the nuggets one at a time, shaking off excess batter. Attach the catfish nuggets to the basket of the Air-fryer. Check the Directions of your Air-fryer for filling the basket in case it requires no over filling of basket.

Toss the oil into a small bowl, dip your basting brush into the oil and baste a small amount of oil onto the top of each catfish nugget. Set your Air-fryer on to 380F and set timer for 17 minutes. Start checking at about 12 minutes.
Detach from basket when done and drain on paper toweling. Attach the next batch to the basket and repeat. **Serve:** when ready and enjoy!

Air Fryer Blackened Fish Tacos

Prep time: 20 minutes **Cooking time:** 25 minutes
Serve: 1

Ingredients

1 (15 ounces) can seasoned black beans, rinsed, and drained
½ teaspoon salt
1 teaspoon Louisiana-style hot sauce (Optional)
¼ cup blackened seasoning
4 (6 inches) corn tortillas
1 tablespoon olive oil
1 tablespoon lime juice
2 ears corn, kernels
1 pound tilapia fillets
cooking spray
1 lime, cut into wedges

Directions

Preheat the oven carefully to 400 degrees Fahrenheit (200 degrees C). Combine black beans, corn, olive oil, lime juice, and salt in a mixing dish. Set aside after gently stirring until the beans and corn are uniformly covered.

Place the fish fillets on a clean work area and pat with paper towels to dry. Spray each fillet lightly with cooking spray and sprinkle with ½ of the blackened seasoning. Turn the fillets over, spray with cooking spray, and season with the rest of the spice.

Place the fish in the air fryer basket in a single layer, working in batches if required. 2 minutes in the oven, cook for 2 minutes more on the other side before transferring to a platter. Cook for 10 minutes, stirring halfway through, in the bean and corn mixture, in the air fryer basket. Fill corn tortillas with fish and top with bean and corn mixture. **Serve:** with lime wedges and spicy sauce on the side.

Baked Fish Fillets

Prep time: 15 minutes **Cooking time:** 25 minutes
Serve: 1

Ingredients

1 tablespoon vegetable oil, or to taste
⅛ tbsp ground black pepper
2 tablespoons lemon juice
1 teaspoon salt
2 pounds mackerel fillets
¼ cup butter, melted
⅛ teaspoon ground paprika

Directions

Preheat the oven carefully to 350°F (175 degrees C). Vegetable oil should be used to grease a baking pan. Season the mackerel fillets in the baking pan with salt and pepper.

Combine the butter, lemon juice, and paprika in a mixing dish. **Serve:** with mackerel fillets. Cook in a preheated oven for 20 to 25 minutes or until the mackerel flakes easily with a fork.

Tamarind Sauce Fish Curry

Prep time: 15 minutes **Cooking time:** 20 minutes
Serve: 1

Ingredients

2 pounds white carp
1 tablespoon vegetable oil
1 cup warm water
1 ½ teaspoons salt
½ teaspoon cumin seeds
1 large onion, minced

2 tablespoons red chili powder
2 tablespoons ground coriander
¼ cup oil
1 tablespoon red chili powder
¼ cup tamarind pulp
1 ½ tablespoon garlic paste
1 pinch salt to taste
1 tablespoon chopped fresh coriander
1 tbs ground turmeric

Directions

Place the fish in a bowl and toss with 1 tablespoon vegetable oil, 1 tablespoon chili powder, turmeric, and 1 1/2 teaspoons salt for about 10 minutes. Pour warm water over the tamarind pulp in a dish.

To obtain the juice from the tamarind, squeeze it. In a pan over medium heat, heat 1/4 cup oil; add cumin seeds and stir. Cook, constantly stirring, until the onion is transparent, 5 to 10 minutes. Cook for 3 minutes after adding the garlic paste.

Cover the skillet and cook the carp for 5 minutes. Bring the fish mixture to a boil with the tamarind juice. Turn the carp pieces over and season with 2 teaspoons red chili powder, coriander, and salt. Cook over low heat for 10 minutes or until the sauce thickens and the oil separates. Garnish with coriander leaves if desired.

Baja Sauce for Fish or Shrimp Tacos

Prep time: 15 minutes **Cooking time:** 25 minutes
Serve: 1

Ingredients

¼ cup sour cream
1 teaspoon lime juice
¾ teaspoon seafood seasoning (such as Old Bay®)
¼ cup mayonnaise
1 tbsp chopped cilantro
¼ teaspoon ground ancho chili pepper

Directions

Combine the sour cream, mayonnaise, lime juice, cilantro, seafood seasoning, and ancho chili pepper in a mixing bowl. Refrigerate for at least 1 hour, covered with plastic wrap.

Homemade Fish Stock

Prep time: 15 minutes **Cooking time:** 20 minutes
Serve: 1

Ingredients

3 pounds fish heads, bones, and trimmings
2 tablespoons unsalted butter
1 rib celery, chopped
1 cup dry white wine
10 whole black peppercorns

2 leeks, white part only, thinly sliced
1 carrot, chopped
2 ½ quarts water
1 bouquet garni
3 thick slices of lemon

Directions

Fish should be washed in cold water and thoroughly drained. Melt the butter in a saucepan over low heat. Cook until the leeks, carrots, and celery are cooked, 5 to 7 minutes. Bring the fish portions, wine, and water to a boil for about 5 minutes. Residuum should be skimmed and discarded. After adding the bouquet garni, peppercorns, and lemon, return to a boil.

Sexy Fish Stew

Prep time: 15 minutes **Cooking time:** 18 minutes
Serve: 1

Ingredients

2 tablespoons butter
salt and pepper to taste
½ cup sliced shallots salt
1 ¼ cups chicken broth
1 pound baby red potatoes, trimmed
½ cup heavy whipping cream
1 tbs chopped fresh tarragon

1 large leek, cleaned and thinly sliced
¾ cup white wine
½ cup thinly sliced fennel bulb
1 pinch cayenne pepper
1-pound boneless rockfish filets, cut into 1-inch pieces

Directions

In a large saucepan over medium-low heat, melt the butter. Cook and stir the leek, shallots, and 1/2 teaspoon salt in the melted butter for 10 to 15 minutes, or until softened. Stir the wine into the leek mixture, turn the heat up to medium and cook for 2 minutes. Bring the chicken broth to a boil. Stir in the fennel and potatoes and cook, occasionally turning, until the potatoes are nearly cooked about 10 minutes. Season with salt, pepper, and cayenne pepper to taste. Stir in the cream to mix.
Cover and heat for 3 minutes after adding the fish and tarragon to the soup. Reduce heat to medium-low, stir gently, and cook until fish flakes easily with a fork, about 6 minutes. Season with salt and black pepper to taste.

Fish and Chips Sliders

Prep time: 15 minutes **Cooking time:** 22 minutes
Serve: 1

Ingredients

cooking spray
3 egg whites
1 tbs. apple cider vinegar
1 pound cod fillets
2 green onions, chopped
1 pinch salt and ground black pepper 8 slider buns

1 (8.5 ounces) bag malt vinegar-and-sea salt chips
½ teaspoon celery seed
⅓ cup plain Greek yogurt
2 tbs honey mustard
3 cups coleslaw mix

Directions

Preheat the oven carefully to 450 degrees Fahrenheit (230 degrees C). Spray a wire rack with cooking spray and place it on a rimmed baking sheet.
Blend the chips in batches until they have the consistency of breadcrumbs. Place the chips on a flat platter.
In a mixing basin, combine egg whites. Place a piece of fish on the prepared rack after dipping it in egg white and coating it with chip crumbs. Rep with the leftover fish. Coat the fish with frying spray. Bake for 15 minutes in a preheated oven. Turn on the broiler and broil
the salmon for 5 minutes, or until it is golden and crispy.
In a large mixing bowl, combine coleslaw mix and green onions while the fish is cooking. Combine the yogurt, honey mustard, vinegar, celery seed, salt, and pepper in a separate dish. Toss the coleslaw mix with the dressing to blend.

Cod Fish Cakes

Prep time: 18 minutes **Cooking time:** 20 minutes
Serve: 1

Ingredients

2 large potatoes, peeled and halved
1 tablespoon grated onion
1 egg

1 tablespoon butter
1 pound cod fillets, cubed
1 tbs chopped fresh parsley
3 tablespoons oil for frying

Directions

Put the potatoes in a large saucepan of water and bring to a boil. Allow the potatoes to simmer until almost tender.
Add the fish to the saucepan and boil until both the fish and the potatoes are tender. Drain well and place the potatoes and fish in a large mixing dish.
Mash together the butter, onion, parsley, and egg in mixing dish

Chicken-Cheese-Fish

Prep time: 18 minutes **Cooking time:** 20 minutes
Serve: 1

Ingredients

2 pounds skinless, boneless chicken breast halves	1 cup shredded Swiss cheese
	4 cups shred Cheddar cheese
4 (3 ounces) cans of tuna packed in olive oil	2 cups heavy whipping cream 4 eggs, beaten
2 cups crumbled feta	1 cup shredded mozzarella cheese
2 cups ricotta cheese	
1 (8 ounces) package cream cheese, softened	3 cups Italian seasoned breadcrumbs
2 eggs, beaten	2 (16 ounces) cans pink salmon, drained
2 tbs butter, cut small pieces	

Directions

Preheat the oven carefully to 350°F (175 degrees C). Fill a large baking dish halfway with chicken breasts. Sprinkle with Cheddar and Swiss cheeses. Layer the tuna and salmon on the cheese in an equal layer. In a mixing bowl, combine the whipped cream and the 4 beaten eggs; pour over the top of the dish.

In a mixing dish, combine the feta, mozzarella, and ricotta cheeses; distribute over the fish. Next, combine the cream cheese, 2 beaten eggs, and breadcrumbs; spread evenly over the cheese. Finally, arrange little slices of butter evenly throughout the entire dish. Wrap with aluminum foil. Bake for 1 1/2 hours, or until cooked through and golden brown on top, in a preheated oven.

Fish Batter with Newcastle™ Brown Ale

Prep time: 15 minutes **Cooking time:** 25 minutes
Serve: 1

Ingredients

1-quart vegetable oil for frying	½ cup flour
½ cup cornmeal	1 pound cod fillets, cut into pieces
½ teaspoon garlic powder	1 teaspoon garlic salt
1 cup brown ale (such as Newcastle™ brown ale)	½ tbsp ground cinnamon

Directions

Heat the oil in a deep fryer to 325°F (165 degrees C). Combine the flour, cornmeal, garlic salt, garlic powder, and cinnamon in a large mixing bowl. Mix in the beer until there are no dry lumps left. Dip the fish into the batter, allowing some of the excess to run out before gently placing it in the deep fryer. Cook for 8 minutes, or until the fish is golden brown and crispy on the exterior and easily flaked. To prevent overcrowding the deep fryer, cook the fish in batches.

Classic Fish and Chips

Prep time: 20 minutes **Cooking time:** 20 minutes
Serve: 1

Ingredients

4 large potatoes, peeled and cut into strips	1 cup all-purpose flour
1 teaspoon ground black pepper	1 teaspoon baking powder
	1 cup milk
1 egg	1 teaspoon salt
1 ½ pounds cod fillets	1-quart vegetable oil for frying

Directions

Place the potatoes in a medium dish of cool water. In a medium-sized mixing basin, combine the flour, baking powder, salt, and pepper separately. Whisk in the milk and egg and continue to stir until the mixture is smooth. Allow the mixture to stand for 20 minutes.

Preheat the oil to 350°F in a big pot or electric skillet (175 degrees C). Fry the potatoes until they are soft in heated oil. They should be drained on paper towels.

Dredge the fish in the batter, one piece at a time, and fry in heated oil. Fry the fish till golden brown. Increase the heat as needed to keep the temperature at 350 degrees F (175 degrees C). Drain well on paper towels. Fry the potatoes for another 1 to 2 minutes to enhance crispness.

Fish and Things Teriyaki Marinade

Prep time: 15 minutes **Cooking time:** 25 minutes
Serve: 1

Ingredients

2 cups soy sauce	¾ cup brown sugar, divided
1 cup honey	
¾ cup white sugar, divided	1 clove garlic, chopped
	4 slices fresh ginger root
8 green onions	

Directions

In a 2-quart saucepan, combine soy sauce, 1/2 cup brown sugar, 1/2 cup white sugar, green onions, ginger, and garlic. Bring the mixture to a simmer. Reduce the heat to low and continue to cook for 15 minutes.

Pour in the remaining whites and brown sugar, as well as the honey. Bring the water to a boil. When the mixture rises and foams and doubles in size, take it from the fire and set it aside to cool.

Twice Fried Fish

Prep time: 10 minutes **Cooking time:** 18 minutes
Serve: 1

Ingredients

1 tablespoon hoisin sauce	1 tablespoon canned
1 tablespoon dry sherry	tomato sauce
1 teaspoon ground black	1 teaspoon white sugar
pepper	1 teaspoon salt
1 ½ pounds cod fillets	3 tablespoons vegetable oil
2 tbs dark soy sauce	1 tablespoon lard
1 teaspoon cornstarch	4 tablespoons water

Directions

Mix hoisin sauce, tomato sauce, sherry, pepper, soy sauce, sugar, and salt in a mixing bowl. Allow for a 20-minute resting period.

1 tablespoon of oil should be rubbed into the filets of fish. Heat the remaining 2 tablespoons of oil in a large pan. Fry the fish for 2 minutes on both sides, then drain on paper towels.

Remove the skillet's oil and replace it with 1 tablespoon of lard. Melt over medium heat and toss in the soy sauce mixture. Dissolve the cornstarch in the water and pour it into the skillet, continually swirling. Cook until the sauce thickens.

Return the fish to the skillet and cook for another minute on each side.

Grilled Tuna Fish Steaks

Prep time: 20 minutes **Cooking time:** 20 minutes
Serve: 1

Ingredients

8 (3 ounces) fillets fresh	½ cup soy sauce
tuna steaks, 1 inch thick	1 tablespoon fresh lime
	juice
⅓ cup sherry	¼ cup vegetable oil
1 clove garlic, minced	

Directions

In a shallow baking dish, place the tuna steaks. Combine the soy sauce, sherry, vegetable oil, fresh lime juice, and garlic in a medium mixing bowl. Turn the tuna steaks in the soy sauce mixture to coat. Refrigerate for at least one hour, covered.

Preheat the grill to high. Grease the grill grate lightly. Place the tuna steaks on the grill and discard the marinade. Grill for 3 to 6 minutes per side, or until done to preference.

Baked Fish Croquettes

Prep time: 15 minutes **Cooking time:** 25 minutes
Serve: 1

Ingredients

2 cups leftover cooked	1 cup soft
steelhead trout	breadcrumbs
½ sweet onion, minced	½ cup mayonnaise
½ cup sour cream	½ lemon, juiced
½ teaspoon	½ teaspoon seasoned salt,
Worcestershire sauce	or more to taste
½ teaspoon garlic powder	½ cup panko
ground black pepper to	breadcrumbs, or as
taste	needed

Directions

Preheat the oven carefully to 425°F (220 degrees C). Then, using parchment paper or aluminum foil, line a baking pan.

Remove the skin, bones, and crust from the trout and flake it with a fork. In a mixing bowl, combine flaked fish, soft breadcrumbs, onion, mayonnaise, sour cream, lemon juice, Worcestershire sauce, salt, garlic powder, and black pepper. Form the mixture into balls, then roll each one in the panko. Place the balls on the baking sheet that has been prepared.

Bake for 15 to 20 minutes, or until the croquettes are gently browned and crispy.

Accidental Fish

Prep time: 15 minutes **Cooking time:** 20 minutes
Serve: 1

Ingredients

4 ounces fillets Mahi Mahi	½ cup salted butter
2 drops Louisiana-style	1 Roma tomato, seeded
hot sauce	and chopped
1 tablespoon lemon juice	1 clove garlic, minced
1 green onion, chopped	2 teaspoons olive oil

Directions

Preheat the oven carefully to 450°F (230 degrees C). Place the mahi-mahi fillets on a baking dish and brush with olive oil. Bake for 20 minutes in a preheated oven or until the fish flakes easily with a fork. Melt the butter in a skillet over medium heat while the mahi-mahi bakes.

Simmer the garlic, lemon juice, and spicy sauce in the melted butter for 1 minute. Cook and stir the tomato and green onion into the butter mixture until heated. To **Serve:**, spoon the sauce over the cooked fish.

Fish Tacos from Reynolds Wrap

Prep time: 15 minutes **Cooking time:** 20 minutes
Serve: 1

Ingredients

Reynolds Wrap® Non-Stick Aluminum Foil
1 teaspoon olive oil
1 tablespoon fresh lime juice
½ teaspoon salt
1 clove garlic, minced
Mango salsa

4 (4 ounces) tilapia fillets, fresh or frozen (thawed)
1 teaspoon seafood seasoning
⅛ teaspoon red pepper flakes
Sliced avocado

Directions

Preheat the oven carefully to 400°F. Line a 13x9x2-inch baking sheet with Reynolds Wrap® Nonstick Foil, nonstick (dull) side up.

Place the tilapia in a pan lined with foil. Combine lime juice, olive oil, seafood seasoning, garlic, salt, and red pepper flakes in a medium mixing bowl. Pour over the fish. Bake for 18 to 20 minutes, or until the salmon flakes easily with a fork. Fill each tortilla with 1/2 fillet, lettuce, salsa, and avocado.

Corn Crusted Red Fish

Prep time: 15 minutes **Cooking time:** 20 minutes
Serve: 1

Ingredients

1 ½ cups fresh corn kernels
1 tbsp red onion, chopped
1 tablespoon cornstarch
1 cup all-purpose flour
1 teaspoon Creole seasoning, or to taste
1 tablespoon vegetable oil

1 tablespoon red bell pepper, chopped

4 (5 ounces) red snapper fillets
3 egg whites, lightly beaten

Directions

Preheat the oven carefully to 350°F (175 degrees C). In a mixing dish, combine corn kernels, bell pepper, onion, and cornstarch; put aside.

Season the red snapper with the Creole seasoning. Dip the fish in the flour, then in the egg whites. Coat both sides of the fish with the corn mixture by pushing it into the egg whites.

In an oven-safe skillet, heat the vegetable oil over medium-high heat. Fry the fillets in the pan until brown, about 5 minutes per side. Place the pan in the preheated oven and cook for another 5 minutes, or until the fish flakes easily with a fork.

Halibut Fish Tacos

Prep time: 15 minutes **Cooking time:** 18 minutes
Serve: 1

Ingredients

1 lime, juiced
¼ cup chopped cilantro
1 jalapeno pepper, diced
¼ teaspoon ground cumin
½ pound halibut fillets
8 corn tortillas
1 cup shredded pepper Jack cheese

¼ cup olive oil
1 tablespoon ground ancho chili powder
salt and black pepper to taste
2 cups shredded cabbage
1 (8 ounces) jar salsa
1 avocado, sliced

Directions

In a large mixing bowl or resealable zip-top bag, combine lime juice, olive oil, cilantro, jalapeño, chili powder, cumin, salt, and pepper. Marinade the halibut for 20 to 25 minutes. Do not over marinate the fish since the lime juice will begin to 'cook' it.

Preheat an outside grill to medium heat and brush the grate gently with oil. Drain marinade and cook fillets for 5 minutes on each side. Cook for another 2 minutes, or until the salmon flakes easily with a fork.

Warm the tortillas on the grill or in the oven. Top tortillas with fish, cabbage, salsa, pepper Jack cheese, and avocado.

Beer Batter for Fish

Prep time: 15 minutes **Cooking time:** 22 minutes
Serve: 1

Ingredients

3 eggs, ¾ cup beer
4 cups pastry flour

½ teaspoon baking soda

.063 teaspoon garlic powder
2 quarts of vegetable oil for frying

1 ½ cups milk
1 tablespoon baking powder
ground black pepper to taste
1 ½ pounds cod fillets

2 tablespoons cornstarch
salt to taste

Directions

Combine flour, baking powder, baking soda, and cornstarch in a medium mixing basin. In a large mixing basin, combine eggs and milk. Pour in the beer.

Mix in the flour mixture. Season with salt, pepper, and garlic powder to taste. Heat the oil to 375 degrees F in an electric deep fryer or a heavy saucepan (190 degrees C).

Coat the fish with batter and place it in the heated oil. Fry for 4 to 5 minutes, or until golden brown. **Serve:**.

Fort Worth Fish Tacos

Prep time: 10 minutes **Cooking time:** 18 minutes
Serve: 1

Ingredients

8 (3 ounces) fillets tilapia
2 tb hot pepper sauce
2 small limes, quartered
2 tbsp chopped fresh cilantro
1 (5.3 ounces) container plain Greek yogurt
1 teaspoon salt
1 cup dark beer
¼ teaspoon ground black pepper

¼ medium head cabbage, finely shredded

2 teaspoons salt
4 ounces cream cheese softened
½ cup mayonnaise
1 tablespoon lime juice
1 cup flour
8 (8 inches) flour tortillas
1 teaspoon garlic powder
cayenne pepper to taste
3 cups peanut oil for frying
(8 ounces) jar prepared salsa
¼ cup chopped fresh cilantro

Directions

Place the tilapia fillets on a platter and season with salt and spicy sauce; cover and chill while creating the cilantro cream sauce. In a small or large measuring cup, combine cream cheese, 2 tablespoons cilantro, mayonnaise, and yogurt; stir well. Mix the lime juice into the cream sauce. Refrigerate, covered.

In a mixing basin, add flour, salt, garlic powder, cayenne pepper, and pepper; stir in beer to produce a smooth batter. Heat the oil in a big, deep-frying pan to 375°F (190 degrees C).

Remove the fish from the refrigerator, dip it in the beer batter, and cook it three times in the heated oil, flipping it until golden (approximately 2 minutes on each side, depending on the thickness). Drain the fish on paper towels and place it on a covered platter to keep warm. Rep with the remaining fillets.

Wrap tortillas in a clean kitchen towel and microwave for 20 seconds or warm. Assemble tacos by laying a heated tortilla on top of a fish fillet. Shredded cabbage properly, a dollop of cilantro cream sauce, a teaspoon of salsa, and a sprinkling of chopped cilantro complete the dish. Each taco should be **Serve:**d with a lime quarter for squeezing.

Snacks, Sides & Appetizers

Root Vegetable Chips with Dill Mayonnaise

(**Ready in about** 40 minutes | **Servings:** 4)

Ingredients

1/2 pound red beetroot, julienned
1/2 pound golden beetroot, julienned
1/2 cup mayonnaise
Sea salt and ground black pepper, to taste
1 teaspoon olive oil
1/4 pound carrot
1 teaspoon garlic, minced
1/4 teaspoon dried dill weed

Directions

Toss your veggies with salt, black pepper and olive oil.

Arrange the veggie chips in a single layer in the Air Fryer cooking basket.

Cook the veggie chips in the preheated Air Fryer at 340 degrees F for 20 minutes; tossing the basket occasionally to ensure even cooking. Work with two batches.

Meanwhile, mix the mayonnaise, garlic and dill until well combined.

Serve: the vegetable chips with the mayo sauce on the side. Bon appétit!

Parmesan Squash Chips

(**Ready in about** 20 minutes | **Servings:** 3)

Ingredients

3/4 pound butternut squash, cut into thin rounds
1 teaspoon butter
1/2 cup ketchup
Sea salt and ground black pepper, to taste
1 teaspoon Sriracha sauce
1/2 cup Parmesan cheese, grated

Directions

Toss the butternut squash with Parmesan cheese, salt, black pepper and butter.

Transfer the butternut squash rounds to the Air Fryer cooking basket.

Air Fryer at 400 degrees F for 12 minutes. Shake the Air Fryer basket periodically to ensure even cooking. Work with batches.

While the parmesan squash chips are baking, whisk the ketchup and sriracha and set it aside.

Serve: the parmesan squash chips with Sriracha ketchup and enjoy!

Mexican Crunchy Cheese Straws

(**Ready in about** 15 minutes | **Servings:** 3)

Ingredients

1/2 cup almond flour
1/4 teaspoon shallot powder 1/4 teaspoon garlic powder
1 ounce Manchego cheese, grated
1/4 teaspoon xanthan gum 1/4 teaspoon ground cumin
1 egg yolk, whisked
2 ounces Cotija cheese, grated

Directions

Mix all Ingredients until everything is well incorporated.

Twist the batter into straw strips and place them inside your Air Fryer on a baking mat.

Cook the cheese straws in your Air Fryer at 360°F for 5 minutes, then flip them over and cook for another 5 minutes.

Before serving, allow the cheese straws to cool. Enjoy!

Greek-Style Zucchini Rounds

(**Ready in about** 15 minutes | **Servings:** 3)

Ingredients

1/2 pound zucchini, cut into thin rounds
1/2 teaspoon oregano
Coarse sea salt and ground black pepper, to taste
Greek dipping sauce
1/2 teaspoon fresh lemon juice
2 tablespoons mayonnaise
1/2 teaspoon dried sage, crushed
1/4 tbs ground bay leaf
1/2 cup Greek yogurt
1 teaspoon extra-virgin olive oil
1/2 teaspoon garlic, pressed

Directions

Toss the zucchini rounds with olive oil and spices and place them in the Air Fryer cooking basket.

Cook in the preheated Air Fryer at 400 degrees F for 10 minutes; shaking the basket halfway through the cooking time.

Let it cool slightly and cook an additional minute or so until crispy and golden brown.

Meanwhile, make the sauce by whisking all the sauce Ingredients; place the sauce in the refrigerator until ready to **Serve:**.

Serve: the crispy zucchini rounds with Greek dipping sauce on the side. Enjoy!

Air Fryer Baby Back Ribs

Prep time: 15 minutes **Cooking time:** 20 minutes
Serve: 1

Ingredients

1 rack baby back ribs
1 tablespoon olive oil
½ teaspoon salt
1 tablespoon brown sugar
½ teaspoon garlic powder
½ teaspoon chili powder

1 tablespoon liquid smoke
flavoring
½ teaspoon ground black
pepper
½ teaspoon onion powder
1 cup BBQ sauce

Directions

Remove the membrane off the back of the ribs and
pat dry with a paper towel. Cut the rack into four
parts. In a small dish, combine the olive oil and liquid
smoke and apply them on both sides of the ribs.
Combine brown sugar, garlic powder, onion powder,
salt, pepper, and chili powder in a mixing bowl.
Season both sides of the ribs well with the seasoning
mixture. Allow the ribs to rest for 30 minutes to allow
the taste to develop.
Preheat an air fryer carefully to 375°F (190 degrees C).
Place the ribs in the air fryer basket, bone side down,
ensure they don't touch; cook in batches if required.
The **Cooking time:** is 15 minutes. Cook for 10
minutes more after flipping the ribs (meat-side down).
Remove the ribs from the air fryer and brush the
bone-side with 1/2 cup BBQ sauce. Return the basket
to the air fryer and cook for 5 minutes. Cook for a
further 5 minutes, or until desired char is obtained,
after flipping the ribs over and brushing the meat side
with the remaining 1/2 cup BBQ sauce.

Roasted Rainbow Vegetables in the Air Fryer

Prep time: 15 minutes **Cooking time:** 18 minutes
Serve: 1

Ingredients

1 red bell pepper
1 zucchini cut in pieces
4 ounces fresh
mushrooms, cleaned and
halved
salt and pepper to taste

1 yellow summer squash,
cut into 1-inch pieces
½ sweet onion, cut into 1-
inch wedges

1 tbsp extra-virgin olive
oil

Directions

Preheat an air fryer carefully according to the
manufacturer's instructions.
Combine the red bell pepper, summer squash,
zucchini, mushrooms, and onion in a large bowl. Toss
in the olive oil, salt, and black pepper to taste.
In the air fryer basket, arrange the vegetables in an
even layer. Cook until the veggies are roasted,
approximately 20 minutes, stirring halfway through.

Air Fryer Flour Tortilla Bowls

Prep time: 15 minutes **Cooking time:** 22 minutes
Serve: 1

Ingredients

1 (8 inches) flour tortilla   1 (4 1/2-inch) souffle dish

Directions

Preheat the air fryer carefully to 375°F (190 degrees
C).
Heat the tortilla in a big pan or directly on the gas
stove grates until warm and malleable. Place the
tortilla in the souffle dish, smoothing it down and
fluting it up the sides.
4 to 5 minutes in the air fryer until the tortilla becomes
golden brown.
Place the tortilla bowl upside down in the basket after
removing it from the souffle dish. 1 to 2 minutes more
air fry until golden brown.

Air Fryer Steak and Cheese Melts

Prep time: 10 minutes **Cooking time:** 18 minutes
Serve: 1

Ingredients

1 pound beef rib-eye
steak, thinly sliced
1 medium onion, sliced
into petals
½ green bell pepper,
thinly sliced
1 tablespoon olive oil
½ teaspoon ground
mustard
4 hoagie rolls
4 slices Provolone cheese

1 tablespoon reduced-
sodium soy sauce
4 ounces sliced baby
portobello mushrooms
½ teaspoon salt
2 tablespoons
Worcestershire sauce
¼ teaspoon ground black
pepper

Directions

Combine the steak, Worcestershire sauce, and soy
sauce in a mixing bowl. Refrigerate for 4 hours to
overnight. Remove from the refrigerator and set aside
for 30 minutes to come to room temperature.
Preheat the air fryer carefully to 380°F (190 degrees
C).
Combine the onion, mushrooms, and bell pepper in a
large mixing basin. Stir in the olive oil, salt, ground
mustard, and pepper to coat. Place the hoagie rolls in
the air fryer basket and toast for about 2 minutes.
Then, place the rolls on a platter.
Place the steak in the air fryer basket and cook for 3
minutes. Cook for 1 minute more after stirring. Place on a
platter.
Cook for 5 minutes in the air fryer basket with the
veggie mix. Cook until softened, approximately 5
minutes more.
Incorporate the meat into the veggie mixture. Place
somewhat overlapping cheese slices on top. Cook for
3 minutes, or until the cheese is melted and bubbling.
Serve: immediately on toasted buns with the mixture.

Rosemary Potato Wedges

Prep time: 10 minutes **Cooking time:** 25 minutes
Serve: 4

Ingredients

3 potatoes, cut into wedges
1 tsp garlic powder
1 tbsp parsley, chopped
Salt

3 tbsp olive oil
1 tbsp fresh rosemary, chopped Pepper

Directions

Preheat the air fryer to 390 F. Soak potato wedges into the water for 30 minutes. Drain well and pat dry with paper towels.

In a mixing bowl, toss potato wedges with parsley, oil, garlic powder, rosemary, pepper, and salt.
Place potato wedges into the air fryer basket and cook for 15 minutes. Stir well and cook for 10 minutes more. **Serve:** and enjoy.

Healthy Mixed Nuts

Prep time: 10 minutes **Cooking time:** 9 minutes
Serve: 4

Ingredients

1/4 cup hazelnuts
1/2 cup pecans
1/4 cup walnuts

1/2 cup macadamia nuts
1 tbsp olive oil
1 tsp salt

Directions

Preheat the air fryer to 320 F. In a bowl, toss nuts with oil and salt. Add nuts into the air fryer basket and cook for 9 minutes. Stir halfway through. **Serve:** and enjoy.

Stuff Mushrooms

Prep time: 10 minutes **Cooking time:** 5 minutes
Serve: 6

Ingredients

9 oz mushrooms, cut stems
6 oz mozzarella cheese, shredded
1/2 tsp salt

1 tsp dried parsley

1 tbsp butter

Directions

Preheat the air fryer to 400 F. In a small bowl, mix together cheese, butter, parsley, and salt until well combined. Stuff cheese mixture into the mushroom caps and place in the air fryer basket and cook for 5 minutes.
Serve: and enjoy.

Crispy Broccoli Popcorn

Prep time: 10 minutes **Cooking time:** 6 minutes
Serve: 4

Ingredients

4 eggs yolks
1/4 cup butter, melted

Salt

2 cups broccoli florets
2 cups coconut flour
Pepper

Directions

Preheat the air fryer to 400 F. In a small bowl, whisk egg yolks with butter, pepper, and salt. In a separate bowl, add coconut flour.

Dip each broccoli floret with egg mixture and coat with coconut flour. Place coated broccoli florets into the air fryer basket and cook for 6 minutes. **Serve:** and enjoy.

Zucchini Bites

Prep time: 10 minutes **Cooking time:** 10 minutes
Serve: 6

Ingredients

1 egg, lightly beaten
4 zucchinis, grated and squeezed
Salt

1 tsp Italian seasoning
1/2 cup parmesan cheese, grated Pepper
1 cup shredded coconut

Directions

Preheat the air fryer to 400 F. Add all Ingredients into the bowl and mix until well combined.

Make small balls from the zucchini mixture and place into the air fryer basket and cook for 10 minutes. Turn halfway through. **Serve:** and enjoy.

Air Fryer Almonds

Prep time: 5 minutes **Cooking time:** 6 minutes **Serve:** 6

Ingredients

1 cup almonds
1 tsp chili powder
1/4 tsp paprika Salt

1/4 tsp cumin
2 tsp olive oil

Directions

Preheat the air fryer to 320 F.
Add almond and remaining Ingredients into the bowl and toss to coat.
Transfer almonds into the air fryer basket and cook for 6 minutes.
Serve: and enjoy.

Air Fryer Cheese-Stuffed Mini Italian Meatloaves

Prep time: 10 minutes **Cooking time:** 18 minutes
Serve: 1

Ingredients

⅓ cup milk
1 egg, lightly beaten
2 ounces small fresh mozzarella balls
2 tablespoons purchased basil pesto
¼ teaspoon ground black pepper
1 pound 90% lean ground beef
⅓ cup Italian-seasoned panko breadcrumbs
½ cup marinara sauce, warmed
1 clove garlic, minced
8 slices pepperoni
1 tablespoon chopped fresh basil

Directions

Combine the milk, pesto, egg, garlic, and pepper in a medium mixing bowl. Next, combine the ground beef and breadcrumbs, being careful not to overmix. Divide the meat mixture into four equal halves. Make a well in the center of each section, leaving a 1/2-inch border around the edge. Fill each well with 2 slices of pepperoni, overlapping to span the whole length of the well. Top with a quarter of the mozzarella balls. Enclose the filling by pressing the meat mixture around it; shape each chunk into an oblong loaf shape. Loaves should be placed in the air fryer basket in batches.
Cook in the air fryer at 370°F (190°C) for 15 minutes, or until an instant-read thermometer inserted into the thickest part of the meat registers 165°F (75°C).
Serve: the meatloaves with warm marinara sauce and fresh basil on top.

Air Fryer Mahi Mahi with Brown Butter

Prep time: 15 minutes **Cooking time:** 25 minutes
Serve: 1

Ingredients

4 (6 ounces) mahi-mahi fillets
⅔ cup butter
salt and ground black pepper
to taste cooking spray

Directions

Preheat an air fryer carefully to 350°F (175 degrees C). Season the mahi-mahi fillets with salt and pepper and coat both sides with cooking spray. Place the fillets in the air fryer basket, leaving space between them.
Cook for 12 minutes, or until the fish flakes easily with a fork and has a golden tint.
Melt butter in a small saucepan over medium-low heat while the fish cooks. Bring the butter to a boil and cook for 3 to 5 minutes, or until it becomes foamy and deep brown. Turn off the heat.
Place the fish fillets on a platter and top with brown butter.

Air Fryer Black Garlic-Cauliflower Patties

Prep time: 18 minutes **Cooking time:** 20 minutes
Serve: 1

Ingredients

1 medium head cauliflower, cut into florets
¼ cup Italian-seasoned breadcrumbs
½ teaspoon ground black pepper to taste
½ teaspoon dried parsley
½ teaspoon dried rosemary
½ teaspoon onion powder cooking spray
½ cup all-purpose flour
2 eggs, beaten
1 teaspoon salt
4 solo black garlic bulbs
½ teaspoon dried basil
2 teaspoons baking powder
½ teaspoon dried oregano
½ tbs red pepper flakes
4 slices Swiss cheese, torn into 4 pieces each

Directions

Combine cauliflower and black garlic; process until finely "riced." Transfer to a mixing basin. In a large mixing bowl, combine the flour, eggs, breadcrumbs, baking powder, salt, black pepper, basil, parsley, oregano, rosemary, red pepper flakes, and onion powder. Stir until everything is completely blended. Preheat an air fryer carefully to 400°F (200 degrees C). Spray the air fryer basket with cooking spray and line it with parchment paper.
Using a big cookie scoop, drop the cauliflower mixture onto the parchment paper and flatten gently with your fingertips.
Cook for 4 to 6 minutes in the air fryer, turn with a spatula, and continue cooking until patties are set, about 1 minute more. Remove each burger from the air fryer and top with 1/4 slice Swiss cheese. Return to the air fryer and cook for 30 to 40 seconds more, or until the cheese is melted.

Air Fryer Tajin Apple Chips

Prep time: 10 minutes **Cooking time:** 18 minutes
Serve: 1

Ingredients

1 apple, cored
½ tablespoon chili-lime seasoning (such as Tajin®), or more to taste

Directions

Preheat the air fryer carefully to 180°F (82 degrees C). Using a mandolin, thinly slice the apple.
Place as many apple slices as you can in the air fryer basket, ensuring they don't touch.
Cook for 12 minutes in the air fryer, working in batches as required. Remove the basket and heat until the apple slices are gently browned on the other side, 8 to 12 minutes longer. Sprinkle with chili-lime seasoning right away.

Classic Zucchini Chips

Prep time: 5 minutes **Cooking time:** 35 minutes
Servings: 6

Ingredients

3 zucchinis thinly sliced   1 teaspoon salt

Directions

Put the zucchini in the air fryer and sprinkle with salt.
Cook them at 350F for 35 minutes. Shake the zucchini
every 5 minutes.

Seaweed Crisps

Prep time: 10 minutes **Cooking time:** 5 minutes
Servings: 4

Ingredients

3 nori sheets   1 teaspoon nutritional
2 tablespoons water   yeast

Directions

Cut the nori sheets roughly and put in the air fryer
basket.
Sprinkle the nori sheets with water and nutritional
yeast and cook at 375F for 5 minutes.

Avocado Sticks

Prep time: 10 minutes **Cooking time:** 14 minutes
Servings: 4

Ingredients

1 avocado, pitted, halves   1 tablespoon coconut
1 egg, beaten   shred

Directions

Cut the avocado halves into 4 wedges and dip in the
egg.
Then coat the avocado in coconut shred and put in
the air fryer. Cook the avocado sticks at 375F for 7
minutes per side.

Mozzarella Sticks

Prep time: 10 minutes **Cooking time:** 4 minutes
Servings: 4

Ingredients

1 egg, beaten   4 tbsp almond flour
9 oz. Mozzarella, cut into
sticks

Directions

Dip the mozzarella sticks in the egg and they coat in
the almond flour. Then put the mozzarella sticks in
the air fryer basket and cook at 400F for 4 minutes.

Lettuce Wraps

Prep time: 10 minutes **Cooking time:** 4 minutes
Servings: 12

Ingredients

12 bacon strips   12 lettuce leaves
1 tablespoon mustard   1 tablespoon apple cider
                             vinegar

Directions

Set the bacon in the air fryer in one layer and cook at
400f for 2 minutes per side.

Then sprinkle the bacon with mustard and apple cider
vinegar and put on the lettuce. Wrap the lettuce into
rolls.

Carrot Chips

Prep time: 10 minutes **Cooking time:** 13 minute
Servings: 8

Ingredients

3 carrots, thinly sliced   1 teaspoon avocado oil

Directions

Set the carrots in the air fryer basket, sprinkle with
avocado oil. Cook the carrot chips for 30 minutes at
355F. Shake the carrot chips every 5 minutes.

Crunchy Bacon

Prep time: 5 minutes **Cooking time:** 8 minutes
Servings: 4

Ingredients

8 bacon slices   1 teaspoon Erythritol
Directions

Sprinkle the bacon with Erythritol and put in the air
fryer basket in one layer. Cook it for 4 minutes per
side or until the bacon is crunchy.

Keto Granola

Prep time: 10 minutes **Cooking time:** 12 minutes
Servings: 4

Ingredients

1 teaspoon monk fruit   1 teaspoon pumpkin pie
2 teaspoons coconut oil   spices
3 pecans, chopped   1 tbsp coconut shred
3 oz. almonds, chopped   1 tablespoon flax seeds

Directions

In the mixing bowl, mix all Ingredients from the list
above. Make the small balls from the mixture and put
them in the air fryer. Cook the granola for 6 minutes
per side at 365F. Cool the cooked granola.

Air Fryer Bacon-Wrapped Scallops with Sriracha Mayo

Prep time: 10 minutes **Cooking time:** 18 minutes
Serve: 1

Ingredients

½ cup mayonnaise	2 tablespoons Sriracha sauce
1 pound bay scallops (about 36 small scallops),	12 slices bacon, cut into thirds
1 pinch coarse salt	1 pinch cracked black pepper
1 serving olive oil	cooking spray

Directions

In a small bowl, combine mayonnaise and Sriracha sauce. Refrigerate the Sriracha mayonnaise until ready to use. Preheat the air fryer carefully to 390°F (200 degrees C). Spread the scallops on a plate or cutting board and wipe dry with a paper towel. Season with salt and pepper to taste. Wrap a third of a slice of bacon around each scallop and fasten with a toothpick.

Cooking spray should be sprayed on the air fryer basket. Place the bacon-wrapped scallops in a single layer in the basket; if required, divide them into two groups.

Cook for 7 minutes in the air fryer. Check for doneness; the scallops should be opaque and the bacon crispy. Cook for an additional 1 to 2 minutes, checking every minute. With tongs, carefully remove the scallops and lay them on a paper towel-lined dish to soak any extra oil from the bacon. Toss with Sriracha mayonnaise and **Serve:**.

Air Fryer Prosciutto and Mozzarella Grilled Cheese

Prep time: 15 minutes **Cooking time:** 20 minutes
Serve: 1

Ingredients

2 tbs unsalted butter	2 slices sourdough bread
2 ounces prosciutto	3 ounces fresh mozzarella

Directions

Preheat the oven to 360° F. (180 degrees C). Butter one side of a slice of bread and set it greased side down on a platter. Top with prosciutto and mozzarella slices in an even layer. Butter the second slice of bread and set it on top, buttered side out. Place in the air fryer and cook for 8 minutes, or until gently browned and toasted.

Air Fryer Beignets

Prep time: 18 minutes **Cooking time:** 20 minutes
Serve: 1

Ingredients

cooking spray	½ cup all-purpose flour
¼ cup white sugar	⅛ cup water
1 large egg, separated	1 ½ teaspoon melted butter
½ teaspoon baking powder	½ teaspoon vanilla extract
2 tablespoons confectioners' sugar, or to taste	1 pinch salt

Directions

Preheat the air fryer carefully to 370°F (185 degrees C). Nonstick cooking sprays a silicone egg-bite mold. Combine the flour, sugar, water, egg yolk, butter, baking powder, vanilla extract, and salt in a large mixing basin. To blend, stir everything together.

In a small mixing basin, beat the egg white with an electric hand mixer on medium speed until soft peaks form. Incorporate into the batter. Transfer the batter to the prepared mold using a tiny, hinged ice cream scoop.

Fill the silicone mold and place it in the air fryer basket.

Fry for 10 minutes in a hot air fryer. Carefully remove the mold from the basket; pop the beignets out and flip them onto a parchment paper circle.

Return the parchment round containing the beignets to the air fryer basket. Cook for another 4 minutes. Remove the beignets from the air fryer basket and sprinkle them with confectioners' sugar.

Air-Fryer Potato-Skin Wedges

Prep time: 15 minutes **Cooking time:** 20 minutes **Serve:** 1

Ingredients

4 medium russet potatoes	3 tablespoons canola oil
1 cup water	1 teaspoon paprika
¼ teaspoon ground black pepper	¼ teaspoon salt

Directions

Fill a big saucepan halfway with salted water and bring to a boil. Reduce the heat to medium-low and cook until the potatoes are fork-tender, about 20 minutes. Drain. Refrigerate in a bowl for 30 minutes or until totally cold.

Combine the oil, paprika, black pepper, and salt in a mixing dish. Toss the quartered cold potatoes into the mixture.

Preheat an air fryer carefully to 400°F (200 degrees C). Place half of the potato wedges in the air fryer basket, skin side down, being careful not to overcrowd.

13 to 15 minutes, or until golden brown. Rep with the remaining wedges.

Air Fryer Salt and Vinegar Chickpeas

Prep time: 15 minutes **Cooking time:** 18 minutes
Serve: 1

Ingredients

1 (15 ounces) can of chickpeas
½ teaspoon sea salt
1 tablespoon olive oil
1 cup white vinegar

Directions

In a small saucepan, combine the chickpeas and vinegar and bring to a boil. Turn off the heat. Allow for a 30-minute resting period.

Remove any loose skins from the chickpeas before draining. Preheat an air fryer carefully to 390°F (198 degrees C). In the basket, distribute the chickpeas equally. Cook for 4 minutes or until the mixture is dry.

Place chickpeas in a heat-resistant bowl and drizzle with oil and sea salt. To coat, toss everything together. Return chickpeas to air fryer and cook for 8 minutes, shaking basket every 2 to 3 minutes, until gently toasted. **Serve:** right away

Fried Green Tomatoes in the Air Fryer

Prep time: 15 minutes **Cooking time:** 22 minutes
Serve: 1

Ingredients

cooking spray
⅓ cup self-rising flour
1 egg, beaten
½ teaspoon ground black pepper
½ cup cornmeal
⅓ cup panko breadcrumbs
1 teaspoon salt
2 green tomatoes, sliced

Directions

Preheat an air fryer carefully to 400°F (200 degrees C). Coat the air fryer basket with cooking spray.
Place the egg in a small dish. Combine cornmeal, flour, panko, salt, and pepper in a second shallow dish. Dip each tomato slice in the egg, then in the cornmeal mixture on both sides.
Place the tomato slices in the prepared basket in a single layer and gently sprinkle the tops with cooking spray.
Cook for 8 minutes in a hot air fryer. Cooking spray should be sprayed on any dry parts after flipping the tomatoes. Cook for 4 minutes more before transferring to a dish lined with paper towels. Repeat with the rest of the tomato slices.

Air Fryer Cajun Crab Cakes

Prep time: 18 minutes **Cooking time:** 20 minutes
Serve: 1

Ingredients

¾ cup panko breadcrumbs
2 teaspoons Worcestershire sauce
½ teaspoon salt
¼ teaspoon ground white pepper (Optional)
3 brioche slider buns (Optional)
¼ cup mayonnaise 1 egg
¾ teaspoon Cajun seasoning
1 teaspoon Dijon mustard
¼ teaspoon cayenne pepper
3 tablespoons remoulade sauce, or to taste
4 ounces fresh lump crabmeat

Directions

According to the manufacturer's instructions, preheat an air fryer carefully to 370°F (188°C).
In a small mixing bowl, combine breadcrumbs, mayonnaise, egg, Worcestershire sauce, mustard, Cajun spice, salt, cayenne pepper, and pepper. Gently fold in the crabmeat.
Using a biscuit cutter, cut out three equal-sized crab cakes. Place the
cakes on a parchment-lined baking sheet and place them in the air fryer basket.
Cook for 6 minutes in a hot air fryer. Cook until browned on the other
side, approximately 6 minutes longer. **Serve:** on slider buns with remoulade sauce.

Desserts Recipes

Homemade Chelsea Currant Buns

(**Ready in about** 50 minutes | **Servings:** 4)

Ingredients

1/2 pound cake flour	1 tablespoons granulated
1 teaspoon dry yeast	sugar
A pinch of sea salt	4 tablespoons butter
1/2 cup milk, warm	1/2 cup dried currants
1 egg, whisked	1 ounce icing sugar

Directions

Mix the flour, yeast, sugar and salt in a bowl; add in milk, egg and 2 tablespoons of butter and mix to combine well. Add lukewarm water as necessary to form a smooth dough.

Knead the dough until it is elastic; then, leave it in a warm place to rise for 30 minutes.

Roll out your dough and spread the remaining 2 tablespoons of butter onto the dough; scatter dried currants over the dough.

Cut into 8 equal slices and roll them up. Brush each bun with a nonstick

cooking oil and transfer them to the Air Fryer cooking basket.

Cook your buns at 330 degrees F for about 20 minutes, turning them over halfway through the cooking time.

Dust with icing sugar before serving. Bon appétit!

Old-Fashioned Pinch-Me Cake with Walnuts

(**Ready in about** 20 minutes | **Servings:** 4)

Ingredients

1 (10-ounces) can crescent rolls	1/2 cup caster sugar
	1/2 stick butter
1 teaspoon pumpkin pie spice blend	1/2 cup walnuts, chopped
	1 tablespoon dark rum

Directions

Start by preheating your Air Fryer to 350 degrees F.

Roll out the crescent rolls. Spread the butter onto the crescent rolls; scatter the sugar, spices and walnuts over the rolls. Drizzle with rum and roll them up.

Using your fingertips, gently press them to seal the edges.

Bake your cake for about 13 minutes or until the top is golden brown. Bon appétit!

Authentic Swedish Kärleksmums

(**Ready in about** 20 minutes | **Servings:** 3)

Ingredients

2 tablespoons Swedish butter, at room temperature	1 egg
	4 tablespoons brown sugar
1 tablespoon lingonberry jam	2 tablespoons cocoa powder A pinch of grated
5 tbs all-purpose flour	nutmeg
	1/2 tbs baking powder
A pinch of coarse sea salt	

Directions

Using an electric mixer, cream the butter and sugar together. Fold in the egg and lingonberry jam until well combined. Mix in the flour, baking powder, cocoa powder, grated nutmeg, and salt until well combined. Pour the batter into a baking dish that has been lightly buttered.

Bake your cake for about 15 minutes, or until a tester inserted into the centre comes out dry and clean. Good appetite!

Air Grilled Peaches with Cinnamon-Sugar Butter

(**Ready in about** 25 minutes | **Servings:** 2)

Ingredients

2fresh peaches pitted halved	2 tablespoons caster sugar
1/4 tbsp ground cinnamon	1 tablespoon butter

Directions

Mix the butter, sugar and cinnamon. Spread the butter mixture onto the peaches and transfer them to the Air Fryer cooking basket. Cook your peaches at 320 degrees F for about 25 minutes or until the top is golden.

Serve: with vanilla ice cream, if desired. Bon appétit!

Chocolate Apple Chips

(**Ready in about** 15 minutes | **Servings:** 2)

Ingredients

1 large Pink Lady apple, cored and sliced

2 teaspoons cocoa powder

A pinch of kosher salt

1 tbs light brown sugar

2 tablespoons lemon juice

Directions

Toss the apple slices in with the remaining Ingredients. Bake at 350°F for 5 minutes, then shake the basket to ensure even cooking and cook for another 5 minutes. Good appetite!

Favorite Apple Crisp

(**Ready in about** 40 minutes | **Servings:** 4)

Ingredients

4 cups apples, peeled, cored and sliced

1 tablespoon cornmeal

1/2 teaspoon ground cinnamon

1/2 cup quick-cooking oats 1/2 cup all-purpose flour

1 tablespoon honey

1/2 cup brown sugar

1/4 teaspoon ground cloves 1/4 cup water

1/2 cup caster sugar

1/2 tbs baking powder

1/3 cup coconut oil, melted

Directions

Toss the sliced apples with the brown sugar, honey, cornmeal, cloves, and cinnamon. Divide between four custard cups coated with cooking spray.

In a mixing dish, thoroughly combine the remaining Ingredients. Sprinkle over the apple mixture.

Bake in the preheated Air Fryer at 330 degrees F for 35 minutes. Bon appétit!

Cocktail Party Fruit Kabobs

(**Ready in about** 10 minutes | **Servings:** 6)

Ingredients

1 pears, diced into bite-sized chunks

2 apples, diced into bite-sized chunks

1 tbs fresh lemon juice

1 tbs ground cinnamon

2 mangos, diced into bite-sized chunks

1 teaspoon vanilla essence

1/2 tbsp ground cloves

2 tablespoons maple syrup

Directions

Toss all Ingredients in a mixing dish. Tread the fruit pieces on skewers. Cook at 350 degrees F for 5 minutes.

Bon appétit!

Peppermint Chocolate Cheesecake

(**Ready in about** 40 minutes | **Servings:** 6)

Ingredients

1 cup powdered sugar

1/2 cup all-purpose flour

1/2 cup butter

2 drops peppermint extract

1 teaspoon vanilla extract

1 cup mascarpone cheese, at room temperature

4 ounces semisweet chocolate, melted

Directions

In a mixing bowl, combine the sugar, flour, and butter. Press the mixture into the bottom of a baking pan that has been lightly greased.

Bake for 18 minutes at 350 degrees F. Set it in the freezer for 20 minutes. Then, combine the remaining

Ingredients to make the cheesecake topping.

Place this topping on top of the crust and place it in the freezer for another 15 minutes to cool. Chill before serving.

Baked Coconut Doughnuts

(**Ready in about** 20 minutes | **Servings:** 6)

Ingredients

1 ½ cups all-purpose flour

1 teaspoon baking powder

A pinch of kosher salt

2 eggs

1/4 tbs ground cardamom

2 tbsp coconut oil, melted

1 teaspoon coconut essence

1 cup coconut flakes

A pinch of freshly grated nutmeg

1/2 cup white sugar

2 tablespoons full-fat coconut milk

1/4 tbs ground cinnamon

1/2 teaspoon vanilla essence

Directions

In a mixing bowl, thoroughly combine the all-purpose flour with the baking powder, salt, nutmeg, and sugar.

In a separate bowl, beat the eggs until frothy using a hand mixer; add the coconut milk and oil and beat again; lastly, stir in the spices and mix again until everything is well combined.

Then, stir the egg mixture into the flour mixture and continue mixing until a dough ball forms. Try not to over-mix your dough. Transfer to a lightly floured surface.

Roll out your dough to a 1/4-inch thickness using a rolling pin. Cut out the doughnuts using a 3-inch round cutter; now, use a 1-inch round cutter to remove the center.

Bake in the preheated Air Fryer at 340 degrees F approximately 5 minutes or until golden. Repeat with remaining doughnuts. Decorate with coconut flakes and **Serve:**.

Authentic Spanish Churros

(**Ready in about** 20 minutes | **Servings:** 4)

Ingredients

1/2 cup water	1/4 cup butter, cut into
1 tablespoon granulated	cubes A pinch of salt
sugar A pinch of ground	1/2 cup plain flour
cinnamon	
1/2 teaspoon lemon zest	1 egg Chocolate Dip
2 ounces dark chocolate	1 teaspoon ground
1/2 cup milk	cinnamon

Directions

Boil the water in a saucepan over medium-high heat; now, add the butter, sugar, cinnamon, salt and lemon zest; cook until the sugar has dissolved.

Next, remove the pan from the heat. Gradually stir in the flour, whisking continuously until the mixture forms a ball; let it cool slightly.

Fold in the egg and continue to beat using an electric mixer until everything comes together.

Pour the dough into a piping bag with a large star tip. Squeeze 4-inch strips of dough into the greased Air Fryer pan.

Cook your churros at 380 degrees F for about 10 minutes, shaking the basket halfway through the cooking time.

In the meantime, melt the chocolate and milk in a saucepan over low heat. Add in the cinnamon and cook on low heat for about 5 minutes. **Serve:** the warm churros with the chocolate dip and enjoy!

Classic Brownie Cupcakes

(**Ready in about** 25 minutes | **Servings:** 3)

Ingredients

1/3 cup all-purpose flour	2 ounces butter, room
1/4 teaspoon baking	temperature
powder	1 large egg
1/2 teaspoon rum extract	A pinch of ground
1/3 cup caster sugar	cinnamon A pinch of salt
3 tablespoons cocoa	
powder	

Directions

In a mixing bowl, combine the dry Ingredients. Combine the wet Ingredients in a separate bowl. Stir in the wet Ingredients gradually into the dry mixture.

Divide the batter evenly among the muffin cups and place them in the Air Fryer cooking basket.

Bake the cupcakes at 330°F for 15 minutes, or until a tester comes out dry and clean. Allow your cupcakes to cool for 10 minutes on a wire rack before unmolding. Good appetite!

Baked Fruit Salad

(**Ready in about** 15 minutes | **Servings:** 2)

Ingredients

1 banana, peeled	1 cooking pear, cored
1 tablespoon freshly	1/4 teaspoon ground
squeezed lemon juice	cinnamon
1/2 teaspoon ground star	1 cooking apple, cored
anise	1/4 cup brown sugar
1/2 teaspoon granulated	1 tablespoon coconut oil,
ginger	melted

Directions

Toss your fruits with lemon juice, star anise, cinnamon, ginger, sugar and coconut oil.

Transfer the fruits to the Air Fryer cooking basket.

Bake the fruit salad in the preheated Air Fryer at 330 degrees F for 15 minutes.

Serve: in individual bowls, garnished with vanilla ice cream. Bon appétit

Red Velvet Pancakes

(**Ready in about** 35 minutes | **Servings:** 3)

Ingredients

1 cup all-purpose flour	1 teaspoon granulated
	sugar
1/8 teaspoon sea salt	1/8 teaspoon freshly
1/2 teaspoon baking soda	grated nutmeg
1/2 cup powdered sugar	2 tablespoons ghee,
	melted
1 small-sized egg, beaten	1 teaspoon red paste food
1/2 cup milk	color
2 ounces cream cheese,	
softened	
1 tablespoon butter,	
softened	

Directions

Thoroughly combine the flour, baking soda, granulated sugar, salt and nutmeg in a large bowl.

Gradually add in the melted ghee, egg, milk and red paste food color, stirring into the flour mixture until moistened. Allow your batter to rest for about 30 minutes.

Spritz the Air Fryer baking pan with cooking spray. Pour the batter into the pan using a measuring cup. Set the pan into the Air Fryer cooking basket.

Cook at 330 degrees F for about 5 minutes or until golden brown. Repeat with the other pancakes.

Meanwhile, mix the remaining Ingredients until creamy and fluffy. Decorate your pancakes with cream cheese topping. Bon appétit!

Clove Crackers

Prep time: 20 minutes **Cooking time:** 33 minutes
Servings: 8

Ingredients

1 cup almond flour	1 teaspoon xanthan gum
1 teaspoon flax meal	1/2 teaspoon salt
1 teaspoon baking powder	1 egg, beaten
2 tablespoons Erythritol	1 teaspoon lemon juice
3 tbs coconut oil, softened	1/2 tbsp ground clove

Directions

In the mixing bowl mix up almond flour, xanthan gum, flax meal, salt, baking powder, and ground clove. Add Erythritol, lemon juice, egg, and coconut oil. Stir the mixture gently with the help of the fork. Then knead the mixture till you get a soft dough. Line the chopping board with parchment. Put the dough on the parchment and roll it up in a thin layer. Cut the thin dough into squares (crackers). Preheat the air fryer to 360F.

Line the air fryer basket with baking paper. Put the prepared crackers in the air fryer basket in one layer and cook them for 11 minutes or until the crackers are dry and light brown. Repeat the same steps with remaining uncooked crackers.

Sage Cream

Prep time: 5 minutes **Cooking time:** 30 minutes
Servings: 4

Ingredients

7 cups red currants	1 cup water
6 sage leaves	1 cup swerve

Directions

In a pan that fits your air fryer, mix all the Ingredients, toss, put the pan in the fryer and cook at 330 degrees F for 30 minutes. Discard sage leaves, divide into cups and **Serve:** cold.

Currant Vanilla Cookies

Prep time: 5 minutes **Cooking time:** 30 minutes
Servings: 6

Ingredients

2 cups almond flour	2 teaspoons baking soda
1/2 cup ghee, melted	1/2 cup swerve
1 teaspoon vanilla extract	
1/2 cup currants	

Directions

In a bowl, mix all the Ingredients and whisk well. Spread this on a baking sheet lined with parchment paper put the pan in the air fryer and cooks at 350 degrees F for 30 minutes. Cool down, cut into rectangles and **Serve:**.

Chocolate Fudge

Prep time: 15 minutes **Cooking time:** 30 minutes
Servings: 8

Ingredients

1/2 cup butter, melted	1 oz. dark chocolate,
2 tbsp cocoa powder	chopped, melted
3 tbsp coconut flour	2 eggs, beaten
3 tablespoons Splenda	Cooking spray
1 teaspoon vanilla extract	

Directions

In the bowl mix up melted butter and dark chocolate. Then add vanilla extract, eggs, and cocoa powder. Stir the mixture until smooth and add Splenda, and coconut flour. Stir it again until smooth. Then preheat the air fryer to 325F.

Line the air fryer basket with baking paper and spray it with cooking spray. Pour the fudge mixture in the air fryer basket; flatten it gently with the help of the spatula. Cook the fudge for 30 minutes. Then cut it on the serving squares and cool the fudge completely.

Cranberries Pudding

Prep time: 5 minutes **Cooking time:** 20 minutes
Servings: 6

Ingredients

1 cup cauliflower rice	1 teaspoon vanilla extract
1/2 cup cranberries	2 cups almond milk

Directions

In a pan that fits your air fryer, mix all the Ingredients, whisk a bit, put the pan in the fryer and cook at 360 degrees F for 20 minutes. Stir the pudding, divide into bowls and **Serve:** cold.

Merengues

Prep time: 15 minutes **Cooking time:** 65 minutes
Servings: 6

Ingredients

2 egg whites	1 tbs lime zest, grated
4 tablespoons Erythritol	1 teaspoon lime juice

Directions

Whisk the egg whites until soft peaks. Then add Erythritol and lime juice and whisk the egg whites until you get strong peaks. After this, add lime zest and carefully stir the egg white mixture. Preheat the air fryer to 275F.

Line the air fryer basket with baking paper. With the help of the spoon make the small merengues and put them in the air fryer in one layer. Cook the dessert for 65 minutes.

Chocolate Banana Packets

Prep time: 5 minutes **Cooking time:** 15 minutes
Servings: 1

Ingredients

Miniature marshmallows (2 tablespoons)
Banana, peeled (1 piece)
Chocolate chips, semi-sweet (2 tablespoons)
Cereal, cinnamon, crunchy, slightly crushed (2 tablespoons)

Directions

Preheat air fryer to 390 degrees Fahrenheit. Slightly open banana by cutting lengthwise. Place on sheet of foil. Fill sliced banana with chocolate chips and marshmallows. Close foil packet. Air-fry for fifteen to twenty minutes.
Open packet and top banana with crushed cereal.

Creamy Strawberry Mini Wraps

Prep time: 10 minutes **Cooking time:** 15 minutes
Servings: 12

Ingredients

Cream cheese, softened (4 ounces)
Powdered sugar (1/3 cup)
Pie crust, refrigerated (1 box)
Strawberry jam (12 tbs)

Directions

Preheat air fryer to 350 degrees Fahrenheit. Roll out pie crusts and cut out 12 squares. Beat together powdered sugar and cream cheese.

Shape each dough square into a diamond before filling with cream cheese mixture (1 tablespoon). Top each with strawberry jam (1 teaspoon) and cover with dough sides. Place mini wraps on baking sheet and air fry for fifteen minutes.

Tasty Shortbread Cookies

Prep time: 25 minutes **Cooking time:** 1 hour 35 minutes
Servings: 4

Ingredients

Powdered sugar (3/4 cup)
Butter softened (1 cup)
Vanilla (1 teaspoon)
Flour all purpose (2 1/2 cups)

Directions

Preheat air fryer to 325 degrees Fahrenheit. Combine butter, vanilla and powdered sugar with flour to form a soft dough. Roll out dough and cut out 4 circles. Place on cookie sheet. Air-fry for fourteen to sixteen minutes.

Heavenly Butter Cake Bars

Prep time: 15 minutes **Cooking time:** 35 minutes
Servings: 12

Ingredients

Butter, melted (1/2 cup)
Cream cheese (8 ounces)
Vanilla (1 teaspoon)
Powdered sugar (1 pound)
Cake mix, super moist, French vanilla (15 1/4 ounces)
Eggs (3 pieces)

Directions

Preheat air fryer to 325 degrees Fahrenheit. Use parchment to line baking dish. Combine cake mix with egg and melted butter to form soft dough. Press into baking dish. Beat together 2 eggs, cream cheese, vanilla, and sugar. Spread on top of cake mix layer. Air-fry for forty-five minutes. Let cool before slicing.

Air-Fried Mini Pies

Prep time: 20 minutes **Cooking time:** 55 minutes
Servings: 4

Ingredients

Pie filling (4 cups)
Egg, whisked (1 piece)
Pie crusts, refrigerated (2 packages)

Directions

Preheat air fryer to 325 degrees Fahrenheit.
Mist cooking spray onto 12 muffin cups.
Roll out pie crust and cut out twelve 4-inch circles. Press each onto bottom of a muffin cup. Cut remaining dough into thin strips. Add pie filling (1/4 cup) to each dough cup. Cover each with dough strips laid in a lattice pattern. Brush whisked egg on tops of pies and air-fry for thirty to forty minutes.

Pumpkin Pie Minis

Prep time: 25 minutes **Cooking time:** 20 minutes
Servings: 12

Ingredients

Nutmeg (1/4 teaspoon)
Brown sugar (3/8 cup)
Heavy cream (1 tablespoon) Egg, large (1 piece)
Pie crust, refrigerated (1 package)
Pumpkin puree (1 cup)
Cinnamon (1/2 teaspoon)

Directions

Preheat air fryer to 325 degrees Fahrenheit. Combine pumpkin, heavy cream, spices, and brown sugar. Unroll dough pieces and cut out twenty-four 2.5-inch circles. Place 12 circles on sheet of parchment. Top each with pie filling (1 tablespoon) and cover with another circle. Press to seal and brush all mini pies with whisked egg (1 piece). Dust all over with mixture of cinnamon and sugar. Air-fry for twenty minutes.

Air Fryer Garlic and Parsley Baby Potatoes

Prep time: 20 minutes **Cooking time:** 25 minutes
Serve: 1

Ingredients

1 pound baby potatoes, cut into quarters	¼ teaspoon salt
½ teaspoon granulated garlic	1 tablespoon avocado oil
	½ teaspoon dried parsley

Directions

Carefully to 350°F (175 degrees C). Toss the potatoes in a basin with the oil to coat. Toss in 1/4 teaspoon granulated garlic and 1/4 teaspoon parsley to coat. Rep with the rest of the garlic and parsley. Place the potatoes in the air fryer basket.

Place the basket in the air fryer and cook, stirring regularly, for 20 to 25 minutes, or until golden brown.

Air Fryer Salmon Cakes with Sriracha Mayo

Prep time: 15 minutes **Cooking time:** 20 minutes
Serve: 1

Ingredients

¼ cup mayonnaise	1 tablespoon Sriracha
1-pound skinless salmon fillets	⅓ cup almond flour
1 ½ teaspoon seafood seasoning	1 egg, lightly beaten
1 green onion, coarsely chopped cooking spray	1 pinch seafood seasoning (such as Old Bay®) (Optional)

Directions

In a small mixing dish, combine mayonnaise and sriracha. 1 tablespoon Sriracha mayo in a food processor; chill the remainder until ready to use To the Sriracha mayo, add the salmon, almond flour, egg, 1 ½ teaspoons seafood spice, and green onion; pulse quickly for 4 to 5 seconds, or until Ingredients are barely mixed but tiny bits of salmon remains. (Be careful not to overprocess the mixture, or it will turn mushy.)

Line a plate with waxed paper and squirt cooking spray on your hands. Transfer the salmon mixture to a dish and shape it into 8 tiny patties. Refrigerate for 15 minutes or until cool and stiff. Preheat the air fryer carefully to 390°F (200 degrees C). Cooking spray should be sprayed on the air fryer basket. Take the salmon cakes out of the refrigerator. Spray both sides with frying spray and place in the air fryer basket, working in batches as required to minimize congestion. Cook for 6 to 8 minutes in a preheated air fryer. **Serve:** with the remaining Sriracha mayo and a small dusting of Old Bay seasoning, if preferred, on a serving dish.

Air Fryer Spicy Dill Pickle Fries

Prep time: 15 minutes **Cooking time:** 18 minutes
Serve: 1

Ingredients

1 ½ (16 ounces) jars spicy dill pickle spears	½ teaspoon paprika
¼ cup milk	1 cup all-purpose flour
1 cup panko breadcrumbs cooking spray	1 egg, beaten

Directions

Drain and pat dry the pickles. In a mixing dish, combine the flour and paprika. In a separate dish, whisk together the milk and the beaten egg. In a third bowl, combine the panko.

Carefully to 400°F (200°C) according to the manufacturer's instructions. Place a pickle on a dish after dipping it in the flour mixture, then the egg mixture, and finally the breadcrumbs. Rep with the remaining pickles. Lightly spray the covered pickles with cooking spray.
Place the pickles in the air fryer basket in a single layer; cook in batches if required to avoid overflowing the fryer. Set a timer for 14 minutes and flip the pickles halfway through.

Air Fryer Brown Sugar and Pecan Roasted Apples

Prep time: 15 minutes **Cooking time:** 22 minutes
Serve: 1

Ingredients

2 tablespoons coarsely chopped pecans	1 teaspoon all-purpose flour
	1 tablespoon brown sugar
¼ teaspoon apple pie spice 2 medium apples	1 tablespoon butter

Directions

Preheat the air fryer carefully to 360°F (180 degrees C).

Combine pecans, brown sugar, flour, and apple pie spice in a small mixing bowl. In a medium mixing bowl, combine apple wedges and drizzle with butter, tossing to coat. Arrange the apples in the air fryer basket in a single layer and top with the pecan mixture.

Cook in a hot air fryer for 10 to 15 minutes, or until apples are soft.

Air Fryer Mini Bean and Cheese Tacos

Prep time: 20 minutes **Cooking time:** 20 minutes
Serve: 1

Ingredients

1 (16 ounces) can refried beans	1 (1 ounce) envelope taco seasoning mix
cooking spray	12 slices American cheese, cut in half 12 (6 inches) flour tortillas

Directions

Preheat the air fryer carefully to 400°F (200 degrees C).
In a bowl, combine the refried beans. Stir in taco seasoning until evenly blended.

1 slice of cheese in the center of a tortilla 1 spoonful of the bean mixture should be spooned over the cheese. On top of the beans, place another piece of cheese. To seal the taco, fold the tortilla over and press down. Continue with the remaining tortillas, beans, and cheese.

Nonstick frying spray should be sprayed on all sides of the tacos. Place tacos in the air fryer basket, ensuring sure none overlap. 3 minutes in the oven cook for 3 minutes longer after flipping the tacos. Rep with the remaining tacos.

Sweet Potato Chips in the Air Fryer

Prep time: 15 minutes **Cooking time:** 25 minutes
Serve: 1

Ingredients

1 teaspoon avocado oil	1 medium sweet potato, peeled and sliced crossways into 1/8-inch slices
½ teaspoon Creole seasoning	

Directions

Preheat the air fryer carefully to 400°F (200 degrees C).
In a large mixing basin, combine the sweet potato pieces. Mix with the avocado oil, covering each piece equally.

Stir in the Creole seasoning until well combined. Spread the slices on the bottom of the air fryer basket in a thin layer.

Cook for 7 minutes in a preheated air fryer. Shake and flip the slices to ensure consistent frying. Cook for another 6 minutes, or until the desired crispness is attained. Allow the potato slices to cool on a rack.

Skinny Air Fryer Funnel Cakes

Prep time: 15 minutes **Cooking time:** 20 minutes
Serve: 1

Ingredients

nonstick cooking spray	1 teaspoon vanilla extract
1 tablespoon almond flour	1 cup almond flour
4 tablespoons erythritol confectioners' sweetener	1 cup nonfat plain Greek yogurt
1 ½ teaspoons baking powder	½ teaspoon salt
1 teaspoon ground cinnamon	

Directions

Carefully to 325°F (165°C) according to the manufacturer's instructions. Line the basket with parchment paper and sprinkle it with nonstick cooking spray.
Combine almond flour, Greek yogurt, 2 tablespoons sweetener, baking powder, cinnamon, vanilla extract, and salt in a mixing dish. Make the dough come together by kneading it with your hands.
Flour your work surface, divide the dough into four equal pieces, and form into balls. Using a bench scraper, cut each ball into 8 equal pieces. Roll each piece in flour and roll into a long, thin rope between your palms. Place all 8 ropes, one by one, into the preheated air fryer basket in a circular mound. Repeat with the rest of the dough balls. Cooking spray should be sprayed on each funnel cake.
5 to 6 minutes in the air fryer until golden brown. Flip each funnel cake over, coat with cooking spray, and continue to air fry for 3 to 4 minutes. Finish with the remaining 2 teaspoons of sweetener.

Air-Fried Jalapeno Poppers

Prep time: 20 minutes **Cooking time:** 25 minutes
Serve: 1

Ingredients

6 medium jalapeno peppers, halved and seeded	1-ounce shredded Cheddar cheese
3 slices salami, dry or hard, pork, beef	6 ounces cream cheese, softened
6 slices bacon, cut in half lengthwise	

Directions

Carefully to 390°F (199°C) according to the manufacturer's instructions.
Fill each half of jalapeño with cream cheese and Cheddar cheese. If
desired, place 1/2 a slice of salami on top of each pepper, wrap with bacon, and fasten with a toothpick. Layer the jalapeño poppers in the preheated air fryer and cook for 10 to 12 minutes, or until the bacon is browned and the cheese is melted.

Easy Air Fryer French Toast Sticks

Prep time: 15 minutes **Cooking time:** 25 minutes
Serve: 1

Ingredients

4 slices of slightly stale thick bread, such as Texas toast parchment paper	2 eggs, lightly beaten
	1 teaspoon cinnamon
	1 pinch ground nutmeg
¼ cup milk	1 teaspoon vanilla extract

Directions

To make sticks, cut each slice of bread into thirds. Then, to fit the bottom of the air fryer basket cut a piece of parchment paper.

Preheat the air fryer carefully to 360°F (180 degrees C).
Combine the eggs, milk, vanilla extract, cinnamon, and nutmeg in a mixing dish until thoroughly blended. Dip each slice of bread into the egg mixture, ensuring sure it is well immersed. Shake each breadstick to remove extra liquid before placing it in the air fryer basket in a single layer. If necessary, cook in batches to avoid overflowing the fryer.

Fry for 5 minutes, then flip the bread slices and cook for another 5 minutes.

Air Fryer Pull-Apart Pepperoni-Cheese Bread

Prep time: 15 minutes **Cooking time:** 20 minutes
Serve: 1

Ingredients

cooking spray	1 ½ pound fresh pizza dough
1tbs grated Parmesan cheese	
1-ounce sliced turkey pepperoni	ground red pepper to taste
dried oregano to taste	garlic
1 teaspoon melted butter	salt to taste
½ cup shredded mozzarella cheese	

Directions

To fit the bottom of your air fryer, shape a big piece of aluminum foil into a pan with 2-inch-high edges. Coat the pan with nonstick cooking spray. Preheat the air fryer carefully to 390°F (200°C) for 15 minutes.

Roll the pizza dough into 1-inch balls and set them in an aluminum foil pan in a single layer. Season with pepperoni, oregano, red pepper flakes, and garlic salt to taste. Brush with melted butter, then top with Parmesan cheese. Cook for 15 minutes with the pan at the bottom of the air fryer. Cook until the mozzarella cheese is melted and bubbling on the bread, about 2 minutes longer. Remove from the air fryer by pulling the sides of the pan up and out of the machine using tongs.

Air Fryer Asian-Inspired Deviled Eggs

Prep time: 20 minutes **Cooking time:** 25 minutes
Serve: 1

Ingredients

6 large eggs	2 tablespoons mayonnaise
1 ½ tbs sriracha sauce	1 ½ tbs sesame oil
1 tbs low-sodium soy sauce	1 tbs finely grated ginger root
1 teaspoon Dijon mustard	1 teaspoon rice vinegar
toasted sesame seeds	1 green onion, thinly sliced

Directions

Place the eggs on an air fryer rack or trivet, leaving enough room between them for air to circulate. Set the air fryer to 260 degrees Fahrenheit (125 degrees Celsius) and the timer for 15 minutes. The air fryer should be closed. Place the eggs in a dish of cold water for 10 minutes after being removed from the air fryer. Then, remove the eggs from the water, peel them, and cut them half. Scoop out the yolks and set them in a tiny food processor. In a mixing bowl, combine the mayonnaise, sriracha, sesame oil, low-sodium soy sauce, Dijon mustard, ginger root, and rice vinegar. Process until the mixture is well blended and creamy, mousse-like consistency. Fill a piping bag halfway with the yolk mixture and evenly spread it into the egg white halves until they are overflowing full; you can also do this with a spoon. Garnish with sesame seeds and green onion, if desired.

Air Fryer Steak Tips and Portobello Mushrooms

Prep time: 15 minutes **Cooking time:** 18 minutes
Serve: 1

Ingredients

¼ cup olive oil	1 tbs coconut aminos
½ teaspoon garlic powder	2 teaspoons Montreal steak seasoning
2 strip steaks	
4 ounces portobello mushrooms, quartered	

Directions

Combine the olive oil, coconut aminos, steak seasoning, and garlic powder in a small bowl. Mix well, then add the steak pieces and marinate for 15 minutes.

Carefully to 390°F (200 degrees C). The perforated parchment paper should line the bottom of the air fryer basket. Remove the meat from the marinade. Fill the air fryer basket halfway with steak and quartered portobello mushrooms.

Cook for 5 minutes in a hot air fryer. Remove the basket, stir the steak and mushrooms around, and cook for 4 minutes.

Sweet Caramel Pineapple

Prep time: 10 minutes **Cooking time:** 12 minutes
Serve: 4

Ingredients
2 cups pineapple slices
1 tbsp butter, melted
2 tbsp maple syrup
1 tsp cinnamon

Directions

Preheat the air fryer to 380 F. In a mixing bowl, mix together pineapple slices, butter, maple syrup, and cinnamon until well coated. Place pineapple slices into the air fryer basket and cook for 12 minutes. Turn halfway through. **Serve:** and enjoy.

Blueberry Cobbler

Prep time: 10 minutes **Cooking time:** 15 minutes
Serve: 2

Ingredients
6 oz blueberries
For topping
½ tsp baking powder
2 tbsp sugar
½ tsp salt
1 tbsp fresh lemon juice
¼ cup milk
¼ cup all-purpose flour
1 tbsp sugar

Directions

Add blueberries, sugar, and lemon juice into the two ramekins and mix well. In a bowl, mix together topping Ingredients and pour over blueberry mixture. Place ramekins into the air fryer basket and cook at 320 F for 12-15 minutes. **Serve:** and enjoy.

Apple Pecan Carrot Muffins

Prep time: 10 minutes **Cooking time:** 10 minutes
Serve: 12

Ingredients
1 egg
½ cup pecans, chopped
1 cup apples, shredded
1 cup carrots, shredded
½ cup yogurt
¼ tsp nutmeg
2 tsp cinnamon
½ tsp salt
1 ½ cups all-purpose flour
½ cup raisins
2/3 cup honey
2 tsp vanilla
1/3 cup applesauce
½ tsp ginger
2 tsp baking powder

Directions

Preheat the air fryer to 350 F. In a mixing bowl, mix together flour, ginger, nutmeg, cinnamon, baking powder, and salt. Add egg, vanilla, honey, yogurt, and applesauce and mix until just combined. Add pecans, raisins, apples, and carrots and fold well.
Spoon batter into the silicone muffin molds. Place muffin molds into the air fryer basket and cook for 10 minutes. **Serve:** and enjoy.

Blueberry Muffins

Prep time: 10 minutes **Cooking time:** 12 minutes
Serve: 8

Ingredients
1 egg
3 tbsp butter, melted
2 tsp vanilla
¼ tsp cinnamon
1 cup self-rising flour
¾ cup blueberries
1/3 cup unsweetened almond milk
¼ cup sugar

Directions

Preheat the air fryer to 340 F. In a mixing bowl, whisk egg with sugar, vanilla, butter, and almond milk.

Add flour and cinnamon and stir until well combined.
Add blueberries and fold well.

Spoon batter into the silicone muffin molds. Place muffin molds into the air fryer basket and cook for 12-14 minutes. **Serve:** and enjoy.

Air Fryer Kale Chips with Parmesan

Prep time: 15 minutes **Cooking time:** 25 minutes
Serve: 1

Ingredients
1 bunch kale
salt and ground black pepper to taste
2 tablespoons grated Parmesan cheese
1 tablespoon olive oil
1 ½ teaspoon chili-lime seasoning

Directions

Carefully to 280°F (138°C) according to the manufacturer's instructions. Wash the kale and separate the leaves from the ribs. Dry the kale leaves
fully before tearing them into pieces. Ribs should be discarded.

In a large mixing bowl, combine the kale leaves and olive oil; toss with your hands until the kale is uniformly and lightly coated. Season with salt and pepper to taste. Mix in the chili-lime seasoning until equally distributed.

Place some kale in the hot air fryer in batches without overlapping. 5 minutes in the oven Shake the basket and continue to air-fry for 3 minutes. Sprinkle with Parmesan cheese to coat, shake, and air-fry for
another 2 minutes, or until crispy. Repeat with the remaining batches, keeping an eye on the air fryer and keeping the temperature low.

Air-Fried Ratatouille, Italian-Style

Prep time: 15 minutes **Cooking time:** 22 minutes
Serve: 1

Ingredients

½ small eggplant, cut into cubes
½ large yellow bell pepper, cut into cubes
½ onion, cut into cubes
1 zucchini, cut into cubes
5 sprigs fresh basil, stemmed and chopped
salt and ground black pepper to taste
1 teaspoon vinegar
1 medium tomato, cut into cubes
½ large red bell pepper, cut into cubes
1 fresh cayenne pepper, diced
2 sprigs of fresh oregano, stemmed and chopped
1 tablespoon white wine
1 clove garlic, crushed
1 tablespoon olive oil

Directions

Carefully to 400°F (200 degrees C).
Combine the eggplant, zucchini, tomato, bell peppers, and onion in a mixing dish. Next, combine the cayenne pepper, basil, oregano, garlic, salt, and pepper in a mixing bowl. To ensure that everything is distributed equally, combine all
Ingredients in a mixing bowl. Drizzle in the oil, wine, and vinegar and toss to cover all veggies.
Place the vegetable mixture in a baking dish and place it in the air fryer basket. 8 minutes in the oven cook for another 8 minutes, stirring occasionally. Stir once more and simmer until tender, 10 to 15 minutes more, stirring every 5 minutes. Turn off the air fryer but leave the dish inside. Allow for a 5-minute pause before serving.

Air-Fried Cauliflower with Almonds and Parmesan

Prep time: 20 minutes **Cooking time:** 25 minutes
Serve: 1

Ingredients

3 cups cauliflower florets
1 clove garlic, minced
⅓ cup finely shredded Parmesan cheese
¼ cup panko breadcrumbs
3 teaspoons vegetable oil, divided
¼ cup chopped almonds
½tsp dried thyme, crushed

Directions

In a medium mixing basin, combine cauliflower florets, 2 tablespoons oil, and garlic; toss to coat. Place in an air fryer basket in a single layer.
Cook for 10 minutes in the air fryer at 360°F (180°C), shaking the
basket halfway through.
Toss the cauliflower with the remaining 1 teaspoon oil in the basin. Toss in the Parmesan cheese, almonds, breadcrumbs, and thyme to coat. Return cauliflower mixture to air fryer basket and cook for another 5 minutes, or until crisp and golden

Air Fryer Corn Dogs

Prep time: 18 minutes **Cooking time:** 20 minutes
Serve: 1

Ingredients

parchment paper
1 (6.5 ounces) package cornbread mix
1 teaspoon white sugar
6 bamboo skewers
⅔ cup milk
1 egg
8 hot dogs, cut in half

Directions

Divide the soaking bamboo skewers into thirds. To properly fit the bottom of the air fryer basket, cut a piece of parchment paper.
Preheat the air fryer carefully to 400°F (200 degrees C).
In a mixing bowl, combine cornbread mix, milk, egg, and sugar until blended; pour into a tall glass.
Insert a skewer into the center of each hot dog piece. Remove the air fryer basket and lay the cut parchment paper on the bottom of the basket. Dip four hot dogs in the batter and set them on top of the parchment paper, alternating the direction of the stick ends.
Cook for 8 minutes in a preheated air fryer without turning, or until desired brownness. Repeat with the remaining hot dogs on a dish.

Air Fryer Salt and Vinegar Fries for One

Prep time: 15 minutes **Cooking time:** 20 minutes
Serve: 1

Ingredients

1 large Yukon Gold potato 1 cup distilled white vinegar
salt and ground black pepper to taste
½ tablespoon light vegetable oil

Directions

Peel the potato and cut it into 1/2-inch sticks lengthwise. For a few seconds, rinse the potato sticks under cold running water. Transfer to a large mixing bowl. Pour in just enough water to cover the potatoes with vinegar. Allow for a 30-minute soak.
Preheat the air fryer carefully to 320°F (160 degrees C).
Drain and pat dry the potatoes. Toss in a bowl with the oil, salt, and pepper and place in the air fryer basket.
Cook for 16 minutes in a hot air fryer until soft but not browned. Shake
the basket and heat it to 355 degrees Fahrenheit (180 degrees C). 6 minutes in the air fryer, shake, and check for doneness. Cook for another 6 minutes, or until the outsides of the fries are crispy and golden

Air Fryer Frog Legs

Prep time: 15 minutes **Cooking time:** 20 minutes
Serve: 1

Ingredients

1 pound frog legs	2 cups yellow cornmeal
2 cups milk	1 cup all-purpose flour
2 tablespoons seafood seasoning	cooking spray

Directions

Pour milk over the top of the frog legs in a dish. Refrigerate for 1 hour, covered. Carefully to 400°F (200°C) according to the manufacturer's instructions. Meanwhile, add cornmeal, flour, and seafood seasoning in a gallon- sized resealable plastic bag. To blend, seal the container and shake it vigorously. Remove 1 frog leg from the milk, allowing the excess to drip into the
dish. Shake the bag with the seasoned cornmeal mixture to coat. Return the frog legs to the cornmeal mixture after dipping them back in the milk. Shake again to coat, then transfer to a dish. Rep with the remaining frog legs.
Cooking sprays the air fryer basket and puts as many frog legs as you can without overlapping. Coat the tops in cooking spray. If necessary, work in bunches. 5 minutes in the air fryer. Cooking spray should be used to remove any chalky patches. Cook for another 3 minutes, or until the bacon is crispy. Repeat with the remaining batches on a platter.

Air Fryer Churros

Prep time: 15 minutes **Cooking time:** 25 minutes **Serve:** 1

Ingredients

¼ cup butter	½ cup milk
2 eggs	1 pinch salt
½ cup all-purpose flour	¼ cup white sugar
½ teaspoon ground cinnamon	

Directions

In a saucepan over medium-high heat, melt the butter. Pour in the milk and season with salt. Reduce the heat to medium and bring to a boil, constantly stirring with a wooden spoon. Add the flour all at once. Continue to whisk until the dough comes together.
Remove from the fire and set aside for 5 to 7 minutes to cool. With a wooden spoon, mix the eggs until the pastry comes together. Fill a pastry bag with a big star tip with the dough. Pipe dough strips directly into the air fryer basket. For 5 minutes, air-fried churros at 340 degrees F (175 degrees C).

Air Fryer Hush Puppies

Prep time: 15 minutes **Cooking time:** 18 minutes
Serve: 1

Ingredients

nonfat cooking spray	¾ cup all-purpose flour
1 ½ teaspoons baking powder	½ teaspoon salt
¼ teaspoon cayenne pepper, or more to taste	1 cup yellow cornmeal
	¼ teaspoon garlic powder
2 tablespoons minced onion	2 tablespoons minced green bell pepper
¾ cup low-fat buttermilk	1 large egg

Directions

Carefully to 390°F (198°C) according to the manufacturer's instructions. Spray the bottom of the air fryer basket with nonfat cooking spray and line with aluminum foil. In a large mixing bowl, combine cornmeal, flour, baking powder, salt, cayenne pepper, and garlic powder. Next, combine the onion and bell pepper.

In a separate dish, whisk together the buttermilk and egg. Mix into the cornmeal mixture. Allow the mixture to sit for 5 minutes. Using a 2-tablespoon cookie scoop, scoop the cornmeal mixture into the foil-lined basket, making sure not to overlap. Coat the pan with nonfat cooking spray.
9 to 10 minutes in a preheated air fryer, until golden brown, crispy, and cooked through. **Serve:** immediately.

Chinese Five-Spice Air Fryer Butternut Squash Fries

Prep time: 20 minutes **Cooking time:** 20 minutes **Serve:** 1

Ingredients

1 large butternut squash	1 tablespoon Chinese five-spice powder
2 tablespoons olive oil	
2 teaspoons sea salt	2 teaspoons black pepper
1 tablespoon minced garlic	

Directions

Preheat the air fryer carefully to 400°F (200 degrees C).
In a large mixing basin, combine the chopped squash. Toss in the oil, five-spice powder, garlic, salt, and black pepper to coat. Cook butternut squash fries in a preheated air fryer for 15 to 20
minutes, shaking every 5 minutes, until crisp. Remove the fries and season with sea salt to taste.

Air Fryer Breakfast Toad-in-the-Hole Tarts

Prep time: 15 minutes **Cooking time:** 20 minutes
Serve: 1

Ingredients

1 sheet frozen puff pastry, thawed
4 eggs
4 tablespoons diced cooked ham
4 tablespoons shredded Cheddar cheese
1 tablespoon chopped fresh chives

Directions

Preheat the air fryer carefully to 400°F (200 degrees C). Unfold the pastry sheet and cut it into 4 squares on a level surface.

Cook 6 to 8 minutes with 2 pastry squares in the air fryer basket. Remove the basket from the air fryer. To make an indentation, lightly push each square with a metal tablespoon. Fill each hole with 1 tablespoon Cheddar cheese and 1 tablespoon ham, then top with 1 egg.

Return the basket to the air fryer. Cook until done, about 6 minutes more. Remove tarts from the basket and set them aside for 5 minutes to cool. Rep with the rest of the pastry squares, cheese, ham, and eggs. Tarts should be garnished with chives.

Air Fryer Roasted Brussels Sprouts with Maple-Mustard Mayo

Prep time: 15 minutes **Cooking time:** 18 minutes
Serve: 1

Ingredients

2 tablespoons maple syrup, divided
¼ teaspoon ground black pepper
⅓ cup mayonnaise
1 tablespoon olive oil - ¼ teaspoon kosher salt
1 pound Brussels sprouts, trimmed and halved
1 tablespoon stone-ground mustard

Directions

Preheat the air fryer carefully to 400°F (200 degrees C).
In a large mixing bowl, combine 1 tablespoon maple syrup, olive oil, salt, and pepper. Toss in the Brussels

sprouts to coat. Arrange Brussels sprouts in an air fryer basket in a single layer, without overcrowded; work in batches if required. 4 minutes in the oven cook until the sprouts are deep golden brown and tender, 4 to 6 minutes longer.

Meanwhile, combine mayonnaise, the remaining 1 tablespoon maple syrup, and mustard in a small mixing dish. Toss the sprouts in a little sauce combination and **Serve:** as a dipping sauce.

Air Fryer Onion Bhaji

Prep time: 15 minutes **Cooking time:** 22 minutes **Serve:** 1

Ingredients

1 small red onion, thinly sliced
1 jalapeno pepper, seeded and minced
1 tablespoon salt
1 teaspoon ground turmeric
4 tbs water, or as needed
cooking spray
1 small yellow onion, thinly sliced
1 clove garlic, minced
1 teaspoon coriander
1 teaspoon chili powder
½ teaspoon cumin
⅔ cup chickpea flour (bean)

Directions

In a large mixing bowl, combine red onion, yellow onion, salt, jalapeño, garlic, coriander, chili powder, turmeric, and cumin. Stir until everything is well blended. Mix in the chickpea flour and water. To make a thick batter, put all
Ingredients in a mixing bowl. If required, add extra water. Allow the mixture to settle for 10 minutes.

Preheat the air fryer carefully to 350°F (175 degrees C).
Nonstick cooking spray should be sprayed on the air fryer basket. Flatten 2 tablespoons of batter into the basket. Repeat as many times as your basket permits without touching the bhajis.

Cook for 6 minutes in a hot air fryer. Cooking spray should be sprayed on the tops of each bhaji. Cook for 6 minutes more on the other side. Transfer to a plate lined with paper towels. Rep with the remaining batter.

Rice & Grains Recipes

Aromatic Seafood Pilaf

(**Ready in about** 45 minutes | **Servings:** 2)

Ingredients

1 cup jasmine rice

1 small yellow onion, chopped

1 bay leaf

4 tablespoons cream of mushroom soup

Salt and black pepper, to taste

1 small garlic clove, finely chopped

1 teaspoon butter, melted

1/2 pound shrimp, divined and sliced

Directions

Bring 2 cups of a lightly salted water to a boil in a medium saucepan over medium-high heat. Add in the jasmine rice, turn to a simmer and cook, covered, for about 18 minutes until water is absorbed.

Let the jasmine rice stand covered for 5 to 6 minutes; fluff with a fork and transfer to a lightly greased Air Fryer safe pan.

Stir in the salt, black pepper, bay leaf, yellow onion, garlic, butter and cream of mushroom soup; stir until everything is well incorporated.

Cook the rice at 350 degrees F for about 13 minutes. Stir in the shrimp and continue to cook for a further 5 minutes.

Check the rice for softness. If necessary, cook for a few minutes more. Bon appétit!

Easy Pizza Margherita

(**Ready in about** 15 minutes | **Servings:** 1)

Ingredients

6-inch dough

1 teaspoon extra-virgin olive oil Coarse sea salt, to taste

2 tablespoons tomato sauce

2-3 fresh basil leaves

2 ounces mozzarella

Directions

Start by preheating your Air Fryer to 380 degrees F.

Stretch the dough on a pizza peel lightly dusted with flour. Spread with a layer of tomato sauce.

Add mozzarella to the crust and drizzle with olive oil. Salt to taste.

Bake in the preheated Air Fryer for 4 minutes. Rotate the baking tray and bake for a further 4 minutes. Garnish with fresh basil leaves and **Serve:** immediately. Bon appétit!

Famous Greek Tyrompiskota

(**Ready in about** 45 minutes | **Servings:** 3)

Ingredients

1 cup all-purpose flour

1 teaspoon baking powder

1/2 cup halloumi cheese, grated

1 egg

1 tablespoon flaxseed meal

1/2 stick butter

1 teaspoon Greek spice blend Salt to taste

Directions

Combine the flour, flaxseed meal, and baking powder in a mixing bowl. In a separate bowl, combine the butter, cheese, and egg. Incorporate the cheese mixture into the dry flour mixture.

Mix with your hands, then stir in the Greek spice blend; season with salt and stir again to combine thoroughly.

Form the batter into a log, wrap in cling film, and place in the refrigerator for about 30 minutes.

Using a sharp knife, cut the chilled log into thin slices. Cook your biscuits for 15 minutes in a preheated Air Fryer at 360 degrees F. Make use of batches.

Good appetite!

Bacon and Cheese Sandwich

(**Ready in about** 15 minutes | **Servings:** 1)

Ingredients

2 slices whole-wheat bread

2 ounces bacon, sliced

1 tablespoon ketchup

1/2 teaspoon Dijon mustard

1 ounce cheddar cheese, sliced

Directions

Spread the ketchup and mustard on a slice of bread. Add the bacon and cheese and top with another slice of bread.

Place your sandwich in the lightly buttered Air Fryer cooking basket.

Now, bake your sandwich at 380 degrees F for 10 minutes or until the cheese has melted. Make sure to turn it over halfway through the cooking time.

Bon appétit!

Baked "Fried" Rice

Prep time: 15 minutes **Cooking time:** 20 minutes
Serve: 1

Ingredients

2 cups long-grain white rice 2 tablespoons canola oil

1 tablespoon sesame oil, or to taste

½ cup sliced green onions

3 cloves garlic, crushed

½ cup diced carrots

1 pinch salt to taste (Optional)

2 teaspoons chili paste

½ cup diced red bell peppers

½ cup green peas

3 tablespoons soy sauce

1 cup diced ham

3 cups chicken broth

Directions

Preheat the oven carefully to 400 degrees Fahrenheit (200 degrees C). In a large baking dish, place the rice. Drizzle canola and sesame oils over rice and toss to cover fully. Combine the garlic, green onions, bell peppers, carrots, peas, and ham in a mixing bowl. Season with salt and pepper. Stir until everything is completely blended.

Combine the chicken broth, soy sauce, and chili paste in a saucepan over high heat. Bring to a boil, stirring constantly. Pour over the rice and give it a quick swirl. Wrap the top securely in heavy-duty aluminum foil. Bake for 32 minutes in a preheated oven. Remove from the oven and set aside for 10 minutes. Remove the lid and fluff the rice with a fork. Seasoning should be tasted and adjusted.

Raise the oven temperature to 475°F (245 degrees C). Return to the oven for 10 minutes or until the rice is toasted and crusted.

Mushroom Rice

Prep time: 15 minutes **Cooking time:** 22 minutes
Serve: 1

Ingredients

2 teaspoons butter

1 clove garlic, minced

1 green onion, finely chopped

½ teaspoon chopped fresh parsley

salt and pepper to taste

6 mushrooms, coarsely chopped

1 cup uncooked white rice

2 cups chicken broth

Directions

In a saucepan over medium heat, melt the butter. Cook the mushrooms, garlic, and green onion until the liquid has evaporated and the mushrooms are tender. Combine the chicken broth and rice in a mixing bowl. Season with parsley, salt, and pepper to taste. Reduce the heat to low, cover, and leave to simmer for 20 minutes.

Island-Style Fried Rice

Prep time: 18 minutes **Cooking time:** 20 minutes
Serve: 1

Ingredients

1 ½ cups uncooked jasmine rice

1 (12 ounces) can fully cook luncheon meat (such as SPAM®), cubed

2 tablespoons canola oil

½ cup chopped green onion 3 tablespoons oyster sauce

2 teaspoons canola oil

3 cups water

½ cup sliced Chinese sweet pork sausage (lap Cheong)

3 eggs, beaten

1 (8 ounces) can pineapple chunks, drained

½ teaspoon garlic powder

Directions

In a saucepan over high heat, bring the rice and water to a boil. Reduce the heat to medium-low, cover, and cook for 20 to 25 minutes, or until the rice is soft and the liquid has been absorbed. Allow the rice to cool fully.

Brown the luncheon meat and sausage in a pan with 2 tablespoons of oil over medium heat. Set aside the beaten eggs and pour them into the heated skillet. Set aside the scrambled eggs.

In a large nonstick pan over normal heat, heat 2 tablespoons of oil and toss in the rice. Toss the rice in the hot oil for approximately 2 minutes, or until cooked through and beginning to brown. Toss the rice for 1 minute longer to enhance the garlic flavor, then add the luncheon meat, sausage, scrambled eggs, pineapple, and oyster sauce. Cook and stir for 2 to 3 minutes, or until the oyster sauce covers the rice and other Ingredients. Stir in the green onions and **Serve:**.

Cindy's Yellow Rice

Prep time: 15 minutes **Cooking time:** 25 minutes
Serve: 1

Ingredients

2 cups water

¼ cup dried minced onion

2 tablespoons olive oil

1 teaspoon ground black pepper

1 cup white rice

1 teaspoon ground turmeric 1 teaspoon garlic powder

1 teaspoon salt

Directions

In a saucepan, bring water to a boil. Combine the rice, onion, olive oil, turmeric, garlic powder, black pepper, and salt in a mixing bowl. Cover the pot, decrease the heat to low, and simmer for 20 minutes, or until the water is absorbed and the rice is tender. With a fork, fluff the rice.

Apple Oats

Prep time: 10 minutes **Cooking time:** 15 minutes
Serve: 1

Ingredients
½ cup gluten-free oats
1 tbsp Greek yogurt
½ tsp cream of tartar
2 tbsp date spread
¼ cup apple, chopped
½ cup unsweetened almond milk
½ tsp baking powder
1 tbsp protein powder

Directions

In a mixing bowl, mix together oats, baking powder, and protein powder. Add yogurt, milk, date spread, and cream of tartar and mix until well combined.

Add apple and fold well. Pour oat mixture into the greased air fryer baking dish. Place baking dish into the air fryer basket and cook at 330 F for 15 minutes. **Serve:** and enjoy.

Peanut Butter Oatmeal

Prep time: 10 minutes **Cooking time:** 15 minutes
Serve: 1

Ingredients
½ cup rolled oats
½ tsp baking powder
1/3 cup unsweetened almond milk
1 tsp maple syrup
¼ tsp vanilla
½ tbsp peanut butter
½ banana
1/8 tsp salt

Directions

Preheat the air fryer to 350 F. Add oats into the food processor and process until get flour like consistency. Add remaining Ingredients and process until well combined. Pour batter into the greased ramekin. **Serve:** and enjoy.

Oats Granola

Prep time: 10 minutes **Cooking time:** 30 minutes
Serve: 8

Ingredients
3 cups old-fashioned oats
3 tbsp brown sugar
½ cup maple syrup
1 tsp vanilla
1 tsp cinnamon
3 tbsp coconut oil, melted
½ tsp salt

Directions

In a mixing bowl, mix together oats, vanilla, cinnamon, brown sugar, oil, maple syrup, and salt until well combined.

Spread oats mixture into the parchment-lined air fryer basket and cook at 250 F for 30 minutes. Stir after every 10 minutes. **Serve:** and enjoy.

Berry Oatmeal

Prep time: 10 minutes **Cooking time:** 8 minutes **Serve:** 4

Ingredients
2 eggs
5 tbsp unsweetened almond milk
1 tbsp vanilla
2 tbsp mixed berries
7 oz banana
2 tbsp honey
2 tbsp Greek yogurt
4.5 oz quick oats

Directions

In a mixing bowl, add banana and mash using the fork.
Add oats, vanilla, honey, yogurt, milk, and eggs and mix until well combined. Add berries and fold well.

Spoon mixture into the four greased ramekins. Place ramekins into the air fryer basket and cook at 400 F for 8 minutes. **Serve:** and enjoy.

Chocolate Oats

Prep time: 10 minutes **Cooking time:** 15 minutes
Serve: 2

Ingredients
1 egg
½ tsp cinnamon
1 tsp vanilla
½ tsp baking powder
½ cup rolled oats
1 tbsp cocoa powder
¼ cup unsweetened almond milk
1 tbsp maple syrup
½ banana Pinch of salt

Directions

Add oats and remaining Ingredients into the blender and blend until smooth. Pour blended oat mixture into the greased ramekins.

Place ramekins into the air fryer basket and cook at 330 F for 13-15 minutes. **Serve:** and enjoy.

Curried Chickpeas

Prep time: 10 minutes **Cooking time:** 18 minutes
Serve: 4

Ingredients
30 oz can chickpeas, drained & rinsed
½ tbsp parsley, chopped
Salt
½ tsp chili powder
2 tbsp curry powder
2 tbsp canola oil

Directions

Add chickpeas and remaining Ingredients into the mixing bowl and toss until well coated. Spread chickpeas into the air fryer basket and cook at 375 F for 15-18 minutes. Stir after every 5 minutes. **Serve:** and enjoy.

Quinoa Fried Rice

Prep time: 20 minutes **Cooking time:** 25 minutes
Serve: 1

Ingredients

1 ½ cups water	2 ½ tablespoons soy sauce
1 ½ tablespoons teriyaki sauce	¾ teaspoon sesame oil
1 tablespoon olive oil, divided	1 cup quinoa salt to taste
3 scallions, chopped, divided 3 cloves garlic, minced	¼ onion, chopped
	2 carrots, peeled chopped
	½ teaspoon minced fresh ginger
½ cup frozen peas	2 eggs, beaten

Directions

Bring the quinoa and water to a boil, season with salt. Reduce the heat to medium-low, cover, and cook for 15 to 20 minutes, or until the quinoa is tender and the water is absorbed. Turn off the heat and put aside for 5 minutes before fluffing the quinoa with a fork. Refrigerate for at least 8 hours and up to overnight.

In a mixing bowl, combine soy sauce, teriyaki sauce, and sesame oil until equally combined. Heat 1 1/2 tsp oil and sauté carrots and onion in a large pan over high heat for 2 minutes. Sauté the remaining 2 scallions, garlic, and ginger for 2 minutes, or until aromatic. Cook until heated through, approximately 2 minutes, with the remaining 1 1/2 tablespoons oil and quinoa.

Cook and swirl the sauce into the quinoa mixture for 2 minutes or evenly covered. In the center of the quinoa mixture, make a well. Pour the eggs into the well; heat and stir for 2 to 3 minutes, or until the eggs are scrambled and cooked through. Cook for 2 to 3 minutes, or until peas are cooked through. Stir in the remaining scallions.

Cinnamon Rice

Prep time: 15 minutes **Cooking time:** 18 minutes
Serve: 1

Ingredients

1 cup uncooked rice	2 tablespoons nonfat milk
2 cups water	5 tablespoons raisins
2 teaspoons margarine	½ teaspoon ground cinnamon
1 teaspoon sugar	

Directions

In a saucepan over medium-high heat, bring rice, water, milk, raisins, and margarine to a boil, stirring periodically. Reduce the heat to low, cover, and simmer for 15 minutes, or until the liquid has been absorbed and the rice is soft. To **Serve:**, combine cinnamon and sugar and sprinkle over rice.

One-Pot Rice and Beef Pilaf

Prep time: 15 minutes **Cooking time:** 20 minutes
Serve: 1

Ingredients

½ cup olive oil	2 cups uncooked white rice
2 pounds bone-in beef pot roast, boned and cubed	4 carrots, peeled and cut into matchsticks
1 onion, peeled, halved, and thinly sliced	2 teaspoons ground cumin salt to taste
2 fresh red chili peppers hot water to cover	1 head garlic, unpeeled (optional)

Directions

Place the rice in a bowl and cover with warm water to soak while the meat cooks. Heat the olive oil in a saucepan over medium-high heat and sauté the bones for 5 minutes, or until gently browned.

Place the bones on a platter. Cook until the onion is tender and translucent, about 5 minutes, in the same saucepan. Brown the meat on both sides, 5 to 10 minutes. Return the bones to the pan and add the carrots. Garnish with cumin. Stir in the entire chili peppers and garlic, then season with salt. Fill the container halfway with boiling water. Bring to a boil, then lower to low heat and continue to cook for 35 to 40 minutes, or until the flavors are fully integrated.

With kitchen tongs, remove the bones and add the rice. Pour in 2 cups hot water and level out the rice to sit flat on top, but do not stir. Cook, covered, over low heat for 20 to 25 minutes, or until tender rice. Before serving, mix everything.

Classic Fried Rice

Prep time: 18 minutes **Cooking time:** 20 minutes
Serve: 1

Ingredients

6 strips bacon, cut into 1/2-inch pieces	8 green onions and tops, sliced
1 egg, beaten	4 cups cold, cooked rice
1 tablespoon minced garlic	3 tablespoons Kikkoman Soy Sauce

Directions

In a large pan over medium heat, cook bacon until crisp. Transfer the bacon to the side of the pan; add the egg and scramble it. Move the egg to the skillet, add the green onions, cook for approximately a minute. Next, stir in the rice, followed by the garlic and soy sauce. Toss until the mixture is properly combined and thoroughly cooked.

Yellow Rice with Meat

Prep time: 15 minutes **Cooking time:** 25 minutes
Serve: 1

Ingredients

1 tablespoon olive oil
2 pork chops
1 onion, diced
2 green bell peppers
4 sprigs of fresh thyme
2 teaspoons cloves
1 (10 ounces) package
yellow rice
1 lemon, cut into wedges
chili sauce

2 boneless, skinless
chicken thighs
2 cloves garlic, finely
chopped
3 bay leaves
1 sprig of fresh rosemary
1 cup peas
1 fresh jalapeno pepper
diced

Directions

In a skillet over medium heat, heat the olive oil. Cook until the pork chops and chicken thighs are browned on both sides, the chicken juices run clear, and the pork chops are done. Set aside after removing from skillet.

Cook until the bell peppers are cooked in the pan, then put aside. Mix in the onion and garlic. Combine rosemary, thyme, cloves, and bay leaves in a mixing bowl. Add rice to the pan, along with the amount of water specified on the rice bag. Cook for another 10 minutes.

Combine the pork chops, chicken, rice, peppers, and peas in a pan. Cook for another 10 minutes, or until the rice is soft. Remove the rosemary, thyme, and bay leaves. To **Serve:**, pour lemon juice over the meats and rice, then top with chopped jalapeño and chili sauce.

Perfect White Rice

Prep time: 15 minutes **Cooking time:** 20 minutes
Serve: 1

Ingredients

2 teaspoons unsalted
butter
2 cups water
½ teaspoon salt

1 cup uncooked long-grain
white rice

Directions

In a medium saucepan over medium heat, melt the butter. Stir in the rice to coat it. Cook for 1 to 2 minutes, or until the rice grains become opaque; do not brown. Pour in the water and salt.

Bring to a boil, then lower to low heat. Allow boiling for 15 minutes, covered. Do not remove the cover. Remove from the heat and set aside for 5 minutes, covered. Before serving, fluff with a fork.

Jeera Rice

Prep time: 20 minutes **Cooking time:** 25 minutes
Serve: 1

Ingredients

1 cup basmati rice
4 whole cloves
4 whole black peppercorns
1 ½ cups water salt to
taste

2 teaspoons vegetable oil
1 teaspoon cumin seeds
1 bay leaf
2 cardamom pods

Directions

Rinse rice three to four times before placing it in a bowl; cover with water and soak for at least 30 minutes.
Cook and swirl cumin in a pan over medium heat until it begins to pop, 2 to 4 minutes. Cook and stir for 1 1/2 minutes, or until the cloves, peppercorns, cardamom pods, and bay leaf are aromatic.

Drain the rice and combine with spice mixture; add 1 1/2 cups water and salt to taste. Cook for 5 minutes, covered, over high heat. Reduce the heat to medium and cook for another 10 minutes. Reduce the heat to low and continue to cook for 15 minutes. Remove skillet from heat and set aside for 15 minutes with the lid on.

Remove the lid and fluff the rice with a fork. Remove the bay leaf, cardamom pods, cloves, and peppercorns from the mixture.

South Indian-Style Lemon Rice

Prep time: 15 minutes **Cooking time:** 20 minutes
Serve: 1

Ingredients

4 cups water

¼ cup raw peanuts
6 tablespoons vegetable oil
½ teaspoon mustard
seeds
¼ cup lemon juice
1 ½ teaspoons salt

2 cups uncooked white
rice
½ teaspoon ground
turmeric
4 green chili peppers,
chopped
15 fresh curry leaves
(Optional)

Directions

Bring water and rice to a boil in a saucepan. Reduce to medium-low heat, cover, and simmer for 20 to 25 minutes, or until the rice is mushy and the water has been absorbed.

In a large skillet over medium heat, heat the oil. Cook and stir the peanuts, turmeric, and mustard seeds for 2 to 3 minutes, or until the peanuts are browned.

Combine the green chili peppers, lemon juice, curry leaves, and salt in a mixing bowl. Fold the cooked rice into the lemon juice mixture.

Chicken and Multi-Grain Stir Fry

Prep time: 20 minutes **Cooking time:** 20 minutes
Serve: 1

Ingredients

1 bag Minute® Multi-Grain Medley, uncooked
½ teaspoon sesame oil
2 cloves garlic, chopped
½ cup snap peas
½ cup broccoli florets
½ cup red bell pepper, sliced
2 cups cooked chicken, shredded

2 large eggs, lightly beaten
1 cup chicken broth
2 tablespoons olive oil, divided
½ cup red onion, thinly sliced
½ teaspoon Chinese five-spice powder (Optional)

Directions

Make Multi-Grain Medley according to package directions
but use broth instead of water. Whisk together the eggs and sesame oil in a small bowl.

12 tbsp olive oil, heated in a large pan at medium-low heat Soft scrambled eggs in a hurry. Remove from skillet and set aside to stay heated. Heat the remaining olive oil in a medium saucepan over medium heat. Sauté for 3 minutes with the garlic, onions, peas, broccoli, bell peppers, and five-spice powder.

Cook for 2 minutes more, or until the chicken, Multi-Grain Medley, and eggs are crisp-tender.

Spent Grain Wheat Bread

Prep time: 15 minutes **Cooking time:** 25 minutes
Serve: 1

Ingredients

1 ¼ cups water
3 tablespoons butter, softened
1 ½ tbsp powdered milk
½ cup rye flour

1 ½ cups bread flour
1 teaspoon active dry yeast

3 tablespoons honey
¼ cup spent grain
1 teaspoon white sugar
1 teaspoon salt
1 ½ cups whole wheat flour
¼ cup vital wheat gluten

Directions

Place the Ingredients in the bread machine's pan in the sequence indicated by the manufacturer. Choose the complete wheat cycle and hit the Start button. Reduce the water by 1 tablespoon if using the delay timer.

Cranberry Pecan Multi-Grain Stuffing

Prep time: 15 minutes **Cooking time:** 25 minutes
Serve: 1

Ingredients

1 tablespoon olive oil
¼ cup chopped celery
½ cup dried cranberries
1 cup chicken broth
½ cup chopped pecans, toasted

½ cup chopped onion
¼ tbs poultry seasoning
1 bag Minute® Multi-Grain Medley, uncooked
1 pinch salt and ground black pepper

Directions

In a medium saucepan, heat the oil over medium heat. Cook for 2 minutes after adding the onion and celery. Combine the chicken seasoning, cranberries, and broth in a mixing bowl. Bring to a boil, then add the Multi-Grain Medley. Cover, decrease the heat to low and cook for 5 minutes. Remove from the heat and set aside for 5 minutes. Season with salt and pepper, if preferred, and stir in the pecans.

Whole Grain Pancakes with Fresh Fruit

Prep time: 15 minutes **Cooking time:** 20 minutes
Serve: 1

Ingredients

1 cup whole wheat flour
1 tablespoon Reddi-wip®
2 tablespoons firmly packed brown sugar
½ teaspoon salt
½ cup Egg Beaters® Original
½ teaspoon vanilla extract
¼ cup honey
No-Stick Cooking Spray
½ cup fresh blueberries
Canola Oil

¼ cup quick cooking rolled oats
1 ½ teaspoons baking powder
¾ cup fat-free milk
¼ cup plain nonfat yogurt
1 tbsp Pure Wesson® PAM® Organic Canola Oil
2 medium bananas, peeled and sliced
Fat-Free Dairy Whipped Topping

Directions

In a large mixing basin, combine the flour, oats, sugar, baking powder, and salt; set aside. Next, combine the milk, Egg Beaters, yogurt, oil, and vanilla extract in a small mixing bowl. Add to the flour mixture and whisk just until combined. (Avoid overmixing.) The batter should still be a little lumpy.)

Coat the skillet with frying spray. Heat over medium heat until hot, or preheat an electric skillet to 400°F. For each pancake, pour roughly 1/4 cup batter onto a heated griddle. Cook for 2 to 3 minutes, or until bubbles appear on the surface and the bottom is golden brown. Cook until golden brown on the other side. Rep with the remaining batter. Drizzle 1 tablespoon honey over each serving and top with fresh fruit. **Serve:** right away.

Whole Grain Carrot Peach Muffins

Prep time: 10 minutes **Cooking time:** 18 minutes
Serve: 1

Ingredients

2 tablespoons butter, slightly softened
1 tablespoon dark brown sugar
½ cup all-purpose flour
1 tbsp ground cinnamon
½ cup oat flour
½ teaspoon baking soda
½ cup white sugar
2 large eggs
1 cup grated carrots
¼ cup rolled oats
1 tbsp all-purpose flour
¼ teaspoon ground cinnamon
½ cup white whole-wheat flour
1 ½ tbsp baking powder
½ cup canola oil
1 teaspoon vanilla extract
1 ½ cups diced peaches

Directions

Preheat the oven carefully to 350°F (175 degrees C). Prepare a muffin tin by lining it with paper liners. Combine the butter, rolled oats, dark brown sugar, 1 tablespoon all- purpose flour, and 1/4 teaspoon cinnamon in a mixing dish. Mix with a fork or your fingertips until the mixture is crumbly.

In a large mixing bowl, combine 1/2 cup all-purpose flour, white whole-wheat flour, oat flour, baking powder, 1 teaspoon cinnamon, and baking soda.

Combine the oil, sugar, eggs, and vanilla essence in a separate dish. Pour into the flour mixture and fold until barely mixed. Next, gently fold in the peaches and carrots.
Fill prepared muffin tins about 2/3 full of batter. Garnish with oat topping.

Bake for 15 minutes, or until a toothpick inserted into the center comes out clean. Cool for 5 to 10 minutes in the pan before transferring muffins to a wire rack to cool fully.

Zucchini Banana Multi-Grain Bread

Prep time: 18 minutes **Cooking time:** 20 minutes
Serve: 1

Ingredients

1 bag Minute® Multi-Grain Medley, uncooked
1 teaspoon vanilla extract
½ cup sugar
3 tablespoons vegetable oil, ¼ cup milk
½ cup walnuts, chopped
3 large eggs, lightly beaten
1 serving Nonstick cooking spray
1 ripe banana, mashed
1 medium zucchini, grated
2 cups baking mix

Directions

Preheat the oven carefully to 400°F. Follow the package directions to make the Multi-Grain Medley. Using nonstick cooking spray, coat a loaf pan.

In a large mixing basin, combine the eggs, sugar, and banana. Stir I the rice, oil, milk, vanilla, zucchini (approximately 1 1/2 cups shredded), and walnuts. Stir in the baking mix until all of the Ingredients are mixed. Pour the mixture into the prepared pan.

45 minutes in the oven, or until a toothpick inserted into the middle comes out clean. Allow to cool for 10 minutes before removing from pan and cooling on a rack.

Special Events

Flavorful Chicken Skewers

Prep time: 10 minutes **Cooking time:** 20 minutes
Serve: 4

Ingredients

1 1/2 lbs. chicken breast, cut into 1-inch cubes
2 tbsp dried oregano
2 tbsp fresh rosemary, chopped
1/2 cup lemon juice
1/4 tsp cayenne Pepper

For marinade
1/2 cup low-fat yogurt
1 tbsp red wine vinegar
1 cup olive oil
4 garlic cloves
Salt
1/4 cup fresh mint leaves

Directions

Add all marinade Ingredients into the blender and blend until smooth. Pour marinade into a mixing bowl.
Add chicken and coat well, cover and place in the refrigerator for 1 hour.

Thread marinated chicken onto the soaked wooden skewers. Place chicken skewers into the air fryer basket and cook at 400 F for 15-20 minutes. **Serve:** and enjoy.

Turkey Meatballs

Prep time: 10 minutes **Cooking time:** 18 minutes
Serve: 6

Ingredients

1 lb. ground turkey
1 tbsp garlic, minced
1 tsp cumin
2 cups zucchini, grated
1 tsp dried oregano
Salt

1 tbsp dried onion flakes
2 eggs, lightly beaten
1/3 cup almond flour
1 tbsp basil, chopped
Pepper

Directions

Preheat the air fryer to 400 F. Add turkey and remaining Ingredients into the mixing bowl and mix until well combined.

Make small balls from the turkey mixture and place into the air fryer basket and cook for 15-18 minutes. Turn halfway through. **Serve:** and enjoy.

Tandoori Chicken Drumsticks

Prep time: 10 minutes **Cooking time:** 15 minutes
Serve: 4

Ingredients

4 chicken drumsticks
1/2 tsp garam masala
1/2 tsp turmeric
1 tbsp ginger garlic paste
1/4 cup yogurt

For marinade
1 tsp chili powder
1 tbsp fresh lime juice
1 tsp salt
1 tsp ground cumin

Directions

Preheat the air fryer to 360 F. In a mixing bowl, add marinade Ingredients and mix until well combined.

Add chicken in marinade and mix until well coated. Cover and place in the refrigerator for overnight. Place marinated chicken drumsticks into the air fryer basket and cook for 15 minutes. Turn halfway through. **Serve:** and enjoy.

Chicken Burger Patties

Prep time: 10 minutes **Cooking time:** 18 minutes
Serve: 4

Ingredients

1 lb. ground chicken
3 oz almond flour
1 tbsp oregano Pepper

2 oz mozzarella cheese, shredded
Salt

Directions

Preheat the air fryer to 360 F. Add chicken and remaining Ingredients into the mixin bowl and mix until well combined. Make four patties from the chicken mixture.
Place chicken patties into the air fryer basket and cook for 18 minutes. Turn halfway through. **Serve:** and enjoy.

Flavorful Stew Meat

Prep time: 10 minutes **Cooking time:** 25 minutes
Serve: 4

Ingredients
1 lb. beef stew meat, cut into strips	1/2 tsp onion powder
1 tbsp garlic powder	1/2 fresh lime juice
1/2 tbsp ground cumin	1 tbsp olive oil
Salt	Pepper

Directions

Preheat the air fryer to 380 F. Add stew meat and remaining Ingredients into the mixing bowl and mix well.
Add stew meat into the air fryer basket and cook for 25 minutes. Stir halfway through **Serve:** and enjoy.

Cheesy Lamb Patties

Prep time: 10 minutes **Cooking time:** 8 minutes **Serve:** 4

Ingredients
1 lb. ground lamb	1/4 cup mint leaves, minced 1/4 cup fresh parsley, chopped
1 tsp dried oregano	
1/2 tsp kosher salt	
1 cup goat cheese, crumbled 1 tbsp garlic, minced	8 basil leaves, minced
	1 tsp chili powder
1/4 tsp pepper	

Directions

Preheat the air fryer to 400 F. Add ground lamb and remaining Ingredients into the mixing bowl and mix until well combined. Make four equal shape patties from the lamb mixture. Place patties into the air fryer basket and cook for 8 minutes. Turn halfway through. **Serve:** and enjoy.

Chipotle Rib-eye Steak

Prep time: 10 minutes **Cooking time:** 10 minutes
Serve: 3

Ingredients
1 lb. rib-eye steak	1/2 tsp coffee powder
1/8 tsp cocoa powder	1/4 tsp onion powder
1/8 tsp coriander powder	1/4 tsp garlic powder
1/4 tsp chipotle powder	Pepper
1/4 tsp paprika	1/4 tsp chili powder
Salt	

Directions

Preheat the air fryer to 390 F. In a small bowl, mix together all Ingredients except steak. Rub spice mixture all over the steak and allow to sit steak for 30 minutes.
Place steak into the air fryer basket and cook for 10 minutes. Turn halfway through. **Serve:** and enjoy.

Yogurt Beef Kebabs

Prep time: 10 minutes **Cooking time:** 15 minutes
Serve: 8

Ingredients
1 1/2 lbs. beef, cut into 1-inch pieces	1/4 cup Greek yogurt
1 onion, cut into chunks	1 tsp garlic, minced
pepper	Salt
	2 bell pepper, cut into chunks

Directions

Preheat the air fryer to 350 F. Add meat and remaining Ingredients into the mixing bowl and mix well. Cover and place in refrigerator for 30 minutes. Thread marinated beef pieces, bell pepper, and onion pieces onto the skewers.
Place meat skewers into the air fryer basket and cook for 15 minutes. Turn halfway through. **Serve:** and enjoy.

Amazing Buttermilk Air Fried Chicken

Prep time: 15 minutes **Cooking time:** 25 minutes
Serve: 1

Ingredients
1 cup buttermilk	½ teaspoon hot sauce
⅓ cup tapioca flour	½ teaspoon garlic salt
⅛ teaspoon ground black pepper	½ cup all-purpose flour
1 ½ teaspoons brown sugar	2 teaspoons salt
	½ teaspoon paprika
1 teaspoon garlic powder	1 egg
½ teaspoon onion powder	¼ teaspoon oregano
¼ teaspoon black pepper	1-pound skinless, boneless chicken thighs

Directions

Add buttermilk and spicy sauce; stir to blend. Shake together tapioca flour, garlic salt, and 1/8 teaspoon black pepper in a resealable plastic bag. In a small dish, beat the egg. In a gallon-sized resealable bag, add flour, salt, brown sugar, garlic powder, paprika, onion powder, oregano, and 1/4 teaspoon black pepper.

Dip the chicken thighs in the following order buttermilk mixture, tapioca mixture, egg mixture, and flour mixture, brushing off the excess after each dipping. Preheat an air fryer carefully to 380°F (190 degrees C). Then, using parchment paper, line the air fryer basket. Fry the coated chicken thighs in batches for 10 minutes in the air fryer basket.

Air-Fried Peruvian Chicken Drumsticks with Green Crema

Prep time: 15 minutes **Cooking time:** 20 minutes **Serve:** 1

Ingredients

olive oil for brushing	1 tablespoon olive oil
2 cloves garlic, grated	1 teaspoon salt
1 teaspoon ground cumin	½ teaspoon smoked
1 tablespoon honey	paprika
½ teaspoon dried oregano	¼ teaspoon ground black
6 (4 ounces) chicken	pepper
drumsticks	1 clove garlic, smashed
1 cup baby spinach leaves,	¾ cup sour cream
stems removed	2 tbsp fresh lime juice
¼ cup cilantro leaves	¼ tbsp ground black
	pepper
½ jalapeno pepper, seeded	¼ teaspoon salt

Directions

Brush olive oil into an air fryer basket. In a large mixing bowl, combine garlic, honey, 1 tablespoon olive oil, salt, cumin, paprika, oregano, and pepper. Toss in the drumsticks to coat. Arrange the drumsticks in the prepared basket vertically, resting against the basket wall and one another.

Cook in the air fryer at 400 degrees F (200 degrees C) for 15 to 20 minutes, or until an instant-read thermometer placed into the thickest section of the drumstick registers 175 degrees F (80 degrees C). To ensure consistent cooking, rearrange the drumsticks using kitchen tongs halfway through.

Meanwhile, mix spinach, sour cream, cilantro, lime juice, garlic, jalapeño pepper, salt, and pepper; process until crème is smooth. Drizzle some cream sauce over the drumsticks and **Serve:** the rest of the crema.

Grandma Egan's Chicken Stock

Prep time: 18 minutes **Cooking time:** 20 minutes **Serve:** 1

Ingredients

1 (8 pounds) chicken	3 stalks celery, chopped
	1 onion, quartered

Directions

In a large stockpot, combine the chicken, celery, and onion. Fill the container halfway with water. Bring the water to a boil.

Remove any extra fat. Reduce the heat to a simmer and cook for 2 to 3 hours. Take out the chicken and veggies. Using a cheesecloth, strain the soup.

Dry-Rub Air-Fried Chicken Wings

Prep time: 20 minutes **Cooking time:** 25 minutes **Serve:** 1

Ingredients

1 tbs dark brown sugar	½ tablespoon kosher salt
1 tablespoon sweet	1 teaspoon garlic powder
paprika	1 teaspoon onion powder
½ tbs ground black	
pepper	
1 tbs poultry seasoning	½ tbs mustard powder
	8 chicken wings, or more
	as needed

Directions

Preheat the air fryer carefully to 350°F (175 degrees C).
In a large mixing bowl, combine brown sugar, paprika, salt, garlic powder, onion powder, poultry seasoning, mustard powder, and pepper. Toss in the chicken wings and work the spices into them with your hands until they are well covered.

Arrange the wings in the preheated air fryer basket, standing up on their ends and resting against each other and the basket wall. Cook for 35 minutes, or until the wings are soft on the inside and golden brown and crisp on the exterior. Place the wings on a dish and **Serve:** immediately.

Mustard Fried Chicken

Prep time: 15 minutes **Cooking time:** 20 minutes **Serve:** 1

Ingredients

5 pounds chicken wings,	2 tablespoons ground
separated at joints, tips	black pepper
discarded	1 tablespoon seasoned salt
2 tablespoons garlic	3 tablespoons prepared
powder	yellow mustard
2 tablespoons onion	
powder	
1-quart oil for frying, or as	3 cups all-purpose flour
needed	

Directions

Season both sides of the chicken wings with seasoned salt, garlic powder, onion powder, pepper, and MSG. I prefer to spread everything out on a large plastic bag for simpler cleanup. Apply a little coating of mustard on each slice. You may use a basting brush or your fingers to apply the sauce. Fill a plastic bag halfway with flour, add the chicken, and shake to coat.
Heat the oil in a deep-fryer or heavy skillet to 350°F (175 degrees C). Cook the chicken for 6 minutes on each side, or until the juices run clear after the oil is heated. Cool for 5 minutes on paper towels before serving.

Air-Fried Breaded Chicken Thighs

Prep time: 15 minutes **Cooking time:** 20 minutes
Serve: 1

Ingredients

4 medium bone-in, skin-on chicken thighs	¼ cup all-purpose flour
¼ cup plain breadcrumbs	1 cup buttermilk
1 teaspoon garlic powder	2 tablespoons grated Parmesan cheese
½ teaspoon ground paprika	1 teaspoon salt
½ teaspoon onion powder	½ teaspoon black pepper nonstick cooking spray

Directions

Combine the chicken thighs and buttermilk in a nonreactive container with a cover or a resealable plastic bag. Marinate for at least 1 hour or overnight in the refrigerator.

Take the chicken out of the refrigerator. Pour out the buttermilk and let the chicken aside to rest while preparing the breading mixture.

In a wide, shallow dish or pie plate, whisk or mix the flour, breadcrumbs, Parmesan cheese, paprika, garlic powder, salt, onion powder, and black pepper until equally blended.

Preheat the air fryer carefully from 375°F to 380°F (190 to 195 degrees C). Lightly coat the air fryer basket with nonstick spray.

Once the air fryer is heated, dip the chicken thighs, one at a time, into the breading mixture, making sure the breading adheres to both sides as much as possible. Then, place gently in the air fryer basket. Repeat until all thighs have been breaded and placed in the basket. They should not be stacked on top of one other.

Set the timer for 25 minutes in the air fryer. When the timer goes off, use an instant-read thermometer to check the temperature. The inside temperature should be 180 degrees Fahrenheit (82 degrees C).

If they aren't quite done but the breading is turning black, simply seal the basket and set them aside to rest or turn the air fryer back on for a few minutes and check again. **Serve:** right away.

Crispy Chicken Salad with Yummy Honey Mustard Dressing

Prep time: 15 minutes **Cooking time:** 22 minutes
Serve: 1

Ingredients

2 tablespoons olive oil	1 ½ cups panko breadcrumbs
¼ teaspoon garlic powder cooking spray	2 tablespoons chopped fresh parsley
½ cup all-purpose flour	¼ teaspoon salt
¼ teaspoon ground black pepper	2 tablespoons water
1 ½ pound skinless, boneless chicken breast halves	2 large eggs
¾ cup mayonnaise	2 large carrots, peeled and sliced diagonally
8 cups mixed spring salad greens	1 cup sliced radishes
4 teaspoons Dijon mustard	3 tablespoons prepared yellow mustard
	3 tablespoons honey
	1 tablespoon lemon juice

Directions

In an extra-large skillet, heat the oil over medium heat. Mix in the panko and garlic powder. Cook, constantly stirring, for 2 to 3 minutes, or until toasted. Allow cooling in a shallow dish for 2 to 3 minutes. Mix in the parsley.
Preheat the air fryer carefully to 400°F and coat the air fryer basket with cooking spray (200 degrees C).

Meanwhile, combine the flour, salt, and pepper in a separate shallow dish. Finally, whisk together the eggs and water in a third shallow dish.

Cut chicken breasts into 1x3-inch strips lengthwise. To coat, dip the chicken strips in the flour mixture, then egg mixture, and finally the panko mixture.

Add the chicken to the prepared air fryer in batches. Cook, rotating once, for 5 to 7 minutes, or until an instant-read thermometer inserted into the thickest sections registers 165°F (74°C). Transfer to a platter, cover with foil and keep warm.

In a large mixing basin, combine salad leaves, carrots, and radishes. In a small mixing bowl, combine the mayonnaise, yellow mustard, honey, Dijon mustard, and lemon juice for the dressing. Salad should be divided among plates, topped with chicken, and drizzled with dressing.

Alphabetical Index

Printed in Great Britain
by Amazon

18191508R00066